# KLEE
## and Nature

# KLEE
# and Nature

Richard Verdi

A. Zwemmer Ltd

Text copyright © 1984 A. Zwemmer Ltd

All works by Paul Klee reproduced
in this book are © ADAGP Paris
and Cosmopress Switzerland 1984

Published by
A. Zwemmer Ltd
26 Litchfield Street, London WC2

ISBN : 0 302 02747 5 CASEBOUND ✓
ISBN : 0 302 02748 3 PAPERBACK

Designed by Christine Charlton
Printed in Great Britain by
BAS Printers Limited, Over Wallop, Hampshire

# Contents

For GJB, naturally.

# Preface and Acknowledgements

One of the first things one notices about a picture by Paul Klee is that the forms which make it up often appear to be treated like living things. Whether one catches sight of the breathing edges of a patch of colour, the nervous energy of a meandering line, or the weathered surface of an entire picture, Klee's means of expression themselves call to mind the very patterns and processes of life – its capacity to grow, to change, and to decay. One of the next things one notices about Klee's art is that it also draws much of its subject matter from the living world and often brings us face to face with the most diverse secrets of nature. From the intimate gropings of a single cell to the more intricate workings of the higher organisms, Klee's curiosity seems to know no bounds; and in this he remains unique among painters. For, although the world of visible nature has inspired artists from the very birth of art itself and the world of invisible nature has often stimulated the creative energies of artists of our own century, Klee explored both of these realms equally in his pictures, and through them sought to penetrate to the deepest mysteries of existence.

This book is an attempt to interpret Klee's pictures in relation to the world of nature and to examine the creative uses to which he put his lifelong explorations of that world. It is not intended as an introduction to Klee or as a chronological account of his development; nor does it concern itself with the many formal, technical, and stylistic innovations of his art. Rather, it is concerned with one important aspect of Klee's subject matter – albeit, perhaps, the most important one. In so varied and inventive an artist as Klee even these restrictions have not been able to prevent me from writing a full-length book despite the fact that Klee would clearly not have wished this. 'People who write full-length books are becoming more and more mysterious to me', he declared in 1917. With all due respect to the equally mysterious Klee, his lifelong pursuit of nature's myriad mysteries would seem to warrant nothing less.

That Klee was an accomplished natural scientist has long been acknowledged and is immediately apparent from his writings, his notebooks, and above all from his pictures themselves. Thus far, however, only isolated attempts have been made to relate Klee's interests in the organic world to the themes of his pictures. This is not surprising, for Klee himself was notoriously reluctant to discuss the content – as opposed to the form – of his pictures, and this in turn has inevitably deterred others from attempting to do so. In addition, Klee's reputation as one of the great fantasists among modern painters has likewise tended to foster the belief that his subject matter and imagery often defy rational explanation. Yet two of the most penetrating writers on the artist have demonstrated that this is not the case: namely, Werner Haftmann in his classic study, *The Mind and Work of Paul Klee*, and Max Huggler in his *Paul Klee, Die Malerei als Blick in den Kosmos*. In revealing the extent to which Klee's works are inspired by the world of nature and the degree to which they often explore the hidden logic and poetry of that world, both of these writers have added immeasurably to our understanding and appreciation of Klee's art; and they have, I confess, provided the chief inspiration for the present work.

More recently, Tilman Osterwold has published two volumes on Klee which group the artist's pictures according to their subjects and themes and will prove to be of inestimable value for future Klee studies.* Both of these provide us with clear evidence that, although Klee was an exceptionally prolific and inventive painter, certain recurring themes and patterns can be discerned among the rich variety of his output and that these in turn may help to bring us closer to some of the central concerns of his art and life. Of these none would appear to have afforded the artist with a greater source of subjects than the world of nature itself. The time may therefore be ripe for an initial exploration of the range and depth of Klee's interests in the living world and of the many forms these took in his pictures.

As the title of this book suggests it is confined to a study of Klee's depictions of organic life; though given that Klee often modelled his own art on the workings of nature it may also prove of some interest to one concerned with his theories of pictorial form. Its format is intended to be as straightforward as possible. The first chapter seeks to survey the general importance of nature in Klee's life and art and to introduce the reader to many of the principal themes and ideas to follow. The next two chapters are concerned with Klee's depictions of animal and plant subjects. Although the former of these are among the artist's most accessible nature paintings they are here given equal treatment with the plants, both for the sake of the balance of the book – and of nature itself. The fourth and fifth chapters consider those works which combine aspects of both these kingdoms and which include some of Klee's profoundest meditations on the natural order. Finally, the last chapter deals briefly with the parallels Klee uncovered between natural and artistic creation and with the relevance of these to his own art. Wherever possible I have made use of Klee's letters, diaries, and pedagogical writings to support my interpretations of his pictures. Notwithstanding the invaluable assistance provided by all of these, the results are offered to the reader essentially as a 'listening-in' to Klee's pictures – to use a term ingeniously coined for this purpose by Werner Haftmann. Klee's creative world remains so private and personal that one often finds oneself reduced to stalking it with one's eyes in much the same way as a piece of 'night music' by Bartók must be stalked with one's ears. In the course of my investigations, then, I have accepted the role of an eavesdropper and have tried to allow Klee's pictures to tell their own story.

---

*Paul Klee, Die Ordnung der Dinge*, ed. Tilman Osterwold, Stuttgart, 1975. Tilman Osterwold, *Paul Klee, Ein Kind träumt sich*, Stuttgart, 1979.

Throughout the study a number of the comparative illustrations have been chosen from books which Klee owned or could have known, though to attempt to establish more precise parallels for certain of his images would seem to be needlessly pedantic when so many books on natural history contain similar illustrations of particular species. For something of the same reason I have deferred a discussion of the background to Klee's art and ideas about nature to a concluding postscript which is offered primarily as a stimulus to further thought and discussion. It is not intended as a comprehensive account of the artistic and theoretical sources of Klee's nature paintings but, rather, as a series of afterthoughts on where such sources may most profitably be sought. In the present state of knowledge about Klee's ideas and imagery so tentative an approach would seem to be the only way forward. Moreover, there is one further reason why I have chosen to defer a discussion of the background to Klee's ideas on nature to the end of the book. As the reader will soon discover from the chapters which precede it, Klee often provides us with the best means of understanding his own works and takes as the themes of many of his pictures those universal truths about nature which would appear to be both logical and self-evident – which is not to say that they have ever before inspired such a rich store of visual images. In this regard Klee's paintings are most fruitfully studied in the context of nature itself and of the artist's own observations on it. While the ideas of others may go some way towards defining the tradition to which Klee himself belongs, they are not intended to explain the origins of his ideas or images. Nature alone best accounts for most of these.

For all the enchantment and appeal of his art, it is not easy to feel close to Klee. His creative universe remains too personal for this; and, rather than seeking to put us in touch with their creator, his pictures often aim to put us in touch with creation itself. For this reason Klee may at times seem an uncomfortably remote and inscrutable painter. As anyone familiar with his writings will know, however, Klee sought long and hard to attain this cosmic and crystalline state in order to explore the eternal secrets of existence in his pictures. This goal is nowhere set out more unforgettably for us than in one of the most illuminating of all Klee's maxims on art: 'Art plays an unwitting game with ultimate things and yet it reaches them'. Klee's own art repeatedly testifies to the importance he attached to this goal and to the sincerity and serenity with which he pursued it. Cautiously extending his own artistic feelers out into the universe he sought constantly to give shape and meaning to the world about us and to make visible its 'ultimate things'. It is a measure of Klee's humility and detachment that these, in the end, have become the true subject of this book.

Like others studying Klee before me, I am indebted to the artist's son, Felix Klee, for the energy and enthusiasm with which he has assisted this project from the start and for the many ways in which he has helped it along. No less indispensable have been the resources of the Paul Klee-Stiftung, Kunstmuseum, Bern, whose able staff and curator, Dr Jürgen Glaesemer, have answered countless queries and performed numerous favours for me in the course of my researches. I am obliged, too, to the many museums and private collectors who have generously agreed to supply me with photographs of works of art in their possession. They are acknowledged individually in the list of illustrations which follows.

Closer to home my warmest thanks are due to the staff of the Morrell Library, The University of York, and especially to Margaret Lawty, for the patience and determination with which she obtained the loan of any number of books needed for my work. With equal courtesy and efficiency David Whiteley, Gordon Smith, and James Merryweather have kindly provided me with many of the comparative illustrations included here. Dr Trudie Berger deserves especial thanks for the care and concern with which she assisted me in attempting to translate Klee's often very cryptic German into something approaching clear English.

Those portions of Chapter V concerning Klee's painting *Fish Magic* were first published in *The Burlington Magazine*, 1974. I am grateful to the Editor of the magazine for permission to reprint them here.

This book would not have been written without the initial support and encouragement of Dr John Golding and Professor Anthony Blunt, who died within days of its completion but who already knew that it was nearly finished.

Once embarked upon this project, I received much valuable advice and assistance from Professor Jacques Berthoud – all of it deeply appreciated. Hugh Haughton and Richard Shone kindly agreed to read the manuscript in its later stages and I remain indebted to them for the many helpful and constructive suggestions they made on its improvement.

Throughout the gestation of this book, I have benefited from the generous guidance of my publisher, Desmond Zwemmer, and of his ever-helpful staff, in particular James Fraser and John Taylor. Christine Charlton deserves the credit – and my sincerest thanks – for the book's design; and I also owe a particular debt of gratitude to Moira Johnston for her careful reading of the final draft and for guiding the text so smoothly through the proof-reading and printing stages.

I would like to thank my parents for the many ways in which they have aided and encouraged me throughout all phases of my work, both before and during Klee. Most of all, however, I am grateful for the comfort and companionship of John and Lucy and of a handful of good friends, without whom – as Klee himself knew – neither life nor work finds a measure of fulfilment. They are Monica and Angelo Bertucci, Mary Darrah, and Andrea and Leonard Patenaude. This book is theirs, too.

# List of Illustrations

Works listed in Klee's own *œuvre* catalogue bear the numbers assigned to them after the date. Klee's catalogue is conserved in the Paul Klee-Stiftung, Kunstmuseum, Bern.

195 *Large Sunflowers II*, by Emil Nolde. 1940. Oil on canvas. 76 × 95 cm. Present whereabouts unknown. Reproduced by permission of the Nolde-Stiftung, Seebüll.

196 *Cross and Spiral Blossoms* (*Kreuz und spiralblüten*), 1925, 9. Watercolour on paper with a coloured paste ground. 25.7 × 32 cm. Present whereabouts unknown.

197 Untitled Watercolour, by Wassily Kandinsky. 1913. 50 × 65 cm. Musée National d'Art Moderne, Centre Georges Pompidou, Paris.

198 *The gramineous bicycle garnished with bells the dappled fire damps and the echinoderms bending the spine to look for caresses*, by Max Ernst. 1920–21. Biological chart altered with gouache. 74.3 × 99.7 cm. Collection, The Museum of Modern Art, New York. Purchase.

199 *Vallisneria spiralis*, from Erasmus Darwin, *The Loves of the Plants*, 1789, Canto I, p. 33.

200 Snow Crystals, from Hans Kayser, *Orpheus, vom Klang der Welt, Morphologische Fragmente einer allgemeinen Harmonik*, Potsdam, 1926, Plate VII, opposite p. 88.

201 Spiral nebula and X-ray of a Snail shell, from Hans Kayser, *Grundriss eines Systems der harmonikalen Wertformen*, Zurich, 1946, Plate 16.

COLOUR PLATES

(appearing between pp. 78–79)

I *Sea-Snail King*, 1933. Kunstmuseum, Bern.

II *Plant-like Strange*, 1929. Kunstmuseum, Bern.

III *Harmony of the Northern Flora*, 1927. Felix Klee, Bern.

IV *Growth of Nocturnal Plants*, 1922. Galerie Stangl, Munich.

V *Sad Flowers*, 1917. Staatsgalerie moderner Kunst, Munich.

VI *Fish Magic*, 1925. Philadelphia Museum of Art, The Louise and Walter Arensberg Collection.

VII *Around the Fish*, 1926. Collection, The Museum of Modern Art, New York, Abby Aldrich Rockefeller Fund.

VIII *Still-life*, 1939–40. Felix Klee, Bern.

IX *Botanical Theatre*, 1924–34. Städtische Galerie im Lenbachhaus, Munich.

X *ab ovo*, 1917. Kunstmuseum, Bern.

XI *Rock Grave*, 1932. Felix Klee, Bern.

xvi

'If you desire to reach out into the infinite,
Move in all directions in the finite.'

J. W. von Goethe, *Gott, Gemüt, und Welt*, 1815.


         Help us to build

Bird – you who sing
Fawn – you who spring
Bloom on the fell
Fish in the well
Worm in the ground
Help us to build
the tower that leads to God

echo 'to God'

         Paul Klee, undated poem.

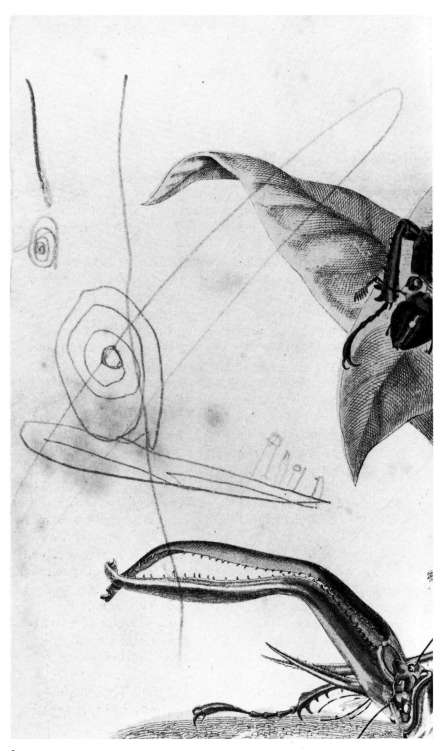

1
*Snails* 1883  Felix Klee, Bern

# 1 · Introduction: **The Artist as Naturalist**

When he was only three or four years old Paul Klee got hold of a neatly coloured print of some rather menacing beetles and inserted between them two pencil sketches of snails, the larger of them complete with its spiralling house, its slowly advancing body, and four prominent antennae (fig. 1). At the even earlier age of two or three years Klee had a dream about the family maid in which her sexual organs were revealed to him. 'They consisted', he later confessed, 'of four male (infantile) parts and looked something like a cow's udder.'[1] Five or six years after this, at the mischievous age of eight, the young Klee stole a dahlia bulb through a gap in the garden fence and transplanted it to his own miniature garden. 'I hoped for pretty leaves and perhaps a friendly flower,' he noted in retrospect, 'but a whole bush grew up, covered with countless deep red blossoms. This awakened a certain fear in me, and I played with the thought of renouncing my possession by giving it away.'[2]

These three incidents from Klee's childhood may appear to have little in common except as they reveal an early interest in art, sex, and nature. But, in fact, their connections go much deeper than this; for in all three of them may be seen a prefiguration of the art of the mature Klee. In the more than five decades which lay before him Klee never lost his fascination for the humble snail, which periodically revisits his easel or drawing-board on more than a dozen occasions from 1895 to 1939 (figs. 6–8, 13, 15–18, 112).[3] Similarly, the friendly or fearsome flower is a constant concern of the man Klee, whose youthful delight in attributing characters or emotions to plants led him to return time and again in later life to depict them as lonely or kindly, heroic or holy (figs. 111, 120, 135, 137).[4] And, as for the infant Klee's frank revelations about the family maid, even these resurfaced in a cryptic watercolour of 1918 entitled *Sexual Recognition of a Youth* (fig. 2). Here, under a cool, omniscient moon, a young boy suddenly enters manhood, his head crowned with a halo of dawning recognition and his raised right arm vigorously proclaiming both his new-found knowledge and his budding sexuality. Plainly visible to the left of the design are the bearers of this revelation – a virile bull, its one eye fixed vigilantly upon us, who jealously guards his chosen mate, her coyly downcast eyes and lashes rhyming with her distended udder and teats. Thus, faithful to his childhood dream even in middle age, the artist still finds the key to sexual understanding in the image of a cow's udder.[5] From all three of these events in Klee's youth and from the art which subsequently grew from them, only one conclusion may be drawn. Nature was with Paul Klee from the start, and it never left him.

In the years immediately following these first initiations into the ways of nature Klee embarked upon a more systematic study of the world about him. In a sketchbook compiled during his tenth and eleventh years he gradually made his acquaintance with a range of beings which were destined to remain a central part of his creative universe.[6] Working now in pencil and watercolour he filled his pages with drawings of fishes, flowers, fruits, and birds, some of them diligently labelled and identified, and all of them prophetic of things to come (figs. 3 & 4); for if one scrambles up these separate sheets of fishes and flowers and jumps thirty-five years in Klee's career one enters the enchanted world of *Fish Magic* (fig. 161), a masterpiece of 1925 which remains one of the artist's profoundest evocations of the mysteries of nature. To be sure, the wisdom and insight which immediately speak to us from the later canvas are nowhere evident in these youthful drawings, but that insatiable curiosity about nature which marks Klee's achievement at every stage surely already is. 'The future slumbers in human beings and needs only to be awakened,' observed Klee in 1901; 'it cannot be created.'[7] But, where Klee and nature were concerned at least, the future would appear to have required no such awakening. For it was never really asleep.

Before Klee could hope to gain a deeper insight into the secrets of nature it was necessary for him to acquire a more intimate knowledge of it on a purely visual level; and this was the task to which he devoted the next phase of his career. Where the animal kingdom is concerned this aspect of Klee's training is amply documented in an extensive series of drawings and watercolours of his teenage years. Isolated sheets of 1892–5 already record his patient study of the intricate anatomy of a butterfly, the skeleton of an eagle, or the flamboyant form of a toucan – all of them rendered with a painstaking attention to detail which calls to mind that coloured print of beetles which the three-year-old Klee had once so irreverently defaced.[8] But an even more remarkable testimony to this growing curiosity about the animal world are three zoological notebooks which Klee compiled between 1895–6 and which remain in the possession of his son. Of these, the first volume is devoted to the molluscs and insects, and the second and third volumes to the birds. In all of these the young artist studiously copied out detailed descriptions of the various classes, orders, and genuses which subdivide these groups and accompanied them with drawings of isolated, individual species or of those portions of their anatomy which might provide a clue to identification. The mouth parts of a beetle, the circulatory system of the insects generally, or the lugubrious exterior of a cuttlefish (fig. 5) – all of these engaged his attention and are recorded in so immaculate and methodical a manner that it becomes easy to see why Klee's patience was occasionally tried during the compiling of these notebooks and the artist led simply to cut out the illustrations of others and paste them onto the appropriate page.

Proudly initialled and dated on one of these pages is Klee's second surviving study of a snail (fig. 6). Carefully exploring this creature from both without and within the artist now presents us with a meticulously drawn and labelled

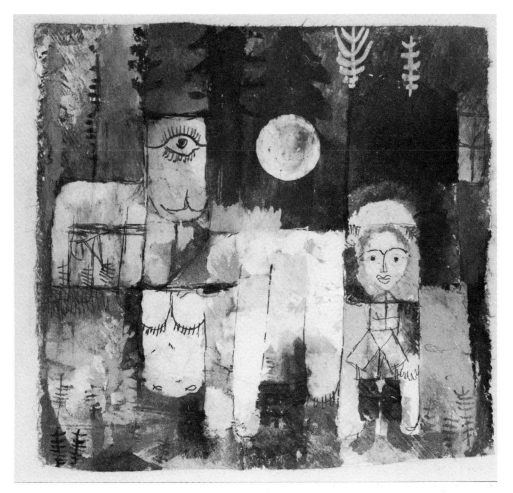

2
*Sexual Recognition of a Youth* 1918 Felix Klee, Bern

account both of its shell and of its labyrinthine internal anatomy. Here too one cannot help but cast one's mind forward to the creations of Klee's maturity; for if we superimpose this notebook drawing of a snail-shell on top of that of its humble resident and deprive both of them of their more purely realistic touches we find ourselves in the world of Klee's *Snail* of 1924 (fig. 8) – a world which no longer concerns itself with an individual species or with literal description but one in which a thorough understanding of the appearance of things in nature has given way to an imaginative recreation of their essence. Only Klee himself could tell us how many snails he had befriended and scrutinized before he found himself able to give birth to such archetypal images of snail-like existence in his mature art. What we do know, however, is that when he began to compile his invaluable catalogue of works in 1911 Klee effectively disowned these early notebook drawings, excluding them from his list of works because they lacked 'creative self-sufficiency'.[9] No one would deny that they do; but they unmistakably pointed the way towards that higher goal.

3

3
*Trout and Perch* 1890
Felix Klee, Bern

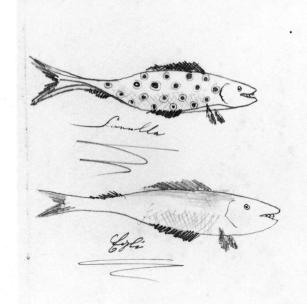

4
*Eight Fruits, Two Flowers*
1889 Felix Klee, Bern

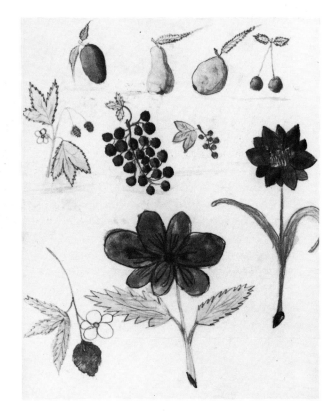

5
*Sepia officinalis* (Common
Cuttlefish) 1895
Felix Klee, Bern

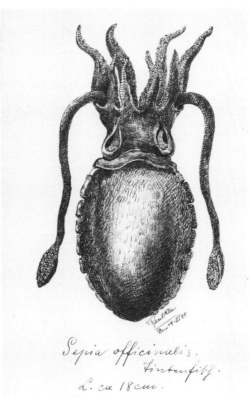

6
*Two studies of snails* 1895
Felix Klee, Bern

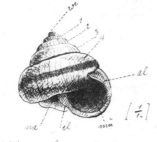

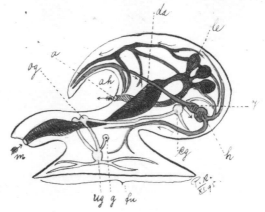

In the years from 1900 to 1914, which were the first in which Klee was to find a measure of 'creative self-sufficiency', such studies after individual objects in nature form a less significant part of his output. When they do occur, however, they already show the artist gradually disengaging himself from the bonds of mere realism to concentrate upon the most essential features of a form. Separate studies of certain of Klee's favourite natural subjects – cats, a pot of asters, or a bed of cactuses[10] – all bear witness to the bolder and more impressionistic leanings of his art during these years. Yet for Klee impressionism was a style no less inimical to true self-expression than the plodding realism of his teenage years; and the task to which he now devoted himself was one of slowly freeing his art from a concern with appearances, whether general or particular, and of finding a style which was truly his own – one which would eventually permit him to say more than nature with fewer means.[11] Working alternately on a series of creations drawn from his imagination and those based on nature, Klee sought a means of reconciling his natural preference for the painting of ideas – that is to say, for poetic subjects – with the plastic (or 'architectonic') means of expression at his disposal;[12] in short, a means of couching his poetic ideas in a pictorial language which paralleled, rather than duplicated, nature's own. Recognizing that he had still not reached this point in 1911, Klee began to catalogue his early works in that year by assigning them the separate letters of 'A' or 'B', according to whether they derived from the imagination ('A') or from nature ('B').[13] Nor can the primacy accorded to works drawn from the imagination go unnoticed here. Klee's avowed desire was always to place nature at the service of his imagination – to be able to evoke its essential beings and processes even with his eyes shut.

A decisive step towards this goal came with Klee's introduction to the *Blaue Reiter* group of artists in Munich in 1911. In the guiding spirits of this group, Wassily Kandinsky and Franz Marc, Klee encountered two painters who shared his conviction that art should seek to penetrate beneath the things of this world, and who can only have reaffirmed his commitment to an art ultimately based on nature; for at this stage in their careers both Kandinsky and Marc still took it as their invariable starting-point. Through this association Klee was suddenly introduced to the most advanced developments in European painting, one of which – Cubism – provided him with a means of forging a new pictorial language, one which was no longer tied to the representation of objects in nature but, instead, to a genuine recreation of them.[14] In this new style, freely floating planes of pure colour, which owed an obvious debt to the formal discoveries of the Cubist painters, could be made to function as true building-blocks in Klee's designs, preserving their structural logic while still making it possible for him to reveal all that was most essential in his chosen subjects. When his picture demanded it, too, this new and more abstract mode of expression could also be placed at the service of Klee's ideas. With this significant step forward, the artist had achieved one of his long-sought ambitions. Henceforth the poetic and the architectonic elements in his art would be indissolubly bound.

A pen-and-ink drawing of 1914 of yet another snail demonstrates this new

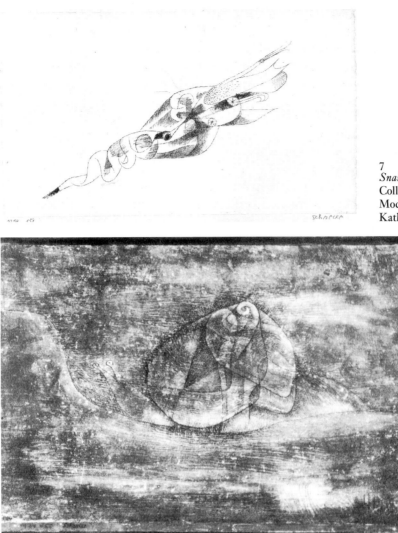

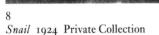

7
*Snail* 1914
Collection, The Museum of
Modern Art, New York,
Katherine S. Dreier Bequest

8
*Snail* 1924 Private Collection

stage in Klee's artistic development at its most characteristic (fig. 7). To one
who has never confronted such a creature this drawing might remain an
irritating enigma. But to one who has, Klee's work could hardly call to mind
anything else – though it can in no way be accused of confining itself to a literal
depiction of this diminutive creature. Rather, it is as though Klee has
decomposed and then re-composed the snail shape from memory. Head, neck,
foot, and spiralling shell are all alluded to, and only the traditional syntax
between these separate areas is obscured. The result is a creation parallel to
nature – one which encapsulates the fundamental features of the snail form
without remaining enslaved to them, and one which strikes us as both original

and truthful. Little wonder that, in the preceding year, Klee had abandoned the classifications 'A' and 'B' in cataloguing his works. From now on everything would simply be Klee. Nature now resided within him, and could be reborn at will in his art.

Everything that one knows about Klee suggests that he stood on uncommonly good terms with nature. Contemporary accounts of his physical appearance even bear this out and note that his mysterious, opaque eyes called to mind those of a deer or that the pale oval of his face resembled a giant egg.[15] Much more important than these, however, are Klee's own self-sought identifications with nature, which very early in life he recognized as his chief refuge and consolation – or, in his own words, as 'the power that maintains'.[16] Seeking to encompass the whole of nature in his life, long before he was able to do so in his art, Klee filled his early diaries and letters with constant reminders to us of the deep bond which he felt uniting him with the rest of creation. Complementing these spiritual links with the world about him, Klee surrounded himself from an early age with a variety of natural companions which made it possible for him to reinforce these links on a purely earthly level.

From his youth Klee already felt a close rapport with the world of animals; and although as a boy he was not above teasing and tormenting certain of the meeker beasts – among them 'large snails'[17] – already with his move to Munich in 1899 he was proudly writing home assuring his parents that one of the chief virtues of his new landlady was that she was a devoted animal lover.[18] So too was Klee, who shared the belief of his friend Franz Marc that animals possessed both an outer and inner purity whereas mankind at best boasted only an outer one.[19] But Klee's attachment to animals was rarely of a silly or sentimental kind. It is true that, in the absence of his fiancée, Lily, he admitted to bestowing his kisses upon 'love-worthy' animals[20] and that, much later in life, he could be heard conducting an entire telephone conversation with his son, Felix, in animal noises.[21] It is also true that as a man of thirty he could still be moved to save the life of a young sparrow[22] and that, even in the midst of the Great War, he found time to record his annoyance over a cat which had callously been turned out to freeze in the night despite the fact that, as Klee saw it, there was something holy in this creature.[23] But if Klee never lost his ability to feel for animals he also recognized that a purely human attachment to them was not enough. For their lives and their ways were subject to laws and impulses different from those of mankind and had to be understood and respected within the broader context of creation as a whole. This was the task that Klee set himself as early as a diary entry of 1905, which briefly outlines what he saw as the noblest feeling one could harbour towards one's fellow creatures. 'Really to love animals,' he wrote, 'that is: to raise them to the same level in relation to what is above.'[24]

In his own day-to-day existence Klee lived in a world dominated by cats. These remained his chosen animal companions for all four decades of his career and their playful antics are lovingly chronicled throughout Klee's diaries and letters. Posing for his camera or sharing his bed, his dinner table, or his studio

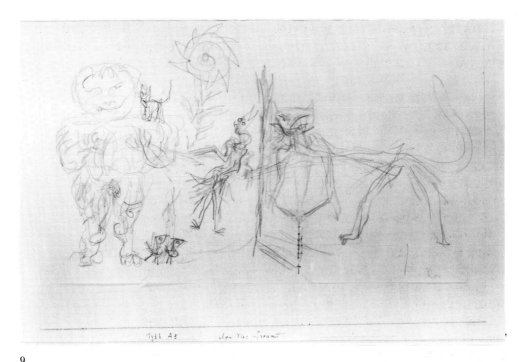

9
*The Animals' Friend* 1933  Present whereabouts unknown

with him, cats provided the artist with relief and recreation from the frictions of his early family life and with comfort and distractions of a perhaps even more welcome kind during the years of his painful last illness.[25] Inevitably, too, they became among the favourite animal subjects of his pictures.[26] But if cats were the preferred pets of Klee's maturity, the young artist also briefly shared his life with an owl and two tortoises.[27] No less silent and secretive than the cats which eventually replaced them in Klee's affections, the owl and the tortoise became – along with the artist's last cat, Bimbo – one of the few identifiable species to enter Klee's late art, where they appear as memories conjured forth from the distant past.[28] In a slightly earlier drawing of 1933 entitled *The Animals' Friend* (fig. 9), which belongs to an unusually personal group of works of this same year,[29] Klee affords us a rare glimpse of the intimate relationship he enjoyed with his favourite cats and birds – and even (as we shall see[30]) with one of his favourite flowers. Yet if such creatures were the only ones regularly to perch on his shoulder or sit at his feet, they were far from the only ones to catch his eye. Whether in the artificial world of the zoo or the natural and exotic habitats of Egypt and North Africa Klee was constantly moved to record his impressions of the most diverse species, from donkeys to dromedaries, and from fornicating toads to ugly baboons.[31] And although he was never destined to become a conventional animal painter – even by the standards of his own century – much of Klee's art and imagery was to find deep inspiration in an ever-growing mental menagerie which was nurtured and nourished by such daily contacts with the world of the beasts.

An even more remarkable testimony to the extent of Klee's identification with nature than his remarks on animals are the frequent analogies with the plant kingdom which he introduces into discussions of his own life – and even of his own, very animal processes. Thus, after an exhausting journey to the Thunersee in September 1901, he writes that he has at last rested and refreshed himself and now has such a clear head 'that my little plant of a soul will soon be able to strike new roots again'.[32] Two years later, and again with reference to a journey to this same region, he notes that if the weather there is favourable he will be ensured of 'much quiet, plant-like and sun-blessed good fortune'.[33] And on a third occasion, having worked long and hard attending to the needs of the plants in his garden in Bern, he confesses that the result of this is that he himself now feels like a plant. 'That is the only way', Klee continues, 'to feel completely at home.'[34] Fleeting and fanciful though these remarks may appear, they clearly reveal a temperament sensitively attuned to the lives and secrets of the plants – one which, even in its late years, could shower pity upon a pair of trees which were trying to bloom outside his Dessau apartment when their efforts were thwarted by an unseasonal mist.[35]

But perhaps the most telling indication of the extent to which Klee explored and explained the events of his own life with reference to those of the plants may be found in those instances when he resorts to a botanical analogy where none would appear to be necessary. Thus, somewhat uncertain of his reactions to a Danish romance which he has just finished reading, he observes of it in February 1902: 'I find in it too many blossoms and too little of the plant's total organism'. Then, quickly switching his analogy to the animal kingdom, Klee adds: 'a mollusk poesy without spine'.[36] And shortly before his marriage to Lily Stumpf in 1906 he cryptically – but somewhat more appositely – begins one of his diary entries with the single sentence: 'The hybrid blossom is an appropriate symbol for a good marriage.'[37] It is a symbol which no experienced farmer or horticulturist would wish to deny him. Finally, mention should also be made here of the most pervasive of all Klee's analogies between an aspect of his own life and that of the plant kingdom: namely, that from his earliest years onwards he repeatedly referred to his own artistic creations as 'fruits'.[38]

But what of Klee's everyday contacts with the world of plants? These, it must be admitted, remain less well documented than his encounters with animals, doubtless because they were necessarily more private and afforded less engaging topics for conversation. To be sure, both his diaries and letters are frequently interspersed with remarks on the state of his garden, on the spiritual rejuvenation he derived from tending it, or on the exotic flora to be marvelled at on his journeys to the tropics.[39] Yet when one considers that the plant kingdom was to furnish Klee with one of his richest sources of imagery and to bring him closer than any other aspect of nature to an understanding of its deepest secrets, such evidence remains disappointingly thin. Certainly there is nothing in Klee's early career to provide us with a botanical counterpart to the three zoological notebooks already discussed; nor is there much evidence that Klee cohabited with plants as readily as he did with certain of his favourite animals. But the reasons for this would appear to be largely circumstantial. At least after his move to Munich in 1906 Klee and his family lived in apartments in major cities and were thereby unable to cultivate a large garden. In place of this Klee tended an ever-growing collection of indoor cactuses, an enthusiasm which he inherited from his father and which clearly appealed to his poetic feeling for nature; for, with a little effort of the imagination, Klee could come to see in these cactuses the hidden forms of men or even of giants.[40] Other than this, however, Klee appears to have relied largely upon regular visits to the countryside and to the parks and gardens of Munich, Weimar, and Dessau to acquaint himself with the world of flowers and plants. On visits to the botanical gardens in Munich he was often accompanied by his son, who recalls that Klee knew the Latin names of every species to be found there and eagerly sought to instil such knowledge in his youthful companion.[41] And that Klee was fully conversant with the rarified language of the taxonomist is confirmed by the deceptive ease with which he could invent fanciful Latin names for the purely fictitious species of plants which occasionally entered his art.[42]

Of those plants and flowers which most frequently entered Klee's life the majority would appear to have consisted of species which were collected on his various outings and subsequently brought home and pressed. Klee is known to have amassed a large collection of such specimens, which he studied and analysed as methodically as he did his collection of zoological drawings and diagrams. Probably the most important surviving evidence of this interest is a group of eight Alpine flowers pressed and preserved on the back of an untitled (and decidedly unbotanical) drawing of 1927 (fig. 10). Its comparatively late date attests to the fact that the artist never ceased to immerse himself in the world about him, even in his full maturity.

Complementing Klee's collection of pressed flowers was his equally extensive collection of natural curiosities – a kind of twentieth-century *Wunderkammer* of all that was most beautiful or bizarre in nature, examples of which Klee collected, mounted, and labelled. Early visitors to his studio often remark upon these anthological gatherings of nature's artistry;[43] and the range of these collections – and thereby of Klee's interests – does appear to have been limitless. Flowers, leaves, roots, and seed-pods; rocks and crystals; algae, mosses, and lichens; corals, molluscs, and butterflies; sea-horses and sea-urchins – all of these found their way into his custody and under his scrutiny. In the one surviving example of these still in the possession of his son (fig. 11) a variety of specimens representing the higher and lower plants are mounted against a black background in a manner which recalls Klee's more mysterious botanical stage landscapes of the 1920s and '30s (figs. 75, 77, 177). Nor may this analogy be as improbable as it seems, for many of the species included in these collections reappear transformed in his own art. Moreover Klee's irrepressible instinct for the poetic is known to have shown itself even in the midst of this most scientific of all his natural pursuits. On at least one occasion he is recorded to have collected specimens of algae during visits to the Baltic and preserved

10
*Eight pressed flowers* 1927
Felix Klee, Bern

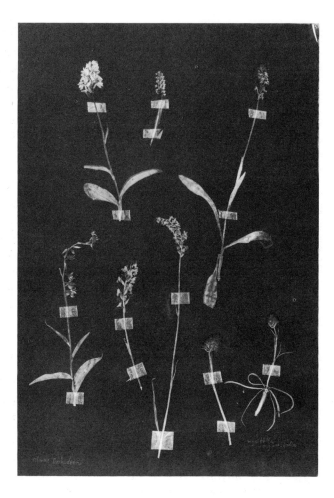

them between sheets of glass in an arrangement which he then rather whimsically entitled *Baltic Forest*.[44] But neither whimsy nor poetry can entirely account for this. Instead, as we shall see, Klee was here expressing one of his central attitudes towards nature, which was forever given to uncovering an image of the whole through a careful study of a mere part, or of discovering entire forests in the workings of a single gathering of cells.[45]

In addition to his deep absorption in the worlds of plants and animals Klee has left us with abundant evidence, both in his art and his writings, of his immersion and identification with nature as a whole, and especially with its changing cycles and moods. As early as 1900 the young artist confessed: 'The comparison of my soul with the various moods of the countryside frequently returns as a motif'[46] – and in fact there are few more pervasive motifs throughout the whole of Klee's writings. Scarcely does a year go by or a season change without the artist making note of this fact and of its inevitable effect upon his own emotional or creative energies. From all of these the impression

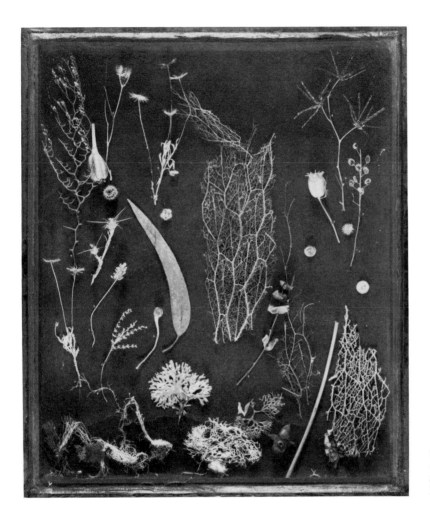

11
*Klee's collection of*
*dried plants* 1931
Felix Klee, Bern

emerges of an individual profoundly susceptible to the changing moods and
patterns of nature – one who felt himself ineluctably bound to its controlling
rhythms and who recognized in nature's vicissitudes a mirror of man's own life
on earth. Thus, whether Klee finds joy or sorrow in the world about him it
remains essentially a comfort – a reminder that the changing fortunes of his
own existence are merely a dim reflection of those of nature as a whole. Indeed,
so fully does Klee seem to have regarded nature as his only true refuge that
more than once in his life he was moved to record his disdain for those works
of man which had sought to encroach upon it. Working out of doors in Munich
in 1899, he wrote to his father that he felt himself so powerfully attracted to
the surrounding landscape 'that with the best will in the world I could no longer
step back on to pavements but wanted as soon as possible to rush back into
the country'.[47] And years later, on a visit to Egypt in 1928, he confessed: 'What
is the whole of civilization, be it good or bad, compared with this water, this
sky, this light?'[48] From such statements as these it is easy to see why the

promise of a blissful union with his fiancée led Klee to compare their future happiness to a garden which would transcend the struggles of this world and in which many seeds of all kinds would be sown.[49] And nearly half-way through their life together it is even more poignant to find him writing to Lily to remind her of the inevitable difference between nature's cycles and those of their own lives. 'The apple trees along the road have just started to bloom,' he observes in May 1918, 'once again another spring and then another one and – one day it must however come to an end, whether one wants it to or not.'[50]

In what Klee himself called his 'poetic-personal idea of landscape'[51] there emerges a distinct progression during his early years – one which initially finds him seeking comfort only in the joys of nature and gradually reveals him to be most at home with its more withdrawn and forbidding moods. Thus, when struck by a spell of personal misfortune in his teens, the despondent Klee seeks refuge in the womb of nature and notes: 'I almost feel as if the best thing, now, would be to lie down for a long sleep, to wake up only on the return of spring'[52] – an idea which, as we shall see, finds expression in any number of his mature paintings.[53] Later in life Klee admitted that, as a young man, he had often identified nature's adversities with his own, but that he had long abandoned such superstitions.[54] Indeed, even before he had left his teens Klee discovered that his own temperament was less volatile than that of nature and that it ultimately bore more in common with the stillness of winter than with the bustle of spring:[55]

In the Egelgasse my emotion reached its climax. In the pond inverted clouds were mirrored. Secret pulsation of the still snow, like breathing in one's sleep. Old trees. The impression of a controlled passion. My portrait. Motion stirs an impulse to act in me, an impulse to experience first. My yearning to wander away, into a springtime. Far out into the land. Away. Ever onward.

If the desire to find solace in the happiness of spring still persists here the passage is chiefly remarkable for its dawning realization that the true Klee was to be a creature of winter – a man of 'secret pulsation' and 'controlled passion'. Indeed, in retrospect it is easy to see that the young Klee had rarely experienced a more clairvoyant vision of his future self than in these musings on the Egelgasse, for in later life he was regularly to find himself at his most comfortable and creative in the silence of winter. Yet this was not his thinking from the start. In a diary entry of 1900 he may still be heard lamenting the arrival of autumn and wondering if the coming winter will make it possible for him to sow his own artistic seeds.[56] Already by 1905, however, Klee was discovering that he was at his most productive when surrounded by frost, snow, and 'everything desolate' and was perversely contemplating moving to Stockholm or Copenhagen in order to maintain his creative energies.[57] Such sentiments are echoed in many other letters with a consistency which forces one to conclude that, if Klee never ceased to exult at the coming of spring, he appears to have found winter-time most conducive to the birth of his artistic fruits. 'It is quiet, the windows are closed, outside there is less life than usual and less noise,' wrote Klee of this season in 1906.[58] Thus, shut out from the world about him he could now get on with the job of discovering it from within.

Far from being a mere idiosyncrasy, Klee's preference for the winter months accords with other aspects of his creative personality, which generally seems to have developed along a path from 'passion' to 'control' and which often found its greatest inspiration in those moments when the world outside was at its most hushed and mysterious, whether in winter, in cloudy weather, or in the depths of the night.[59] At such times, when nature was at its most uncommunicative, Klee apparently found himself freer to probe beneath its quiet exterior and to discover its cosmic import; whereas in the heat of the day or the full flush of spring the temptation to describe nature from a purely earthly point of view became irresistible. But so limited a vision was never to be the self-styled goal of the mature Klee, whose determination to disengage himself from the world of both the senses and of sentiment is movingly charted throughout his earliest writings and paintings. Figuratively speaking at least, both of these reveal a transition from the warmth of springtime to the chill of winter.

Only very early in Klee's career does one find him declaring his ambition to be the expression of a kinship with all of earthly existence. This occurs in a letter to his mother of 1900.[60] Within two years, however, he is acknowledging a new goal for himself – one which was to remain his chosen one and which is here outlined with remarkable precision and foresight, long before Klee had discovered any means of realizing it on an artistic level:[61]

> Affect the world, but not as part of a multiplicity like bacteria, but as an entity, down here, with connections to what is up there. To be anchored in the cosmos, a stranger here, but strong – this, I suppose, will probably be the final goal. But how to reach it?? To grow, for the time being simply to grow.

Further entries in both Klee's diaries and letters mark this quest for a position which would eventually permit both the man and the artist in him to transcend the boundaries of this world; and in charting his progress towards this goal Klee resorts to a series of images which gradually transform him from a fleshly human being into an ember – or a crystal. A creature of springtime thus gives way to one of winter.

Already in 1901 Klee avows his desire to free himself from the fetters of the earthly and admits to hating his own body except when he pauses to remember that 'better part' of him which depends upon it.[62] Four years later he confesses that a truthful self-portrait would now show him sitting 'like a kernel in a nut' – an 'allegory of incrustation', as he calls it, though to us it may seem more of an allegory of impenetrability.[63] In the next year he may be found dreaming of being 'borne to places where one no longer seeks voluptuousness';[64] and having gradually attained this state of creative and emotional disembodiment, he describes himself as follows in 1915:[65]

I am armed, I am not here,
I am in the depths, am far away . . .
I am far away . . .
I glow amidst the dead.

In the same year Klee writes of himself as one who has deserted the realm of the 'here and now' for 'a realm of the yonder where total affirmation is possible' and proudly describes himself as the 'crystalline type'.[66] 'Abstraction' and 'cool Romanticism' now characterize his view-point on life; and, although Klee foresees that this state may never be one of complete invulnerability, for the moment it protects him. 'That is how it is today,' he observes, 'but then: the whole crystal cluster once bled. I thought I was dying, war and death. But how can I die, I who am crystal? I, crystal.' Alienated and detached from the ebbings and flowings of a purely earthly existence Klee now sees himself as a creature released from an undue concern with the things of this world and elevated to a position of cosmic understanding. It is almost as though he resembles a large, omniscient eye looking down upon nature – a motif which may often be found in his art of these years (fig. 160) and which remains perhaps the most truthful of all his self-portraits.[67] Summing up this changed relationship to the world about him Klee offers us the following undated couplet, which clearly cannot be very early:[68]

All and everything I loved
and now I am a cool, cool star.
(*Alle alle hatt ich gern*
*und jetzt bin ich kühler Stern.*)

Essentially poetical though many of the above-quoted passages may seem they are amply justified by the exalted goal which Klee set for himself and by the arduous struggle he endured to attain it. Moreover, they are fully vindicated by the best of the works of art which resulted from Klee's efforts to transcend the earthly. For although many of Klee's best-loved paintings and drawings appeal to us primarily through their wry humour, their beguiling simplicity, or their sheer beauty, others penetrate much deeper than this and strike us with all the force of a blinding revelation, as though transmitted by some distant intelligence. And this in fact is exactly what Klee set out to do. As a 'cool star' floating above our own sullied planet he could proceed from this lofty and remote vantage point to reduce its myriad complexities to order, and to reveal those underlying bonds between nature's most diverse creations which remain concealed from those empowered with a merely earthly vision. The greater the distance, the profounder would be the truths disclosed to the artist. And in time entire forests would appear from a random collection of cells gathered from the slime of the sea.

Nowhere is Klee's approach to nature in his maturity more fully set out for us than in the lecture *Ways of Studying Nature*, which he delivered at the

Bauhaus in 1923;[69] and since a consideration of this text is a necessary preliminary to the study of his paintings and drawings of natural themes, it would be well to examine carefully the goals which Klee outlines for the pictorial artist in this key essay.

Klee opens his discussion with one of the most oft-quoted of his many familiar maxims on art: 'For the artist, dialogue with nature remains a *conditio sine qua non*.' 'The artist', he continues, 'is a man, himself nature and a part of nature in natural space'. Thus from the start Klee acknowledges that the artist's role is one of exploring the world about him and that the way to do this is by entering into a true dialogue with nature – that is to say, through an exchange of views between artist and object rather than through a mere monologue in which nature speaks and the artist listens, learns, and imitates what he 'hears'. The latter path, Klee notes, sufficed for earlier generations of artists, who directed their creative efforts to a 'painfully precise investigation of appearance'. 'In this way excellent pictures were obtained of the object's surface filtered by the air; the art of optical sight was developed', observes Klee, 'while the art of contemplating unoptical impressions and representations and of making them visible was neglected.' Although Klee's own art had reached this stage by the time he wrote these lines, the reader need hardly be reminded that he too had served his artistic apprenticeship by engaging in a simple monologue with nature after the manner of those masters of 'optical sight', the Realists and Impressionists, to whom he is obviously alluding above.

As Klee sees it, the way to a deeper understanding of the invisible face of nature comes through the recognition that the artist is part of a totality much greater than that which meets the eye. 'The artist of today', he remarks, 'is more than an improved camera; he is more complex, richer, and wider. He is a creature on the earth and a creature within the whole, that is to say, a creature on a star among stars.' His true goal, Klee continues, should therefore be to instil a 'sense of totality' into his conception of any object in nature – in other words, to divine its place and purpose in the grand scheme of things as though seeing it from the most remote point in the universe, from a distant star.

But for Klee the key to such a cosmic understanding of creation is not to be found simply in distancing oneself and in dreaming or musing on the things of this world. Rather it is firstly to be found in knowing them intimately, not merely as they appear but as they actually *are*. 'The object grows beyond its appearance through our knowledge of its inner being,' observes Klee, 'through the knowledge that the thing is more than its outward aspect suggests.' This process, which Klee calls 'visible penetration', consists of dissecting or visualizing the inner workings of an object until one has grasped its essence. Only when its form and function are fully known on this level will the artist find himself capable of recreating it in his art without the stimulus of the object itself. At this stage we are in the world of Klee's two *Snails* of 1914 and 1924 (figs. 7 & 8), which concern themselves with no individual organism in nature but with an entire class of beings, and which have so fully penetrated to the essence of their subjects that they may now offer us an imaginative recreation of those features which pervade all of snail-like existence and which distinguish it from all other forms of life.

Having once acquired such intimate knowledge of an object in nature, Klee proceeds to outline two ways in which the artist may relate it to the rest of creation, both of them (as he puts it) 'non-optical'. The first of these is the way of 'intimate physical contact, earthbound, that reaches the eye of the artist from below'; while the second is that of 'contact through the cosmic bond that descends from above'. As these two goals imply, the first seeks to place the object in the context of the rest of earthly creation and the second, in a larger, cosmic one. The result will be an image of the macrocosm glimpsed through the careful study of an element of the microcosm, which was Klee's preferred way with nature throughout his life. This explains why his art so often strikes us as uncovering a transcendental reality through the patient scrutiny of those beings and objects familiar to us from our own everyday lives.

'All ways meet in the eye and there, turned into form, lead to a synthesis of outward sight and inward vision,' Klee continues:

It is here that constructions are formed which, although deviating totally from the optical image of an object yet, from an overall point of view, do not contradict it.

Through the experience that he has gained in the different ways and translated into work, the student demonstrates the progress of his dialogue with the natural object. His growth in the vision and contemplation of nature enables him to rise towards a metaphysical view of the world and to form free abstract structures which surpass schematic intention and achieve a new naturalness, the naturalness of the work. Then he creates a work, or participates in the creation of works, that are the image of God's work.

Klee accompanies his discussion with a diagram which summarizes the three pathways – the optical, the earthly, and the cosmic – which he deems necessary for the fullest possible understanding of any object in nature (fig. 12). Whether intentionally or not, this diagram in itself evokes all three of these pathways and at once calls to mind the form of an eye, an orbiting planet, and an entire solar system. This analogy between the role of the artist and that of a distant, cosmic intelligence – all-seeing and all-knowing – is confirmed in the conclusion to his lecture, quoted above, where the artist's creations are compared with those of the original creator. Having immersed himself in the totality of creation, the artist may now hope to give birth to works which possess a naturalness which parallels, but in no way duplicates, those of God himself.

Nowhere in his discussion of these three levels of understanding does Klee offer his readers examples of them in practice. His art of the time, however, demonstrates these in abundance – even if, for the sake of convenience, we confine ourselves once more to his renderings of the lowly snail.

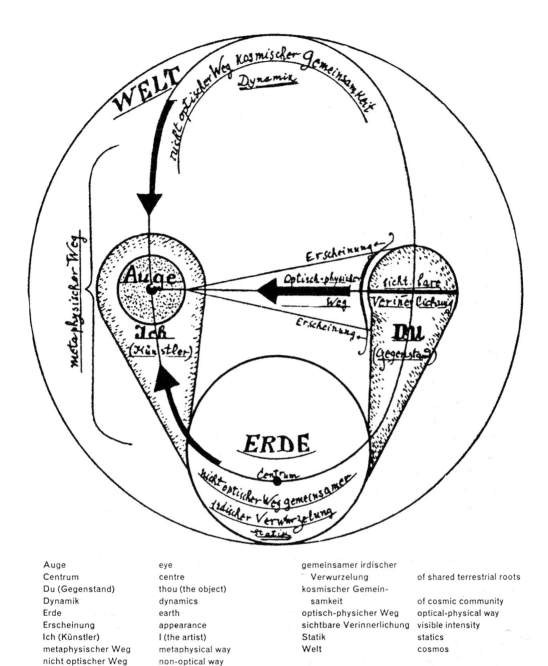

| Auge | eye | gemeinsamer irdischer | |
| Centrum | centre | Verwurzelung | of shared terrestrial roots |
| Du (Gegenstand) | thou (the object) | kosmischer Gemein- | |
| Dynamik | dynamics | samkeit | of cosmic community |
| Erde | earth | optisch-physicher Weg | optical-physical way |
| Erscheinung | appearance | sichtbare Verinnerlichung | visible intensity |
| Ich (Künstler) | I (the artist) | Statik | statics |
| metaphysischer Weg | metaphysical way | Welt | cosmos |
| nicht optischer Weg | non-optical way | | |

12
The Artist's Eye, from *Ways of Studying Nature* 1923

We have already seen how the study and analysis of the form of this simple
creature during his early years gradually enabled Klee to create works which
afford us an image of the archetypal snail; that is to say, of the common
denominators which rest, invisible, beneath the countless varieties of such

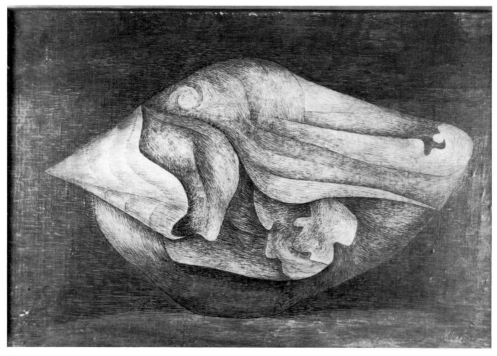

13
*Sea-Snail King* 1933 Kunstmuseum, Bern

creatures one encounters in nature. But to proceed this far was still only to have
arrived at the essence of an object in nature and not yet to be able to relate
it to other things of this world. However, both in his art and his teachings Klee
took this next step by further reducing the snail form to a simple spiralling or
meandering line which then invited comparisons with the most diverse facets
of creation. Ignoring the head, antennae, and body of this organism, as though
to suggest that none of these was its uniquely distinguishing feature, Klee
concentrated instead upon the lines described by its shell; and from there it
was but a small step to relate these to the unfurling spiral of a blossoming
flower, to the convoluted structure of the mammalian abdomen and umbilical
cord, or to the layers of nutrient flesh which surround the seed in a large fruit
(figs. 13, 14, 104, 105). The last of these analogies particularly appealed to Klee,
who regularly introduced comparisons between an apple and a snail-shell into
his classroom teachings.[70] But, far from being comparisons of a fanciful or
purely formal kind, the relations described to us here make visible a profound
truth about nature's inner workings; for in both the snail-shell and the apple
such layers serve to protect their respective inhabitants, whether they be docile
snail or dormant seed. Indeed, even the analogies with unfurling blossoms and
with the abdomen and umbilical cord may be seen as essentially protective in
nature, the one over the heart of the flower – and thereby over its procreative
centre – and the other over the developing foetus. As such the spiral pattern

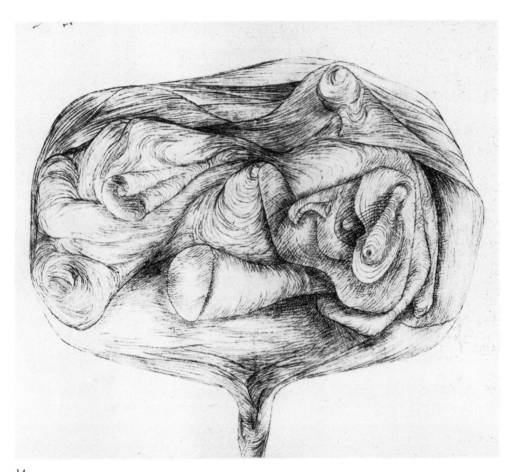

14
*Calix abdominis (Belly Bud)*, 1934 Present whereabouts unknown

may be seen to pervade the most diverse facets of life for similar reasons. Whether in the fruit, the flower, the snail, or the mammal, nature appears to have invented it as a means of sheltering certain of its most helpless creations.[71]

But what of the snail shape when viewed from beyond the earth – in short, from a distant star? Here one moves to what Klee himself admitted to be a metaphysical level of understanding, one in which the philosopher and the poet in him take over from the scientist. On this level Klee most often introduces the snail shape into his art as a floating body in the heavens, where it literally forms a link between earth and cosmos (figs. 15, 112).[72] Its distinguishing spiral still plainly visible, it now serves to evoke the whirling motions of clouds or nebulae or the orbiting relationship generally throughout the solar system. Such a transformation of the tiny snail into an immense planet may ultimately strike us as more poetical than plausible. Yet it is worth remembering that the orbiting pathways of the planets themselves indicate a position of dependence and protection comparable to that which the snail enjoys from its cosy shell.

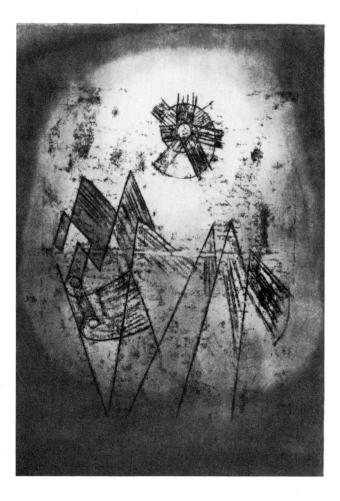

These three levels of understanding, whether with regard to the snail or to any other motif in Klee's art, are not to be seen as marking a chronological progresssion throughout the course of his career. Rather, once having mastered the visual aspects of any form the way was open for Klee to explore its essential kinship with other facets of life as the spirit moved him. Although it is generally true that his understanding of such relations deepened with age, it is also the case that, at any point in his maturity one may encounter the same object treated from several points of view, from the purely comic to the truly cosmic. The difference depended upon the vantage point which Klee unconsciously adopted in the course of creation. By his own admission Klee felt 'at home with all things under, on, and over this earth';[73] and from moment to moment – or at least picture to picture – his chosen view-point upon nature was thereby subject to change.

'. . . all things under, on, and over this earth.' There could hardly be a better description of Klee's own art, which is seemingly limitless in its range of subjects and themes. Probably no one has ever counted the proportion of the artist's more than 9,000 works which take nature as their subject, but a conservative estimate would put these at between one-quarter and one-third of the whole. And even this would not include those works in which nature's most complex creation – man – is Klee's true subject, any more than it would include the large number of works in which aspects of the non-living world are presented to us in a guise which ultimately owes its inspiration to nature. What it would include, however, would be a body of works in which few facets of the living world are left entirely unexplored and in which many never explored before by a creative artist are here made visible to us for the first time. From the amorous escapades of the mammals and birds to the procreative instincts of a single cell; and from the emotions of the fishes to those of the flowers – Klee's curiosity, accompanied by his brush or pen, encompassed all of these. No wonder that he was once moved to write of himself: 'I am God. So much of the divine is heaped in me that I cannot die.'[74] Much of the divine was indeed 'heaped' in Klee and is vouchsafed to us in his finest pictures. In these, as we shall see, Klee appears to have put himself in closer touch with the patterns and processes of creation than any other artist of our time. Like a medieval monk tending his kitchen garden – half mystic and half scientist – Klee left no stone in nature unturned and explored its every mystery and its slightest vibration without ever losing sight of the whole.

Few generalizations can be made about the course of Klee's development where his treatment of natural imagery is concerned; for once he had found his mature style virtually nothing was beyond his reach. For this reason most of his favourite natural themes may be found throughout his career and do not confine themselves to specific periods. There are, however, a few exceptions to this. Although Klee was the most impersonal of painters, occasionally facets of his own life may be found reverberating in his art. For instance, during the 1920s, when the form and behaviour of fishes so often served him as a useful pedagogical example, he created many of his most important fish pictures.[75] Similarly, Klee's depictions of fruits tend to fall into the following decade, when his own creative fruitfulness was a major preoccupation.[76] Sometimes, too, even the most trivial events in his life could affect the pattern of his art. Thus, among Klee's depictions of lions nearly one-third may be dated to 1933. This is explained by the fact that in this year the artist was living next to the Düsseldorf Zoo and was repeatedly awakened by the howling of these beasts at night.[77] But such coincidences are rarely to be discovered in Klee's art, which, at least until the last years of his career, obeys an internal logic which transcends the vicissitudes of his own life.

There are, nonetheless, some very broad trends which one may discover in this logic. Probably the most important of these is Klee's clear preference for the typical – rather than the individual – in nature. This was a preference which obviously accorded with his cosmic vantage point upon creation and which, appropriately enough, accounts for much of the universal appeal of his art. It explains why the birds which find their way into Klee's pictures are almost invariably just 'birds' and not 'sparrows' or 'peacocks', or why the word 'fruit' occurs as many as seventy times among the titles of his works and the words 'apple' or 'pear' no more than a dozen each.[78] Moreover, this was a preference which arose inevitably from Klee's search for the unifying characteristics which underlay the many subtly differentiated species of plants and animals one encountered in nature.

Yet another general trend which may be observed in Klee's art is his gradual progression from a macroscopic to a microscopic view of creation. This reveals itself in a tendency to concentrate upon the broader themes and patterns in nature during the 1910s and '20s and upon the individual elements of those themes in the following decade. Hence Klee's renderings of parks, gardens, and landscapes in general tend to predominate during the former period, whereas the separate inhabitants of those parks and gardens – the flowers, leaves, seeds, and fruits – tend to concern him during the later years of his career. Other than this, however, it would be unwise to attempt to put too rigid a framework around Klee's lifelong dialogues with nature except to note that they were truly encyclopaedic in range and encompassed the entire hierarchy of life. This will become immediately apparent in the next chapter, when a gradual progression down the evolutionary ladder of the animal kingdom will require us to stop at nearly every stage along the way.

Inseparable from Klee's many paintings and drawings of natural subjects was the central place occupied by nature in his teachings. By the artist's own admission his appointment to the Bauhaus in 1921 forced him to clarify and communicate ideas and methods which he had previously been applying unconsciously in his art;[79] and, as such, his pedagogical writings afford us a welcome insight into the theoretical principles which underlay many of his paintings of these years. Although many branches of knowledge or experience were at one time or another introduced into his teachings, the example of nature was always at the forefront of his thoughts and was regularly called upon to illuminate the most diverse problems in pictorial composition. As the greatest of all creators nature itself remained the best teacher – or, as Klee preferred to call it, 'the best school'.[80] But not far behind it was Klee himself, whose ability to instil into his students a sense of both wonder and respect for nature is attested to in countless tributes to his teachings.[81] Many of these remark upon the artist's rare ability to make his students see nature afresh – as though for the first time – from a view-point which (as one such testimony puts it) was 'exactly scientific' and yet 'thoroughly Klee-like'.[82]

In another account of Klee's classroom methods, Marianne Ahlfeld-Heymann recalls an instance when the artist requested his Bauhaus pupils to draw the form of a leaf. 'Several students smiled indulgently,' she notes, 'over this extremely simple exercise':[83]

Pacing slowly up and down, Klee said a few words, softly and with long pauses; thereupon all of us felt that we had never before seen a leaf, or rather *the* leaf, the essence of the leaf. He made us sense how life streamed through its main and subsidiary veins, how its form was determined by this, and how the cellular tissue embroidered itself lightly and yet firmly

like a net around the veins. . . . We felt this so strongly that the pencil
in our hands became heavy and we had to admit that the first thing we
had to do was to learn to see before we could draw another line.

Although Klee's desire to make his students penetrate to the essence of an
object in nature is already familiar to us, the passage quoted above also
introduces another of the central concerns of both his art and his teachings –
one which cannot be ignored in any account of Klee's approach to creation,
whether natural or otherwise. This was the stress which he placed upon
formation rather than form, or upon the forces and processes which ultimately
gave rise to a finished form in nature. For Klee all of creation was essentially
a matter of forming – of building and shaping primordial elements or ideas.
This alone was a living process, whereas the end result was, by comparison,
dead. To be sure, a careful study of nature's finished forms could often reveal
much about the processes which had brought them into being. But for the
creative artist the true lessons were to be learned by retracing the steps that
nature itself had taken in giving birth to its creations and by discovering those
factors, both internal and external, which had conditioned these.[84]

On one level Klee's concern with the phenomenon of formation arose from
a desire to introduce a temporal dimension into his art. For, to Klee, the visual
arts – like music – were essentially modes of expression which unfolded in
time;[85] and, as we shall see, any number of his pictures seek to encapsulate
more than one temporal moment in their treatment of a natural subject.[86] But,
on another level, Klee's desire to peer through a finished form to uncover the
forces which had shaped it arose from his firm conviction that all of nature's
inventions were ultimately composite creations and that, by reducing these to
their separate parts, one could come closer to an understanding of nature's
creative methods and apply these to one's own. Only in this way would the
relations between the parts and the whole of any organism be revealed to the
artist; and only in this way too would the relations between different organisms
disclose themselves to his inner eye. Through an analysis of the patterns and
principles which nature applied in building its forms the artist could thereby
come closer to understanding the economy and consistency which underlay
even the most diverse creations, from an apple to a snail-shell.

In his art, as in his teachings, Klee's search for the constituent parts of any
organism typically led him to reduce his own forms to a series of rhythmically
repeated units – to the visual equivalent, at least, of the single cell in nature.
The separate petals of a flower, the scales of fishes, the segments of a worm,
or the spirals of a snail (fig. 16) – in all of these Klee gleaned and laid bare
the structural blueprint which nature had followed in creating such forms.
When applied to his own pictorial methods Klee referred to this practice as
'Gliederung' or 'articulation' and proceeded to build up his works through the
varied repetition of basic, germinal elements, with the result that his pictures
often strike us as both disarmingly simple and endlessly inventive.[87] Like
nature itself, Klee's means remain economical and yet capable of infinite

variation, thus ensuring that he will produce works which possess a unity and diversity which mirrors that of the world about him.

Given Klee's belief that the deepest secrets of nature were only revealed when one penetrated to the primordial units out of which it had fashioned its own creations it is hardly surprising that he was most attracted to those organisms which revealed these with the greatest clarity. Unlike all other painters of nature before him Klee is most at home with the lowest forms of life. To be sure, nature's more complex and composite creations – trees, the higher mammals, or man himself – frequently occupy his creative attentions. But it is only when Klee descends below these – to a plant, a leaf, a snail, or a fish – that he succeeds in bringing us closest to the heart of creation. Here alone may nature's artistry be glimpsed in its purest state. And, accordingly, both in his art and his teachings Klee preferred to concern himself with those organisms which revealed most plainly to the naked eye the processes which had shaped their being. As the formative impulses in the living plant are more visible than those in even the lowest animals, these were preferred. But even within the animal kingdom itself there were distinctions to be made. For instance, the finished form of a worm or a fish revealed more of its formative history to Klee than did that of the higher animals. This explains why Klee's greatest meditations on nature often take as their subject the simplest beings. For the lower down the hierarchy of life Klee descended the closer he seems to have felt himself approaching the very centre of things – the moment of Genesis. And in one way or another all of Klee's approaches to nature were designed to bring him as close as possible to the day of creation itself. His search for the essence rather than the appearance of things; his quest for the invisible archetype behind the countless visible species to be found in nature; his desire to discover the unifying features linking even the most diverse beings; and his emphasis upon the processes of formation which had given rise to any living organism – all of these were directed towards returning him to 'the womb of nature, at the source of creation, where the secret key to all lies guarded'.[88]

Devoted student of nature though Klee undoubtedly was, the aim of all of these efforts was never an end in itself. Rather it was one which might eventually be turned to his own creative purposes, as Klee himself admitted in the practical advice which he offered to the teacher of a group of young art students in 1930. In addition to retracing the course of his own creative apprenticeship, Klee introduces us here to the greatest benefit which he imagined to be awaiting any artist from a lifelong descent into the 'womb of nature':[89]

As their talent develops guide your pupils towards Nature – into Nature. Make them experience how a bud is born, how a tree grows, how a butterfly unfolds so that they may become just as resourceful, flexible, and determined as great Nature. Seeing is believing – is insight into the workshop of God. There, in Nature's womb, lies the secret of creation.

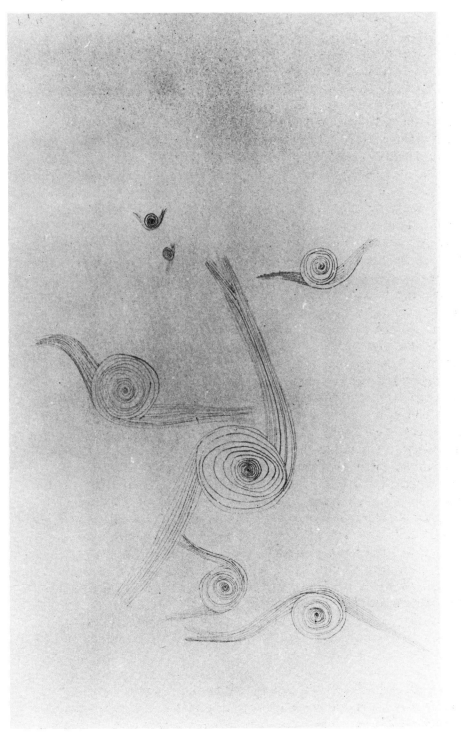

16
*Snails* 1926 Present whereabouts unknown

From this it may be seen that the true goal of Klee's explorations of the living world was that he might be able to create like it and to mirror in his own works something of nature's own resourcefulness and determination. This was an objective which he recurrently outlined for himself from his earliest years and which finds frequent expression throughout his writings. Perhaps the most obvious of these is Klee's favourite comparison between his own creations and nature's fruits. But scarcely less familiar are his many references to the similarities between birth in nature and in art, between the growth of a seed and that of a picture, and between the phenomenon of genesis as it underlies both creative realms.[90] In all of these Klee seeks to discover and apply laws which appear to him common to both nature and art. Having thus probed to the heart of the living world he now strives to emulate it in his own works and to give birth to pictures which are inspired not simply by nature itself but by that animating impulse which originally brought it into being.

Klee's most lucid account of this relationship is probably the famous comparison between the development of a tree and that of an artist in his lecture *On Modern Art*.[91] The artist, he observes, has studied the world about him and acquired a sense of direction within it. 'This sense of direction in nature and life, this branching and spreading array,' notes Klee, 'I shall compare with the root of the tree':

From the root the sap flows to the artist, flows through him, flows to his eye. Thus he stands as the trunk of the tree. Battered and stirred by the strength of the flow, he moulds his vision into his work. As, in full view of the world, the crown of the tree unfolds and spreads in time and in space, so with his work. Nobody would affirm that the tree grows its crown in the image of its root. Between above and below can be no mirrored reflection. It is obvious that different functions expanding in different elements must produce vital divergences. But it is just the artist who at times is denied those departures from nature which his art demands. He has even been charged with incompetence and deliberate distortion. And yet, standing at his appointed place, the trunk of the tree, he does nothing other than gather and pass on what comes to him from the depths. He neither serves nor rules – he transmits. His position is humble. And the beauty at the crown is not his own. He is merely a channel.

From this it is apparent that the role which Klee envisages for the creative artist is in many respects that of a disinterested purveyor of truth – of a philosopher or a scientist. Rooted and nourished by the world about him, he acts as an intermediary, giving rise to works which are shaped by his experiences of life and reflect these on a higher plane. In the process, however, he simply transmits – or, more properly, transmutes – the essential truths of nature into those of his own works, acting as a kind of medium through which the creations of nature may be filtered and reborn as art.

There can be no better reminder of the detached and crystalline stance which

Klee assumed in front of nature in his maturity than this comparison between the artist and that 'humble mediator',.[92] the trunk of the tree, whose task it is to convey substances from one realm to another, where they may give rise to new life. In Klee's very last years, however, much of this detachment is visibly broken down in a series of late images of nature which take a decidedly more personal turn. In these the once-crystalline Klee may now be seen to 'bleed', his invulnerability shattered by precisely those two adversaries he had feared and foreseen more than twenty years before – 'war and death'.[93] In the shadow of these Klee embarked upon the most urgent and productive phase of his entire career, creating more than 2,500 works during his last five years. In addition to reflecting the tragic course of his last illness and his growing premonitions of death, many of these also remind us that Klee's own despair and demise coincided with that of the world about him. Indeed, so fully does the artist himself appear to have sensed this that in 1933 – the very year in which the Nazis forced his exile from Germany – autobiography re-entered his art.[94] The mask had dropped. Henceforth the growing crisis both without and within would become the true substance of Klee's art. 'Is Europe limping or am I?' he enquired just a year after this, now safely resettled in Bern.[95] The truth is that both were – arm in arm.

That the works which Klee created during these years remain the most moving of his entire career – and among the most profound late works by any artist of our century – has rarely been disputed. But precisely because of their altered vantage point upon things they must be considered separately in any examination of Klee's art. Much that is already familiar to us from the earlier Klee is, to be sure, still to be found here. But, where the natural world in particular is concerned, many of Klee's favourite images are now refracted through so aberrant a lens as to emerge wholly new and, more often than not, deeply disturbing. Although Klee is too varied and resourceful an artist to invite sweeping generalizations, a confrontation with these final creations of his brush or pen makes it easy to see why one critic was moved to describe them all as 'Variations on the theme – "The End – period"'.[96]

It is not hard to interpret the style of the late Klee from an autobiographical point of view. Afflicted with an insidious and degenerative disease of the skin which slowly robbed him of his manual dexterity, he was gradually moved to work on an increasingly large scale and to evolve a means of expression of the utmost boldness and simplicity. Thus, in any number of the late paintings thick, black, hieroglyphic shapes lie fractured and strewn against a coloured background like dice cast to the winds (figs. 102, 107, 154). And in the even more numerous late drawings a terse and lumpy line slowly traverses the page to give birth to the ripe 'fruits' of Klee's late imaginings. In either case the abiding impression is one of a ruthless economy and of a new monumentality. A final testament couched in a language so powerful and portentous that it speaks to us of hitherto undisclosed truths and imprints itself indelibly on the memory.

And what is the message of these truths where Klee and nature are concerned? As will be seen from the ensuing chapters, these take many forms

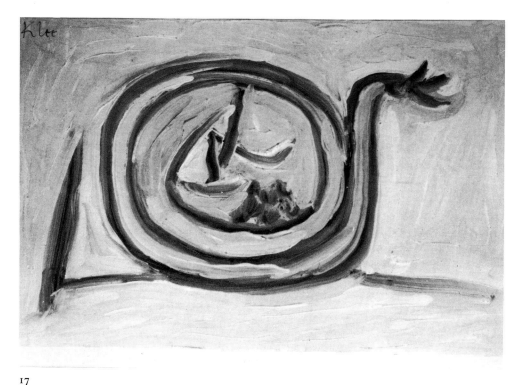

17
*Snail Post* 1937 Galerie Rosengart, Lucerne

and are not easily summarized. But a certain *tone* at least may be detected
running through them; and this is best characterized as a sudden awareness
of the more irrational elements and impulses in nature. Thus, whereas Klee's
earlier dialogues with the world about him had so often been directed towards
uncovering its underlying logic and reason, an overwhelming proportion of the
late works speak to us of the contrary. In one way or another Klee now
unleashes a demonic element in nature and seems to stand in awe – or even
terror – of it in his works. Nature's cruelty, its monstrousness, and its
mercilessness now become the artist's chosen preoccupations. Mutations and
metamorphoses of the most alarming kinds suddenly erupt onto his easel or
drawing-board; and in the process many of Klee's most beloved beings and
images now take on a dark and threatening shape.

Nowhere is this better demonstrated than in one of the artist's final
renderings of a snail (fig. 17). Now even this supremely harmless creature
appears transformed into an object of terror and malice as it strides the
landscape like a giant steamroller, relentlessly destroying everything in its path.
In yet another of Klee's late depictions of snails the shell of a conch lies broken
and scattered over the sheet, its parts slowly metamorphosing themselves into
ominously clenched fists (fig. 18). And, in an even later work of 1940 entitled
*Everything runs after!* (fig. 19), many of the artist's other favourite natural
companions appear similarly transformed. Here trees and fruits sprout legs and
feet and eagerly join the birds, beasts, and fishes in pursuit of a human victim

30

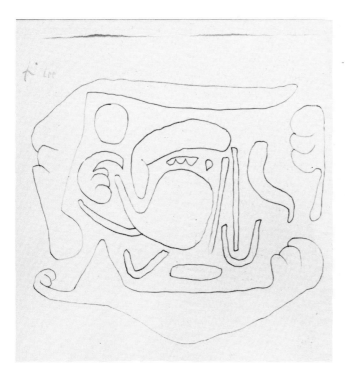

18
*Conch Still-life I* 1939
Kunstmuseum, Bern

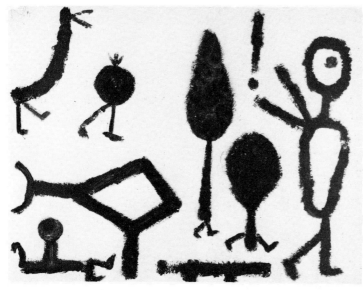

19
*Everything runs after!* 1940
Kunstmuseum, Bern

who struggles vainly to escape from them. When one remembers that these
selfsame beings were among Klee's chosen partners and playmates in his 1933
*The Animals' Friend* (fig. 9) it is impossible not to view this work as a distressing
sequel to that earlier drawing and to recognize in it a decidedly altered view
of life. Although it would be far too simple to characterize this new attitude
as one of fear, dread, or mere disillusionment, it was surely one of resigned
acceptance – acceptance of the fact that nature's laws and reason would forever

defy human understanding. Klee himself implies this in two lines added to his last painting just before his death in 1940: 'Should all therefore be known?' he asks. 'Oh, I think not!'[97] In the context of his profoundly valedictory late art these lines reflect that same mood of philosophical resignation before the mysteries of life as those appended by Beethoven to the concluding movement of his last string quartet: 'Must it be? It must be'.

If Klee's late art presents us with a new and sombre vision of the incomprehensibility of nature, his late writings remind us that he continued to find comfort in it to the last. Although such testimonies are often as terse as the pictorial language of the late Klee they leave one in little doubt that, even in the midst of those 'days of great struggle'[98] which his illness brought upon him, he never lost his delight in the unfolding spectacle of nature. Thus, in 1936 – a year in which the severity of Klee's condition made it impossible for him to create more than a handful of works – he wrote to Lily from Tarasp, where he was convalescing:[99]

> Yesterday we went to the Ofenpass and enjoyed the view down into the Münster valley. The flora of this early spring was simply delightful. Nature has not been disturbed there, not even dried wood has been collected. The animal world too is left to itself. To tell the truth there weren't many animals to be seen, though on the return journey we met two foxes in an exposed territory. The first of these was very beautiful, indignant over the disturbance and moved about three or four metres away and waited there until we – having stood still – had a good look at him. A crow was also close by.

In such a passage as this that ceaseless curiosity which had marked Klee's involvement with nature from the start remains fully in evidence – so much so that the passage could just as easily have come from the pen of the youth of fifty years before – the one who, in his turbulent adolescence, had confessed: 'Nature *does* love me! She consoles me and makes promises to me'.[100]

Right up to the end nature continued to make such promises to Klee, for whom the advent of a new year brought with it a fresh opportunity to free oneself from uncertainty and to turn one's strengths to 'fruitfulness'.[101] Eternal worshipper of the world about him, Klee even found time to record his delight in nature as he greeted his final change of season, in June 1940, at the end of what was to be his last journey to the sanatorium at Muralto-Locarno. 'I have travelled fairly well,' he writes, 'but I was grateful for the car in Bellinzona, especially as it was very humid there. From the north side I enjoyed the most enchanting pictures of spring.'[102] Just over two weeks later Klee died while gazing at one of the 'fruits' of that last spring – a bouquet of carnations, which subsequently became the only flowers to accompany him in death.[103]

# 2 · The Animal Kingdom

Franz Marc kept a large white sheep dog; his close friend Paul Klee, a succession of cats. According to Kandinsky, Marc's dog boasted a 'manner, strength of character, and mildness of disposition' which made him 'an exact four-legged copy of his master'.[1] Klee, on the other hand, was constantly being bemused and outsmarted by the wily antics of his beloved cats.[2] In their art, too, both men showed distinct preferences where the animal world was concerned. Thus Marc preferred to paint horses and deer, and Klee birds and fishes – or, among the higher animals, cats and camels. These clear differences between a temperament which sought strength and solace in nature and one which sought wonder and mystery were fully understood by Klee. In an entry in his diaries, written shortly after Marc's untimely death in 1916, he compared his own attitude towards nature with that of his departed friend and in the process provided us with one of the most illuminating of all accounts of his chosen vantage point upon creation. Marc, he observes:[3]

> is more human, he loves more warmly, is more demonstrative. He responds to animals as if they were human. He raises them to his level. He does not begin by dissolving himself, becoming merely a part in the whole, so as to place himself on the same level with plants and stones and animals. In Marc, the bond with the earth takes precedence over the bond with the universe.

In contrast, Klee admits that his own spirit is less warmly human and prefers to follow the latter course:

> What my art probably lacks, is a kind of passionate humanity. I don't love animals and every sort of creature with an earthly warmth. I don't descend to them or raise them to myself. I tend rather to dissolve into the whole of creation and am then on a footing of brotherliness to my neighbour, to all things earthly. I possess. The earth-idea gives way to the world-idea. My love is distant and religious.

> . . . I place myself at a remote starting point of creation, whence I state *a priori* formulas for men, beasts, plants, stones and the elements, and for all the whirling forces . . . There is no sensuous relationship, not even the noblest, between myself and the many. In my work I do not belong to the species, but am a cosmic point of reference.

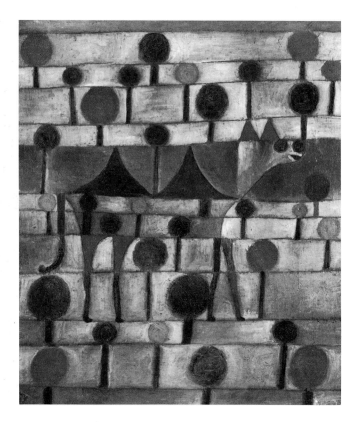

20
*Camel in a Rhythmic Tree
Landscape* 1920
Kunstsammlung Nordrhein-
Westfalen, Düsseldorf

In the art of these two masters this distinction between the earthly Marc and the cosmic Klee is apparent both in their choice of animal subjects and in their treatment of them. Where the first of these is concerned it need only be said that, whereas Marc confines himself almost exclusively to the higher and gentler beasts – that is, to those which may most readily be raised 'to his level' – Klee embraces a far wider range of creatures, moving from the highest to the very humblest types and showing a distinct preference for those species which are *least* susceptible to arousing warm and human sympathies. Thus, if the centre of Marc's animal universe rests with the docile, hooved mammals – the horses, cows, and deer – Klee's resides instead in the depths of the sea or the realm of the air, with the anonymous and mercurial fishes and birds. Marc's dog and Klee's cats here reveal much of the character of their respective owners; for whereas Marc derives comfort and companionship from his chosen pet, Klee is fated to a cold and piercing gaze which scrutinizes and yet keeps its distance – in short, to one which mirrors his own preferred outlook upon things. Little wonder, then, that Klee would hear nothing of keeping a dog for fear that he would become enslaved to it – or, as he himself put it, become merely 'a dog to one's dog'.[4]

These differences are also evident when the two artists treat similar subjects, as a comparison between Klee's *Camel in a Rhythmic Tree Landscape* of 1920 and Marc's *Mountain Goats* of 1913 will show (figs. 20 & 21). Even without

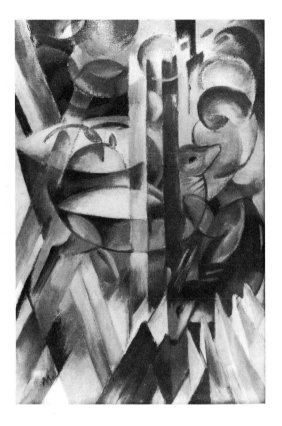

knowing anything of Marc's attitude towards nature it is hard to suppress an
empathetic response to his goats, with their generously swelling curves, their
soulful eyes, and their supplicating poses and expressions. As in all of the artist's
most characteristic works of these years, Marc's animals here appear ineluctably
bound to the rhythms of nature. Meekly and uncomprehendingly, they
surrender their destinies to its controlling laws and submit to a force which all
but dissolves them in their surroundings. Whether one finds this union between
creature and creation saddening or consoling, there can be no mistaking the
deep humanity of its author. 'I try to intensify my sensitivity for the organic
rhythm of all things,' wrote Marc of his artistic aims in 1908, 'I seek pantheistic
empathy with the vibration and flow of blood in nature – in the trees, in the
animals, in the air . . .'[5]

But what of Klee's *Camel*? Among his mature paintings it is as close as he
ever came to emulating Marc's many renderings of animal existence embedded
in the very fabric of nature. And although it is not as typical of Klee's art as
a whole as Marc's *Goats* is of his, its approach to this subject is fully in keeping
with Klee's more objective outlook upon creation. Thus, rather than presenting
us with a pantheistic rendering of the animal's oneness with its surroundings,
Klee transports his camel from its normally arid habitat to the middle of an
orderly grove and proceeds to uncover an ingenious series of visual puns
between portions of the camel's anatomy and features of the surrounding

landscape. Humps are now made to double as mountains, and eyes and legs to rhyme with the crowns and trunks of trees. Far from empathizing with this beast as it coexists with nature Klee prefers instead to turn a coolly analytical eye towards all aspects of his scene, penetrating beneath their very different exteriors to reveal their underlying similarities. To be sure, the result may here impress us more as an exercise in wry pictorial humour than as a solemn expression of Klee's philosophy of nature. But it at least demonstrates how the artist's reluctance to respond to animals in a purely earthly manner led him to confront them from a 'cosmic point of reference' – one which permitted him the maximum of visual and intellectual insight into his subject, and of emotional neutrality. Accordingly, if Marc's *Goats* immediately prompts us to wonder how his animals *feel*, Klee's *Camel* encourages us instead to consider how his animals *figure* in the broad and bewildering pattern of nature's creations to which they belong.

Klee's *Camel in a Rhythmic Tree Landscape* is also characteristic of the artist's general approach to the world of the higher animals in its very lack of profundity. Although Klee was to show a steady interest in animal subjects throughout his career, only rarely do they become a major concern of his art and, in further contrast to Marc, almost never do they provide him with the subjects of his most penetrating explorations of the world of nature. Given Klee's lifelong search for the archetypal in creation it is perhaps inevitable that this role was accorded instead to the lower animals and the plants, which appear to approach the more irreducible forms of life and which rarely invite those decidedly human responses so often lavished upon their higher relations. Fully aware of this temptation where the higher animals were concerned, Klee readily yielded to it in his art and preferred to depict such creatures as beings endowed with character, personality, and unashamedly human urges and emotions. Often, indeed, the higher animals enter Klee's art as mere substitutes for mankind itself. In such instances the artist typically draws his inspiration from those realms and activities where the human and animal meet, whether in the bustling surroundings of the circus or carnival or in the more sinister world of human bestiality. Sacred and performing animals, lecherous and malevolent animals abound in Klee's work.[6] But in all of these the artist prefers to remain more comic than cosmic in character, creating works which belong to what Grohmann called the 'outer circle' of Klee's levels of inspiration[7] – that is to say, ones which do not concern themselves with what the artist himself regarded as 'ultimate things'.

When one surveys the range of Klee's depictions of the higher animals several surprises present themselves. Considering the curiosity and fantasy which so often mark his works, Klee's interest in the mammalian world is both very limited and very orthodox. Moreover, it is also full of surprising omissions. For example, for an artist so fond of uncovering analogies between man and the other animals Klee pays little attention to the most nearly human of all beasts, the monkeys and apes.[8] For a native of Bern, he largely ignores the bears which gave his city its name and which still remain among its chief tourist attractions.

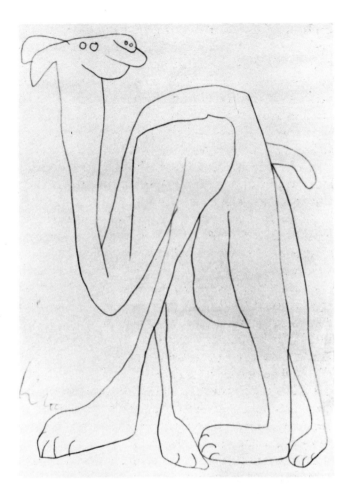

And for one renowned for his inexhaustible inventiveness Klee rarely concerns
himself with nature's more unusual inventions among the higher beasts. To be
sure, the occasional lion or elephant may be found in his work. But more often
Klee's desire to reveal nature at its most typical leads him to favour ordinary
domestic animals – horses, dogs, cows, and (above all) cats – and to cast these
familiar creatures in unfamiliar roles rather than to depict the unfamiliar itself.
A notable exception to this, however, is the camel, which we have already met
in a painting of 1920 and which is one of the few exotic species to make regular
appearances in Klee's art, beginning with his epoch-making Tunisian visit of
1914, when the artist drew at least one such beast.[9] Thereafter Klee showed
a recurring fascination with this creature and especially with its ungainly hump,
which seems to have appealed to him as an invention both supremely practical
and comical. Like another of Klee's favourite animal parts, the snail-shell, the
camel's hump distinguished this creature as a rare example of fortitude and
dogged self-sufficiency among nature's inventions. But in at least one later
drawing of this subject, the 1939 *And still a Camel* (fig. 22), Klee presents us
with a more searching account of this cumbersome creature, whose sunken

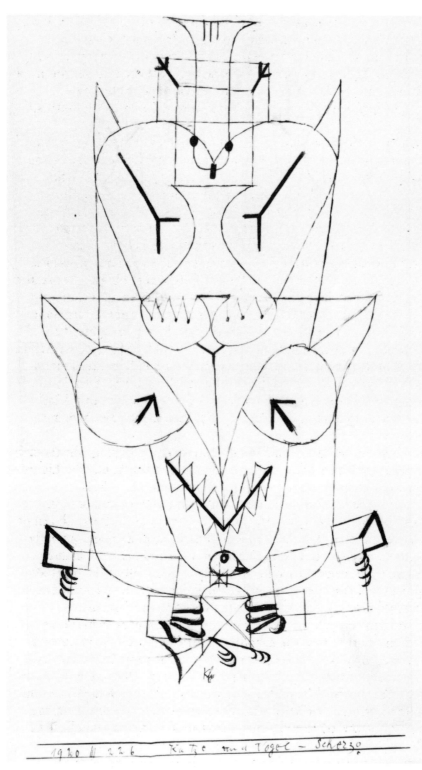

23
*Cat and Bird Scherzo* 1920 Kunstmuseum, Bern

hump and haunches now meet as it straddles the page, and who turns to view its dilapidated chassis as though preparing to bestow upon it one last lick – a kind of Rosinante among camels.[10] At a time in his art when so many earlier images were resurfacing metamorphosed into strange and alien shapes the artist may well have derived some comfort from the reappearance of this old companion of his Tunisian days, its constitution now flagging but its spirit still hopeful.

If Klee's delight in the droll silhouette of the camel owed itself to a specific event in his life the same cannot be said of his many depictions of cats. As one who is reputed to have worshipped his own cat as an Egyptian god,[11] who so readily admitted to giving his heart away to a mere 'mouser'[12] – and who confessed to wishing to be reborn a cat if forced to choose another life[13] – it is not surprising to find Klee celebrating this creature as everything from an idol to a confidant in his art. Yet far from always showing his cats in a favourable light Klee also acknowledged their cruel obsession with birds and, on several occasions, depicted them literally with birds on the brain in a manner reminiscent of the 1905 etching *Threatening Head*.[14] In one example, the 1920 pen drawing *Cat and Bird Scherzo* (fig. 23), two such feline persecutors come together to perform a malicious duet, one (at the top) lost in thoughts of an innocent bird which has already penetrated its skull; while below, its hands join forces with those of its partner to work the wings of a second feathered victim as though playing an accordian or reading a piece of sheet music. Even in so merely witty an invention as this Klee's objectivity before nature leads him to put aside all personal preferences in order to do justice to the true character of his chosen subject.

Apart from Klee's undeniable fondness for certain of the higher animals such creatures also figure more generally in a number of recurring themes in his art – themes which, while in no way central to his achievement, do at least demonstrate the diversity of his responses to mankind's closest relations in nature. Of these probably the least important is the motif of the horse and rider, a favourite preoccupation of Klee's childhood drawings, when it appears to be inspired by an infatuation with circuses and merry-go-rounds.[15] This theme re-emerges in the years around 1910 in a number of essentially light-hearted works, now presumably inspired by Klee's association with the *Blaue Reiter*, which took its name from the horse and rider subject,[16] and with his preparations for illustrating Voltaire's *Candide*, where the horseman theme provides one of the leitmotifs of the narrative.[17] Finally, it returns at the end of Klee's career in a remarkably synoptic drawing of 1940 entitled *When I rode on a Donkey* (fig. 24), with its poignant image of a solitary rider who now appears barely distinguishable from his steady mount. Although the title of this work once again suggests an earlier memory returning to haunt the artist, the theme of the journey towards an unknown destination is in fact a familiar one in late Klee.[18]

Far more important than the horse and rider subject are Klee's many renderings of the higher animals as symbols of the maternal and sexual instincts

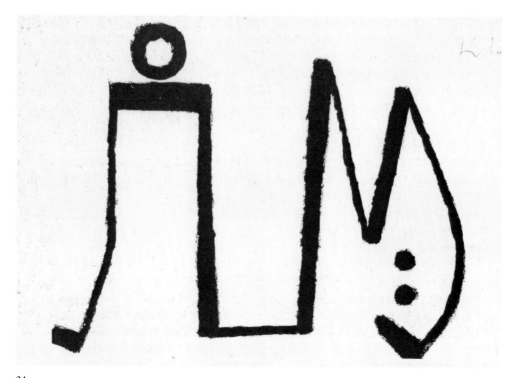

24
*When I rode on a Donkey* 1940 Private Collection, Rome

in nature. In these works, which begin early in Klee's career and may be found
intermittently to his very last years, familiar animals such as horses, dogs, and
bulls are typically accorded roles which mirror or caricature those of mankind
itself and thereby permit the artist to explore the essential animality of much
of human behaviour. Where the theme of maternity is concerned, this analogy
is only made explicit in such late pictures as the 1937 *Mother Animal* (fig. 25),
in which a dog-like creature dons both teats and human breasts and thereby
becomes an image of the maternal instinct as it pervades the mammalian world.
But a similar theme is already implicit in such earlier works as the 1906 *Beast
suckling her Young*[19] or the 1927 *Mother Dog with three Litters* (fig. 26). In both
of these a telling mixture of patience and vigilance in the tending of their infant
charges converts these creatures of ostensible bestiality into ones of pure
charity.

Bestiality, however, becomes the underlying concern of another notable
group of Klee's works involving the higher animals. This consists of those early
etchings and drawings in which fawning, lascivious beasts – half-hound and
half-stag – stand in for the male pursuer in a sexual relationship, courting the
attentions of half-modest females who offer them roses while coyly withholding
even greater prizes.[20] Klee's employment of this motif, which derives from
nineteenth-century images of saintly womanhood defiled by the bestial male,[21]

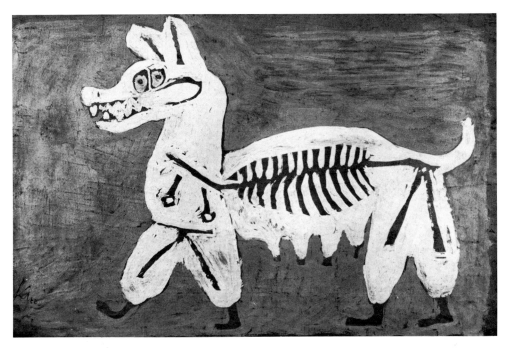

25
*Mother Animal* 1937 Kunstmuseum, Bern

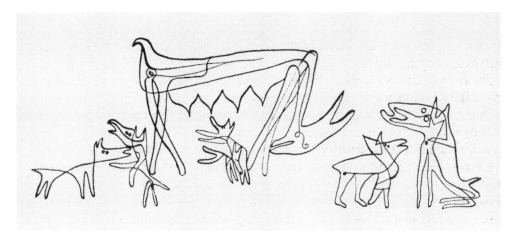

26
*Mother Dog with three Litters* 1927 Private Collection, New York

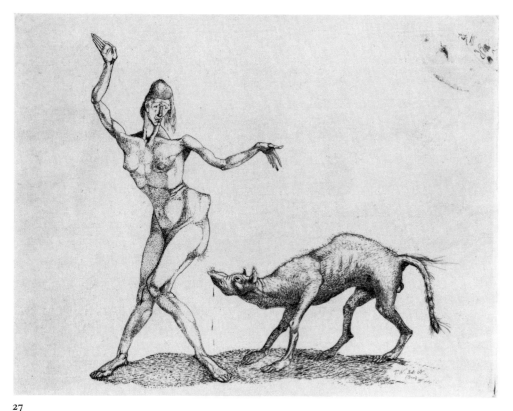

27
*Woman and Beast I* 1903 Etching

is aptly summarized in his own account of the 1903 etching *Woman and Beast* (fig. 27). 'The beast in man pursues the woman, who is not entirely insensible to it. Affinities of the lady with the bestial. Unveiling a bit the feminine psyche. Recognition of a truth one likes to mask.'[22]

Generally speaking Klee succeeded in masking this truth in his mature creations, when his own outlook on both art and life had significantly altered and when the procreative instincts in nature had come to have much deeper significance for him. Nevertheless, it does surface occasionally in such drawings as the 1926 *Stallion Taming* (fig. 28) and the 1929 *What a Horse!*,[23] where there can be little doubt that the figurative stallion of both works is none other than the lusting human male himself. But in what is perhaps Klee's last word on this subject – the 1937 *Donkey eating out of Hand* – the aged artist adopts a more conciliatory tone and prefers to celebrate the potential partnership, rather than the proverbial battle, between the sexes.[24]

Finally, among Klee's most characteristic roles for the higher animals there is one which may be directly related not to his own personal preoccupations but to those of his time. In the years immediately preceding the outbreak of the Great War the artist frequently drew wild beasts openly insulting, attacking,

42

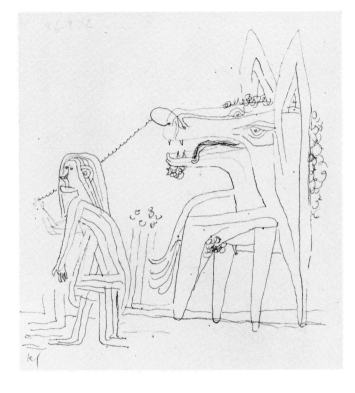

28
*Stallion Taming* 1926
Kunstsammlung Nordrhein-
Westfalen, Düsseldorf

and devouring their human victims, thereby converting a man-made disaster into a natural one and thinly disguising his own fears and hostilities at a moment of impending tragedy throughout Europe (fig. 29).[25] Unprepossessing though many of these works are they must be seen as Klee's own modest – but nonetheless deeply-felt – contribution to that general concern with the destructive impulses in nature through which so many artists of his time sublimated their own fear and despair on the brink of war. Rarely disposed to making autobiography the substance of his art Klee here couched his own anxieties in images of the eternal conflict between man and beast. But his message is nonetheless clear and speaks to us with redoubled force through its very unpretentiousness. Time and again in these works it becomes apparent that the artist wishes us to substitute mankind itself for these predatory beasts.

   With the coming of the Second World War, however, Klee forsook these unassuming exercises in anger made into art and gave vent to his feelings in a series of unashamedly personal works. One of these – the innocently entitled *Animal Fable* of 1933 (fig. 30) – takes as its subject the legendary Minotaur, which was also a favourite subject of Picasso during these years.[26] To be sure, the Minotaur was topical for other reasons in 1933; for it was in that year that the Surrealists first issued their journal *Minotaure* and, a year later, Klee himself was to become a contributor to the first *Minotaure* exhibition in Brussels.[27] Yet this coincidence alone may not account for the artist's sudden interest in this fabulous creature, which Picasso had seen as an image of either violence and

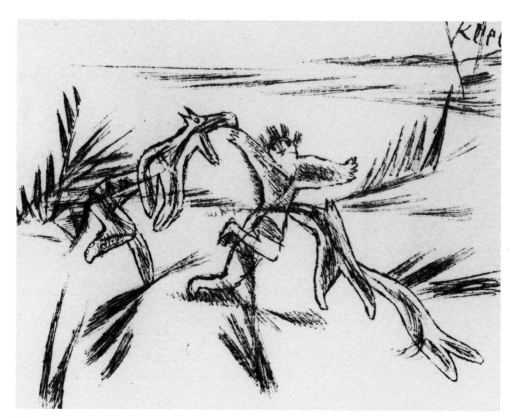

29
*Doing Battle with Beasts of
Prey* 1913
Private Collection, Switzerland

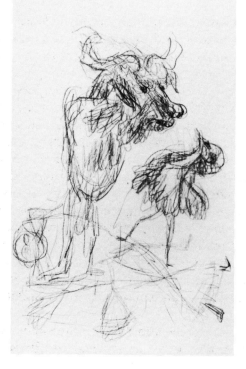

30
*Animal Fable* 1933
Kunstmuseum, Bern

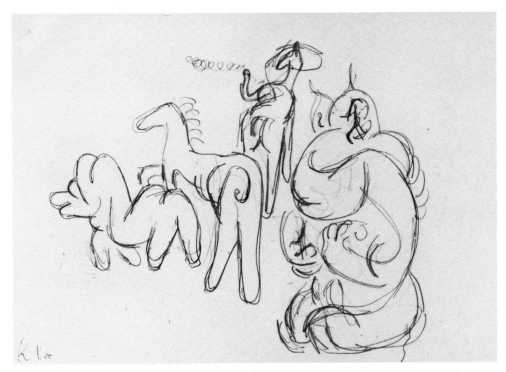

31
*Forgotten by Noah* 1939 Kunstmuseum, Bern

brutality or gentle domestication in nature. In Klee's own drawing, which was
made in the very year of his dismissal from the Düsseldorf Akademie, the
legendary beast crushes one victim and turns threateningly towards another,
leaving us in little doubt as to which view of the Minotaur is intended.

In Klee's late art, with its joint preoccupation with the realms of both heaven
and hell, the world of the higher animals plays a relatively small part. Yet in
his treatment of such subjects alone may be traced in miniature the growing
pessimism and disquietude of these concluding years. A drawing of 1939
entitled *Forgotten by Noah* (fig. 31) may serve to introduce us to the prevailing
mood of any number of these works. In this, four unidentifiable species – part-
hound and part-horse, part-lion and part-man – huddle together and gaze upon
nothingness. Stranded by the ark, they have now only to await the rising waters
of the Flood. Such mutant and composite animal types are characteristic of the
late Klee, whose art abounds in hybrid beasts – dog-lion-monkeys and bull-like-
cats[28] – which poignantly aspire ever higher on the evolutionary ladder and
yet appear destined instead only for an early extinction. As freak experiments
of nature they remain forgotten not only by Noah but by the original creator
himself.

Nowhere is Klee's preoccupation with such unfit species more apparent than
in his many late renderings of massive and literally tank-like animals, whether

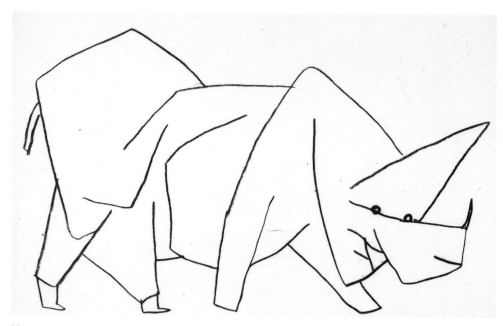

32
*Masked Rhinoceros* 1940 Felix Klee, Bern

real or imagined – creatures such as the rhinoceros (fig. 32), the steer, or the unnamed protagonist of *Entrepreneurial Beast*.[29] But this theme finds its fullest expression in a series of fourteen drawings of 1939–40 which take as their subject the now-extinct European aurochs, a wild ox which roamed the continent until the early seventeenth century, and which was described by Julius Caesar as showing mercy to neither man nor beast.[30] As such it would appear a fitting subject for an artist who once again found himself surrounded by a terrible war. But the drift towards death within Klee himself took precedence over such external events and led him to shower his customary late mercy upon this most merciless of beasts. Instead of presenting us with a brutal and fiercely combative creature Klee offers us a poignantly vulnerable one, preferring to depict the aurochs as fleeing or ageing, listening or indecisive, descending a mountain or tending its young – the last of these even calling to mind a Madonna and Child group (fig. 33).[31] In the face of its legendary power and ruthlessness, the artist – himself facing imminent extinction – thus concedes to this most belligerent of creatures qualities and frailties which had eluded its earlier chroniclers.

This new mood of compassion and tenderness is often to be met with in Klee's late art and gives to it precisely that quality of 'passionate humanity' which the artist himself had admitted to be lacking in the more cosmic and crystalline creations of his maturity.[32] And at least where the world of the higher animals is concerned this deep humanity is rarely more movingly

46

33
*URCHS and Offspring* 1939
Kunstmuseum, Bern

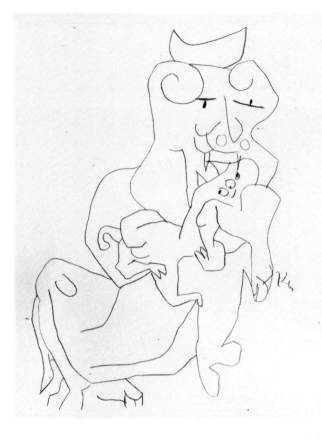

34
*An Animal will soon be happier*
1940 Kunstmuseum, Bern

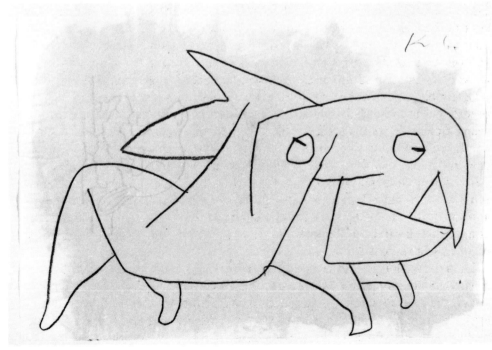

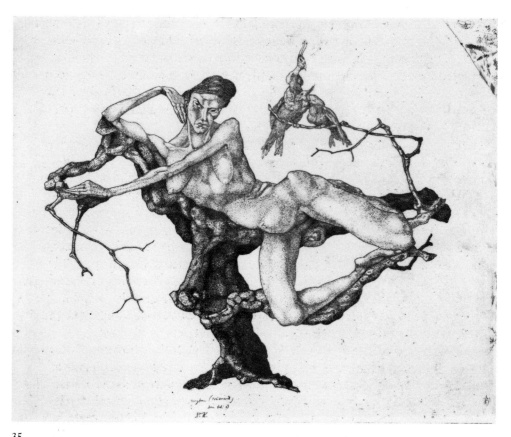

35
*Virgin in a Tree* 1903 Etching

expressed than in the ironically entitled *An Animal will soon be happier* of 1940
(fig. 34). For all its formidable defences, its imposing bulk, and its purposeful
gait, the anguished expression of this Panzer-cum-rhinoceros confesses to us
that the only happiness it will ever know will be that of being unburdened of
life itself. With images such as this Klee's lifelong explorations of the relations
between man and beast have come full circle. For having initially discovered
so much of the beast in man the aged artist has here come to uncover at least
as much of man in the beast.

When one moves from Klee's treatment of the world of mammals to that
of the birds one basic difference immediately presents itself; and as might be
expected from Klee it is one ultimately derived from nature itself. For all their
marvellous array of shapes and sizes birds must be admitted to share more in
common with one another than do their mammalian relations. Thus the general
body-type of a hummingbird or a blackbird more closely resembles that of an
ostrich than does the form of a mouse or a mole resemble an elephant.
Accordingly, whereas mammals are usually rendered as individual types or
species in Klee's art, the same is not so for birds. Here the artist prefers to

resort to two 'a priori formulas', one denoting the perching variety (with short legs and neck) and the other a more aquatic type (with longer legs and neck) – though, to be sure, there are variations within these. But rarely does Klee designate individual species of birds; and, as with the mammals, rarely does he show any interest in the more exotic or unusual varieties. Rather he prefers to treat the bird kingdom generically and jealously safeguards the essential anonymity of its members in his creations.

That nature itself encourages one to think of birds in this way may partly explain why Klee's depictions of them arguably surpass his renderings of mammals in both quality and interest. As creatures whose form and behaviour invite a more universal treatment, birds were to become (along with fishes) Klee's preferred animals – truly cosmic creatures whose bird's-eye view of the world perfectly accorded with the artist's own. But, in addition to this, Klee's involvement with the realm of the birds may be explained in much simpler terms. The artist's son, Felix, has admitted that his father was bewitched by birds and flowers[33] – two themes which inspired some of his greatest paintings. Nor may Felix's pairing of these two facets of creation be purely fortuitous; for Klee's art often suggests to us that he regarded birds as the flowers of the animal kingdom – as bright, beautiful, elusive, and invariably good.

Birds figure prominently in Klee's art as early as his first drawings from nature.[34] Thereafter, in the 1903 etching *Virgin in a Tree* (fig. 35), a pair of birds wilfully indulge their sexual appetites in ironic contrast to the sexual self-deprivation of Klee's atrophied virgin – a contrast which the artist himself described as a 'critique of bourgeois society'.[35] Such a work cannot help but recall the reclining nymphs of Cranach, an artist whom Klee had especially admired on a visit to the Uffizi in 1902.[36] Like Klee's virgin, these proudly proclaim their own chastity while at their feet a pair of those allegedly most over-sexed of birds, the partridges, give the lie to such protestations.[37]

In another early etching, *Hero with a Wing* of 1905, Klee mocks man's attempts to fly like the angels[38] just as, at the opposite end of his career, in *More Bird than Angel* of 1939,[39] he would contrast the merely earthly powers of flight in birds with those of their divine counterparts. Yet for Klee even a semblance of such powers was sufficient to earn for the birds – more than for any other of nature's creations – a place close to the angels. This is made clear to us in two closely related paintings of 1934, *Aviatic Evolution* and *Angel in the Making* (figs. 36 & 37).[40] In these the raw materials out of which either birds or angels may be born take on a similar shape, with only the head and arrow of Klee's embryonic bird and the cross and sun of his future angel distinguishing between a creature destined to a corporeal and essentially earthbound existence and one which will be elevated to the realm of pure spirit. When one remembers that Klee himself sought a final resting place 'beside an angel of some kind',[41] it may not be too fanciful to suppose that he envied the birds, whose wings made it possible for them to ascend at least half-way to heaven. Certainly their ability to free themselves from earthly constraints had already won Klee's admiration as early as this poem of 1902:[42]

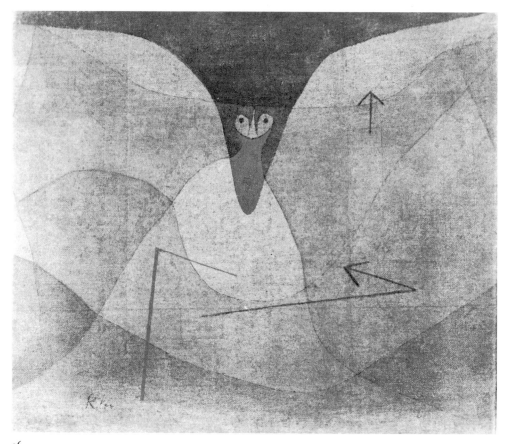

36
*Aviatic Evolution* 1934 City Art Museum of Saint Louis

At the sight of a tree
One envies the birds
They avoid
Thinking of trunk and roots
And self-complacently swing with agility the whole day long
And sing on the topmost branches.

With the formation of his mature style Klee employs birds even more freely and imaginatively, though not always without obvious symbolic intent. Thus, in 1917, in the midst of the Great War, he devotes a series of works to the favourite bird of the German lyric poets, the nightingale, which also figures in a poem by Klee of this year.[43] In both his poem and his pictures Klee follows his Romantic predecessors and discovers a bitter-sweet mixture of solace and sorrow in the nightingale's soothing song. Yet at the same time as Klee was seeking refuge from the war in the image of this bird 'not born for Death' he was also acknowledging the birds in general as one of the indirect causes of the

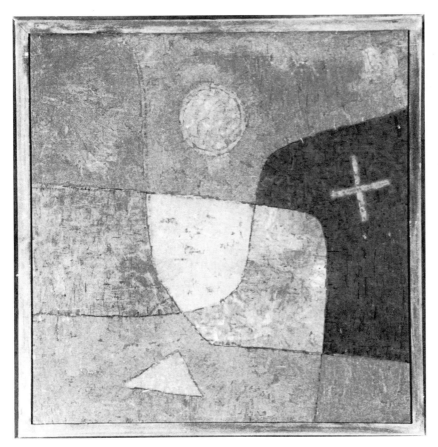

37
*Angel in the Making* 1934 Felix Klee, Bern

holocaust surrounding him. In 1918, shortly after leaving the air corps, he paid
tribute to these creatures as an inspiration to the development of the airplane
in such works as *Bird Planes*;[44] and, in an even more sinister drawing of the
following year entitled *Battle in the Sky* (fig. 38), Klee turned his bird-planes
against their very begetters – the plain-birds – and depicted them remorselessly
piercing their innocent victims through the heart. The hidden irony of both
of these works only becomes apparent when one compares them with the more
beneficial roles to which Klee was putting his diving birds during these same
years. One of these is the supremely hopeful *Flower Myth* of 1918 (fig. 39) in
which a strikingly similar bird descends upon a seductive blossom which
proffers a large, ripe fruit – the whole inevitably calling to mind the bounty
and harmony of nature. Now no longer employed as an instrument of death
and destruction Klee's bird here fulfils its more natural role as a begetter of
new life.

    Also in 1918, the traditional role of the dove as a harbinger of peace becomes
the subject of *Descent of the Dove* (fig. 40), with its radiant image of a white

38
*Battle in the Sky* 1919
Present whereabouts unknown

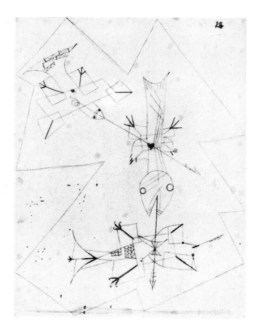

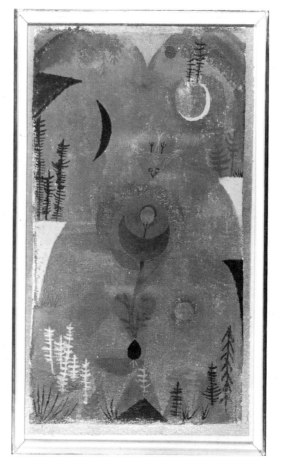

39
*Flower Myth* 1918
Kunstmuseum, Hannover

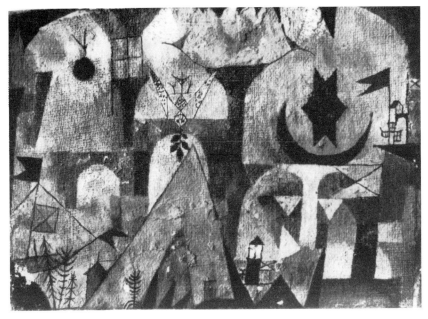

40
*Descent of the Dove* 1918 Present whereabouts unknown

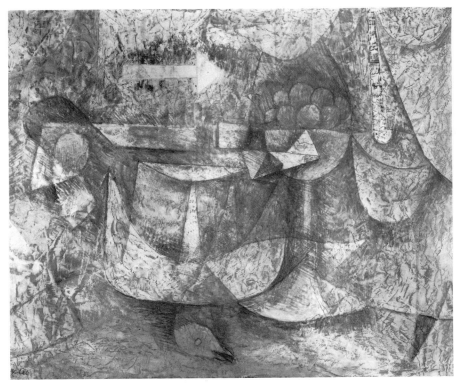

41
*Still-life with a Dove* 1931 Private Collection, USA

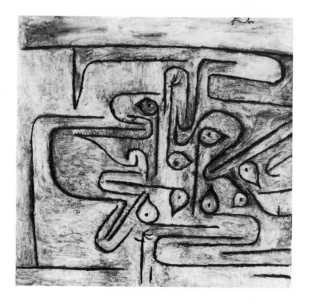

42
*War of the Birds* 1935
Private Collection, Switzerland

dove swooping down upon a welcoming landscape and bearing an olive branch
in its beak to restore peace to Europe in the year of the Armistice. But, by 1931
– the year of Klee's own enforced flight from Dessau – the warlike theme
returns in the deeply moving *Still-life with a Dove* (fig. 41). Now the dove's
descent is tragically interrupted by an arrow which shoots through the air and
brings its victim down mortally wounded, its head already blue with the pallor
of death – a horrifying premonition of countless fallen to come. And Klee
pursues this theme in his 1935 *War of the Birds* (fig. 42), where the
dismembered bodies of a community of birds lie embedded in thick paint like
dead soldiers in the mud. 'When even the traditionally peaceable birds choose
to make war,' the artist seems to ask, 'is there any hope left for man?'

Apart from these more obviously topical uses for birds Klee's interest in them
tends to centre around their gregarious habits and their miraculous powers of
flight and song. The former, for instance, is made the subject of any number
of depictions of travelling and migratory birds;[45] though on occasion it is
fleeing – rather than flying – that really seems to concern the artist.[46] Closely
related in style, though not in meaning, to these light-hearted burlesques on
the ways of the birds is an extraordinary drawing of 1922 entitled *Attempt at
a Development of Flight* (fig. 43).[47] In this Klee appears to retrace the
evolutionary history of the birds from a cumbersome and flightless ancestor
through two intermediary stages until he has sufficiently simplified and stream-
lined their anatomy to make them fully air-worthy. Although Klee's evident
interest here in the origins of nature's creations was one shared by certain of
his contemporaries, his unique understanding of the evolutionary process which
gave rise to the birds becomes clear when one compares his 1922 drawing with
André Masson's *Birth of the Birds* of 1925 (fig. 44).[48] In the latter, which is
a prime example of the 'automatic' drawings of the Surrealists, feathered
existence arises out of nothingness, as though created from the chaos of Genesis

54

43
*Attempt at a Development of Flight* 1922
Present whereabouts unknown

44
*Birth of the Birds* by André Masson 1925
Collection, The Museum of Modern Art, New York, Purchase

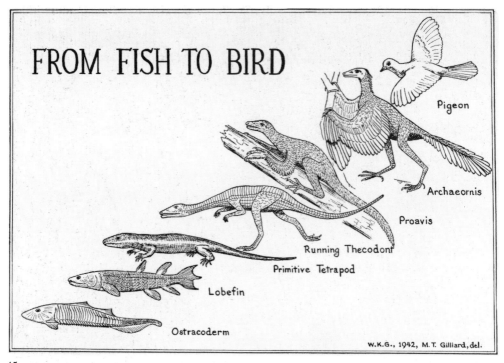

FROM FISH TO BIRD

Pigeon

Archaeornis

Proavis

Running Thecodont

Primitive Tetrapod

Lobefin

Ostracoderm

W.K.G., 1942, M.T. Gilliard, del.

45
*From Fish to Bird* Photo courtesy of The American Museum of Natural History

rather than through a logical process of natural selection and variation. As such, Masson's image evokes that state of ferment which preceded the very birth of nature itself. Klee, on the other hand, shuns such a theory of spontaneous generation for the birds and prefers one based on sounder scientific evidence. Thus his birds arise not out of a primordial ether but by a process of gradual evolution from their nearest relations, the land-bound reptiles. To be sure, Klee's drawing might still find no place in a textbook on the origin of the species. But, as is so often the case with his works, the principle which it outlines would be immediately recognizable to the writers of such works (fig. 45).

Perhaps Klee's most characteristic treatment of birds is as the garrulous and gregarious inhabitants of an enchanted sea- or landscape, where they serve as bright, scattered accents against the duller tones and repeated rhythms of their surroundings. Among such works are *Water Birds* of 1919, *Exotic River Landscape* of 1922, and *Bird Garden* of 1924.[49] The masterpiece of this group, however, is probably the well-known *Landscape with Yellow Birds* of 1923 (fig. 46), an elegantly decorative work which artfully transcends the bounds of mere decoration through two small, and probably last-minute, additions. Painted on two sheets of paper laid side by side, this little picture cunningly gives over the small space between them to its two most fanciful and realistic

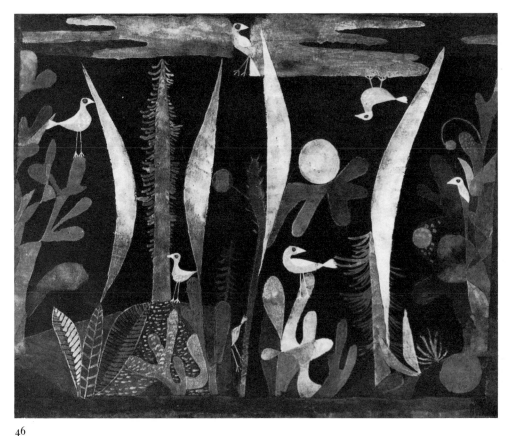

46
*Landscape with Yellow Birds* 1923 Private Collection

touches. At the top a bird has strayed into thin air, its spindly legs apparently resting on nothing, and is held in place only by the edges of paper to either side. And at the bottom another bird slips unceremoniously out of view, its legs and tail only just visible – a motif which adds a slightly ominous note to the proceedings. No longer just an enchanted landscape, the pristine setting of Klee's picture now seems to pose a threat for its innocent and unwary visitors. Admittedly, this is here very much underplayed. But the same cannot be said for the 1939 sequel to this picture, *Birds in a Water Park* (fig. 47), where, despite the innocuous title, it is hard not to see this landscape as fraught with perils. Now three birds wander aimlessly amidst trees whose leaves and branches have become almost obscenely humanoid breasts and limbs, seemingly lying in wait to engulf their hapless victims.

Along with any number of the works already discussed Klee's *Birds in a Water Park* suggests that the artist regarded birds not only as among the most gifted and innocent of nature's creations but also as among the most victimized – whether by cats, arrows, trees, snakes, or man. Where the last of these is

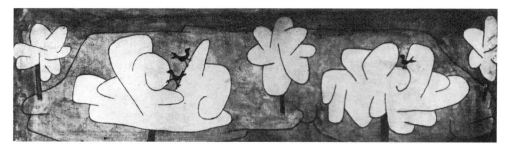

47
*Birds in a Water Park* 1939 Present whereabouts unknown

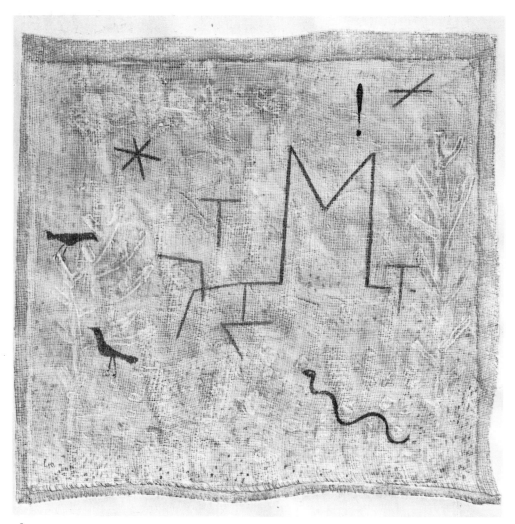

48
*Garden Gate M* 1932 Kunstmuseum, Basel

concerned it is worth noting that the adolescent Klee was himself not above inventing traps for the birds – though, once caught, he would always set them free.[50] Years later Klee devised a bird trap of another kind in the form of that quartet of mechanical birds which adorn his famous – and only superficially humorous – *Twittering Machine* of 1922.[51] As Maurice Shapiro has observed,[52] these wire birds are nothing other than decoys placed above a trap and programmed to warble in the hope of luring real birds to their deaths below. And, as for the theme of snakes and birds, these figure in the unnerving *Garden Gate M* of 1932 (fig. 48). Here a pair of birds play in a garden paradise oblivious to the presence of a serpent which stealthily advances towards them to commit that murder (*Mord*) which has given this garden its name. The whole inevitably calls to mind that very first garden – Eden – and those original victims of the serpent's wrath, Adam and Eve.

In Klee's late works birds make infrequent appearances in many of the guises already discussed, whether as lovers, sociable beings, or merely attractive adornments to a background of land or sea.[53] Occasionally, too, as in the 1939 drawing *The Vulture has Him*,[54] they take on a more malevolent role as predators upon man and thereby reflect the doom-laden atmosphere of so much of late Klee. In a no less disturbing drawing of this same year entitled *Earth-Sky Amphibian* (fig. 49) Klee returns to the theme of avian evolution, previously

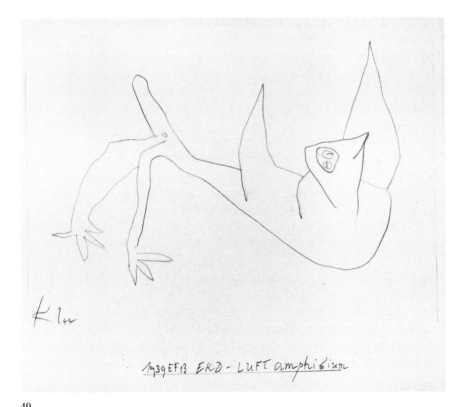

49
*Earth-Sky Amphibian* 1939 Kunstmuseum, Bern

set out so logically for us in the 1922 *Attempt at a Development of Flight*. Now, however, the monster which greets our eyes bears more in common with those tragically mis-shapen and malformed late mammals of these same years – a creature whose head and torso yearn to soar heavenwards but whose feet remain firmly implanted in the ground. The result is a being of neither progress nor privilege, but only of unbearable pathos.

As with his late renderings of mammals, Klee's late birds frequently reveal a preoccupation with extinct and degenerate species and especially with types which now wear their feathers more as a burden than as a passport to freedom. Thus, in two works of 1937 – *Water Tower Bird* and *Extinct Bird* (fig. 50)[55] – Klee portrays a species which most closely resembles the present-day pelican. With their thick necks and heavy limbs such creatures seem to represent a dying breed comparable to the aurochs which the artist was also depicting during these years – in short, a creature whose sheer bulk ultimately rendered it more defenceless than defensive. Indeed, a glance at either of these works or at the related *Water Birds* of 1939 (fig. 51) immediately suggests that, whereas the young Klee had so often equated the realm of the birds with that of the air and the airplane, the dying artist now sees them instead as mere vessels adrift on the sea. The comparison with boats and ships, which are a constant concern of Klee's final years,[56] is unmistakable and lends to these works an added poignancy. For, having previously revelled in the apparent victory of the birds over the forces of gravity, the late Klee now grounds his birds, firmly rooting them to the constraints and vicissitudes of a life confined to either land or sea.

In addition to birds Klee's single greatest love among the animals was the fishes, which furnished the subjects for a large body of works spanning his entire career, many of them among his supreme masterpieces.[57] Nor may this relationship be purely coincidental, for birds and fishes share certain general features usually denied to their higher relations. For one, they are typically much more colourful and thus might understandably have appealed to one of the finest colourists among modern painters. In addition, both birds and fishes inhabit realms traditionally denied to man and the higher beasts; and, given Klee's love of the more esoteric aspects of nature it is not surprising to find him relishing the opportunity to don feathers or fins through his art and thereby to cohabit, however briefly or vicariously, with these privileged inhabitants of the air or sea. Moreover, such a privilege may also have appealed to the artist on a more purely aesthetic level, for it is well known that Klee sought to free not only himself but his creations from 'earthly bonds'[58] and to endow them instead with a sense of truly dynamic movement – that is to say, of movement not subject to the laws of gravity. As the artist himself admitted such movement was possible in the atmospheric and watery zones.[59] These alone brought one into closer contact with cosmic space through their liberation from the forces of gravity – a belief which may well have fostered Klee's love of the inhabitants of these two zones and led him to endow them with truly cosmic significance in his art.

50
*Extinct Bird* 1937
Kunstmuseum, Bern

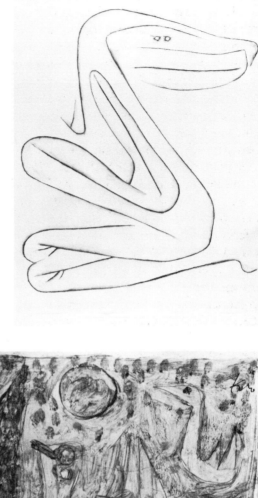

51
*Water Birds* 1939
Present whereabouts unknown

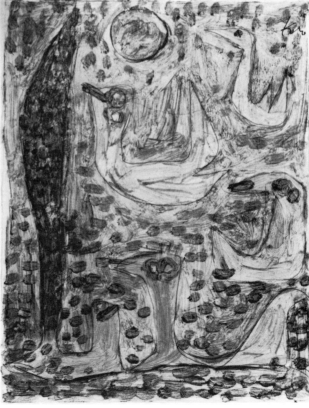

52
*Fishes and Birds* 1915  Present whereabouts unknown

Beyond this, Klee's affection for birds and fishes may owe something to the
fact that both classes of beings share an apparent simplicity of outer shape
together with an equally apparent anonymity which it is harder to attribute to
the higher animals but which would understandably have appealed to Klee's
detached and crystalline vantage point upon nature. This aspect of their appeal
is made ingeniously apparent to us in a drawing of 1915 entitled *Fishes and Birds*
(fig. 52) in which the same basic shape serves to evoke both classes of beings
and a mere change of direction suffices to distinguish them. Finally, where
fishes at least are concerned, there is a much less hypothetical reason for Klee's
attachment to these creatures: namely, that for much of his life he was a keen
fisherman and that, from at least as early as his visit to the Naples Aquarium
in 1902, he was an equally keen observer of undersea life.

One year before this visit, in the spring of 1901, Klee created a series of
boldly designed watercolours on the theme of fishes and fishing which are his
earliest works to be devoted to any single group of animal subjects.[60] Although
the sinuous linear rhythms of these works owe much to the inspiration of both
Japanese art and the *Jugendstil*, the treatment of the fishes themselves is already
pure Klee. With that sardonic wit so often encountered in his early works,
Klee's fishes here emerge as drolly human creatures – scowling, leering, kissing,
or simply indulging in one last meal before being wrenched from the sea to
provide a meal for another (fig. 53). Indeed, in several of these pictures one
can already detect a concern with that general theme of the interdependence
of the species which was to form the basis of certain of Klee's most mature
and symbolic fish pictures.[61] Thus, the presence of a baited worm or a smaller
fish which itself provides food for a larger one together with the inclusion of
the hook and tackle establishes a three-stage progression from worm to fish and
fish to man which appears with such consistency throughout this group of works
that it can hardly be accidental. Underlying even such seemingly witty creations
as these, then, Klee may well have concealed a darker message.

Klee's tendency to describe these early fishes in purely human terms also
characterized his first great revelations of undersea existence at the Naples
Aquarium in March 1902. Suddenly overwhelmed by the beauty and

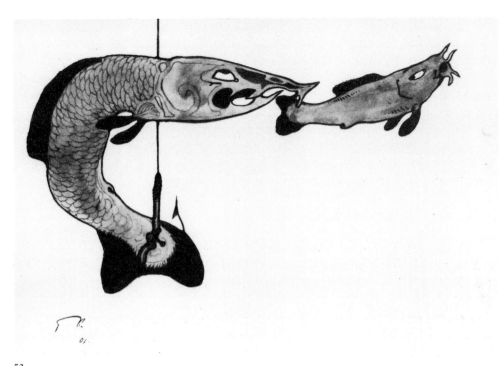

53
*Two Fish, one on the Hook* 1901 Felix Klee, Bern

strangeness of the world there unfolded to him, he was initially led to see it
only in relation to his own. An octopus stared out at him like an art dealer with
'compromising familiarity, as if I were a new Böcklin and he a second Gurlitt';
and sedentary species covered to their ears in sand reminded him of 'humanity
sunk in its prejudice'.[62] But as the wonders of this new realm of polyps and
starfishes revealed themselves to him, Klee gradually came to see them more
objectively. A blissful creature bathed in light swam towards him and seemed
'purer than any being I could have imagined in Paradise'. 'At length my
thoughts turned to religion,' Klee continued, 'and I admired the extravagance
of its god-like fantasy while questioning the purpose of such forms and colours
in a realm denied to man. That was arrogance.' It was an arrogance of which
the mature Klee was never to be guilty. Abandoning his own rod and tackle
in mid-life, when he apparently found the notion of catching and killing fishes
abhorrent,[63] Klee moved now to regard them as creatures possessing a place,
purpose, and dignity all their own. And increasingly that place came to be at
the very centre of things.

Among Klee's more straightforward fish pictures the majority form an
obvious counterpart to his many sea- and landscapes with birds. As in the latter,
a group of luminously painted fishes are depicted against a sombre background
as colourful and animated blossoms of an alien realm. In such works his
principal delight in these creatures seems to be with their relatively simple

shapes and with their tendency to swim in groups – a feature of fish behaviour which readily lent itself to the creation of works of great decorative beauty. Hand in hand with such works, however, Klee also devoted a number of his most mysterious paintings to fishes, among them *The Goldfish* and *Fish Magic* of 1925 and *Around the Fish* of the following year (figs. 161, 162, 169). As these deeply symbolic works far transcend Klee's more orthodox images of animal life, they are best discussed elsewhere.[64] But even from a glance at them here it becomes apparent that Klee accorded to fishes a very special place amongst nature's creations. Simple of shape and bold of hue, seemingly unhampered in their movements, and passing their secretive lives out of sight of much of the rest of nature, they appear to have been seen by the artist as among the most fortunate and liberated of beings.

Although Klee was never moved to set out his ideas on fishes in writing it is tempting to imagine that, had he done so, they would have taken a form similar to that put forward by Walter in Robert Musil's *The Man without Qualities*. For Walter every human being had his correspondence in an animal – some in birds and others in fishes. Walter identified himself with the latter, though Klee might well have chosen either. But Walter's reasons for being particularly drawn to fishes would surely have been appreciated by Klee:[65]

> Today he would perhaps have been able to answer that the magic of fish lay in the fact that they did not belong to two elements, but rested entirely in one. Again he saw them before him, as he had often seen them in the deep mirror of the water, and they did not move as he himself did, upon solid ground, along a surface that was its own frontier to the empty sphere of the second element. ('At home neither here nor yonder!' Walter mused, elaborating the thought in this direction and that, 'belonging to an earth with which one shares no more than just that little space taken up by the soles of one's feet, and with all the rest of one's body rearing up into air – an element through which the unsupported body would fall, an element one has to displace in order to be there at all!') No, fishes' ground and air and drink and food, their fear of enemies, and the shadowy passing of their loves, and their grave – it all enclosed them. They moved in that by which they were moved, in a way that man experienced only in dreams, or perhaps in the yearning desire to be restored to the sheltering tenderness of the maternal womb . . .

Cynics like Walter's wife Clarisse might well reply that such features simply made fishes 'the great middle class of the watery kingdom'. But for Walter and (one suspects) for Klee they would appear to have been seen instead as the great middle class of creation itself. Coming just half-way up the hierarchy of animal beings, they could be regarded as ideal representatives of this entire kingdom – as whole, pure creatures whose self-contained and unspectacular lives made them perfect embodiments of average nature.

In keeping with this attitude towards fishes Klee was rarely if ever disposed

54
*Underwater Garden* 1939
Private Collection, Switzerland

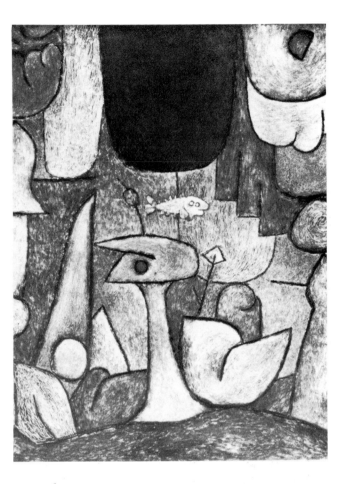

to treat them individually in his mature art. But the same cannot be said of his last fish pictures. Now, in his more personal late manner, Klee frequently presents us with one or two fishes boldly filling the picture space and depicted literally 'out of water' and thereby already dead.[66] Indeed, even when he returns his late fishes to the sea the ominous mood prevails. In *Underwater Garden* of 1939 (fig. 54), for instance, Klee penetrates to the bottom of the sea to spy on the life of a single, lonesome fish. One's sympathies are immediately aroused at the sight of this spindly creature lost in a world whose surroundings seem to conceal a lurking danger. Painted in a raw and easily detectable pink Klee's solitary fish uneasily navigates its way through an undersea garden so overgrown and so overpoweringly blue that it gives the impression of being an elaborate trap set by nature itself to lure and ensnare those seduced by its intoxicating richness and beauty. Along with any number of Klee's other late renderings of nature the setting of his *Underwater Garden* is so hypertrophied in form as to remind us less of natural than of monstrous growth. Adding to this impression are its vivid and yet lacklustre hues, which ultimately strike the eye as simply toxic.

The protagonist of this picture is also representative of any number of Klee's

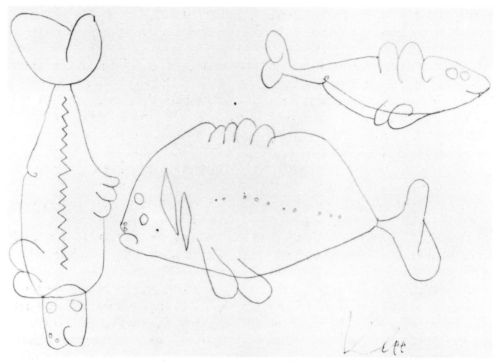

55
*Three Fishes* 1939 Kunstmuseum, Bern

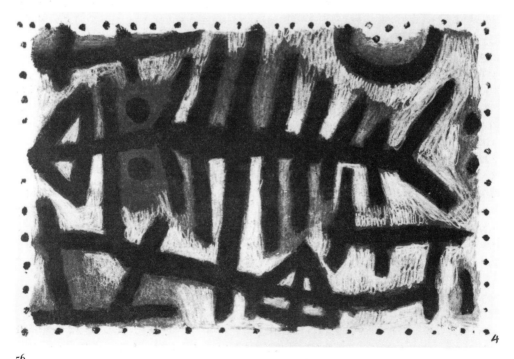

56
*Mud-Louse Fish* 1940 Private Collection, Switzerland

66

late fishes through its very primitiveness. Although Klee had seldom been moved to designate the species of his fishes throughout his career, in his last works the most frequently encountered types are those degenerate varieties one associates with the unexplored regions of the deep-sea bed. Bloated, armoured, and spiky in form, they most readily call to mind such living fossils as the coelacanth, and in this respect they parallel the aged artist's obsession with extinct species and call to mind the origins, rather than the aspirations, of the fish kingdom as a whole (fig. 55).[67] This preoccupation is confirmed in a handful of late works – among them *Caterpillar Fish* and *Mud-Louse Fish* of 1938 and 1940 (fig. 56)[68] – where, as the titles themselves suggest, Klee creates a transitional race of creatures, part-fish and part-insect. Although such organisms can never have existed the artist's fascination with such primitive creatures is consistent with much that we have already seen. Moreover, the notion of a degenerate species which perished through a cruel and yet inevitable process of natural selection was one which was tragically relevant to Klee himself at this time.

Other than birds and fishes Klee's favourite artistic subjects among the lower animals were snakes, snails, and certain types of insects. Although it would be wrong to assume that all three of these groups appealed to him for the same reasons, it is worth noting that they do bear certain features in common which an artist of Klee's leanings might have found especially intriguing. Like many of the lower animals their external anatomy reveals – or at least appears to reveal – a good deal about their internal structure; and given Klee's desire to penetrate to the essence, rather than merely the appearance, of objects in nature they may well have struck him as notable examples of organisms in which essence and appearance were virtually the same. For all three appear to be composed of a series of repeated units or segments which render them relatively self-explanatory and make it seemingly easy to retrace the course of their development. Indeed, when viewed externally at least, snakes, snails, and Klee's favourite insects – lice – all give the impression of having evolved solely through a process of accretion; that is to say, of increasing in size or length merely by the duplication of like parts. Once again this is something which cannot be claimed for mammals and birds but which has a parallel in one of the central tenets of Klee's art: namely that a form should always reveal the processes of its formation and that ultimately formation is more important than form.[69]

But with these significant differences aside Klee would seem to have had very different reasons for repeatedly depicting snakes, snails, and lice. As we have seen, snails had already entered the art of the infant Klee and were to reappear periodically throughout the rest of his career, when their spiralling shells and their radial principles of organization would appeal to Klee primarily on a formal level. In contrast to his evident affection for these simple creatures nothing could be less endearing than Klee's treatment of snakes and lice in his art. As traditionally less lovable animals in any case, these were eventually made the subjects of some of his most harrowing images, nearly all of them dating from the very last years of his life.

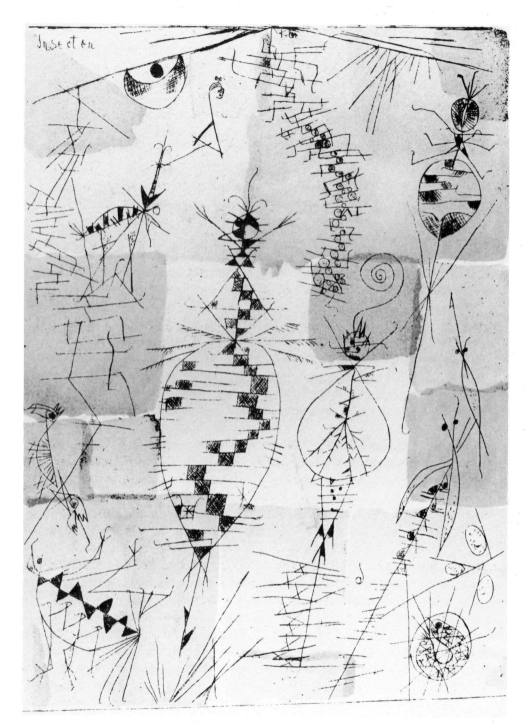

57
*Insects* 1919 Colour lithograph

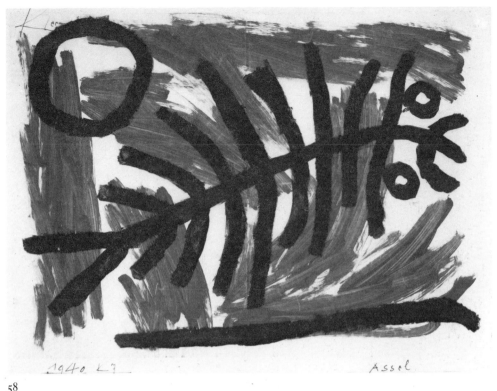

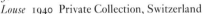

58
*Louse* 1940  Private Collection, Switzerland

Insects in general had already occupied the artist during the middle years of his career, when their bewildering variety of types and underlying similarity of structure had clearly caught the eye of the insatiably curious Klee. Depicted in all shapes and sizes they yet invariably display that regular pattern of rhythmically articulated markings which characterizes so many of the lower animals (fig. 57). Although the majority of these creatures are unidentified, a few are designated by the artist as beetles or plant-lice, the former shown camouflaging themselves on the leaves of a host plant and the latter already penetrating deep into the flesh of their vegetable victims to drink their life's-blood.[70] But lice only become a genuine obsession during Klee's late years, when they are made the focus of his single most important group of insect pictures.[71] With their segmented skeletons rendered in slashing black strokes, these creatures fill the picture spaces of a number of powerful and nightmarish late works, their threatening presence belying their small size (fig. 58). As these works are typically confined to thick black strokes seen against an oozing pool of red, it is hard not to see these late lice as harbingers of doom, with their menacing black bodies resembling prison grating and their blood-red surroundings, an open wound. Indeed, how better to account for Klee's sudden preoccupation with these loathsome creatures except as they may have come to symbolize for him those insidious forces which were slowly sapping his own vital juices and preparing him for an eternal confinement?

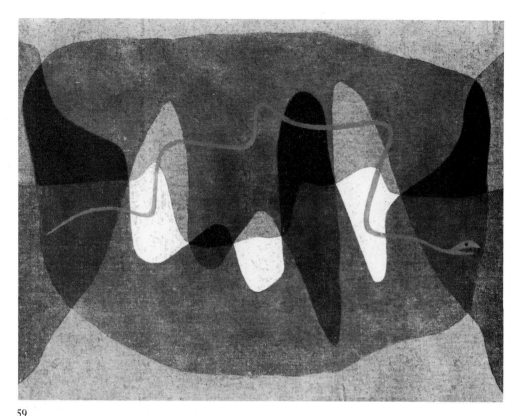

59
*Snake Paths* 1934 Private Collection, Switzerland

If anything, snakes occur with even greater frequency during Klee's late years; and once again his sudden obsession with these most maligned of all God's creatures is scarcely anticipated earlier in his art. In a handful of works of the early 1930s, however, Klee employs the form of a slithering serpent as a linear arabesque set against a coloured background; and at least one of these, the 1934 *Snake Paths* (fig. 59), provides us with a clue as to his initial reasons for portraying such creatures. With the form of the serpent depicted against a background of its recent movements Klee here reminds us that the snake is one of few animals in nature to retrace its entire form as it journeys along. In this respect its whole body functioned for Klee as a 'giant foot'.[72] Seen in this way the snake afforded Klee with a ready-made example of one of his highest artistic goals – namely, the combination of a spatial and a temporal view of the same subject.

In *Dead Cataract* of 1930[73] Klee alludes to the more traditional role of the serpent as the author of the Deluge in much the same way as he was to acknowledge it as the author of sin itself in the aforementioned *Garden Gate M* of two years later (fig. 48). And it is in these guises that the serpent returns to haunt Klee in his final years and speaks to us of his primal fears. Now snakes

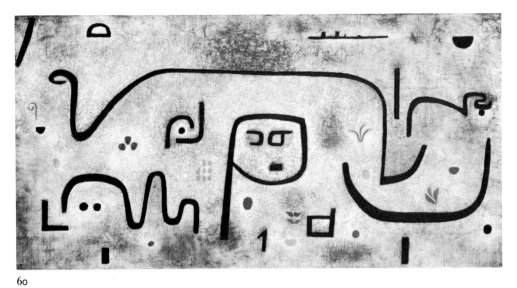

60
*Insula Dulcamara* 1938 Kunstmuseum, Bern

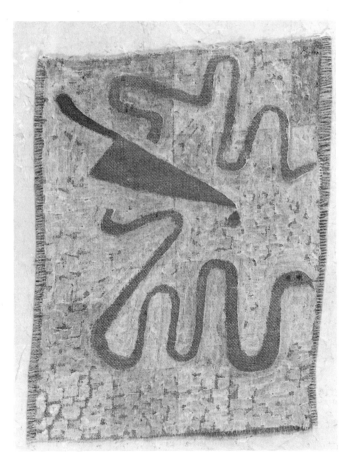

61
*Severing of the Snake* 1938
The Solomon R. Guggenheim
Museum, New York

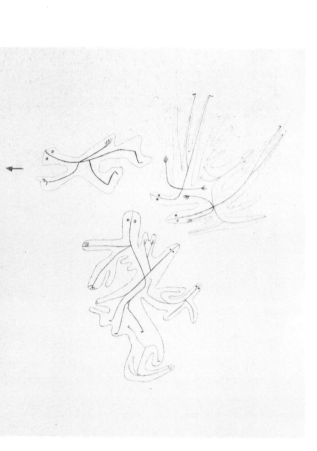

62
*Spirits of the Air* 1930
Fitzwilliam Museum,
Cambridge

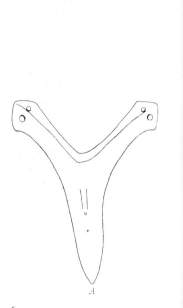

63
*Double-headed Planaria*

appear either as blatant symbols of evil, as bearers of doom and destruction,
or as seductive temptresses whose attractions – like those of their biblical
ancestor – are in every way fatal. Such a serpentine presence forms part of one
of the artist's major works of these years, the 1938 *Insula Dulcamara* (fig. 60)
– an evocation of a 'bitter-sweet', powdery-hued paradise infested with serpents
and presided over by a ghostly death's-head.[74] Nor can one fail to notice the
many ways in which Klee seeks to destroy the snakes in any number of his late
pictures – either by cutting them in half (fig. 61), blasting them with armoured
tanks, attacking them with arrows, or simply bending them around the page
in agonized postures.[75] Like Poussin at the end of his life Klee prepared the
way for his own death with an obsessional concern with that creature ultimately
responsible for bringing death itself into the world.

When one moves from the reptiles, insects, and molluscs to the very lowest
animals one would appear to find Klee losing interest; and, indeed, no one class
of these can claim to have furnished him with as much inspiration as those
already considered. But certain primitive species do make an appearance in his
work, though often only in a disguised form. For instance, the formal
inspiration for the strange beings which inhabit Klee's misleadingly entitled
*Spirits of the Air* of 1930 (fig. 62) will be readily recognizable to any biologist
as deriving from that group of fresh-water flatworms which includes the well
known laboratory animal *Planaria*. Like Klee's 'spirits' these simple creatures

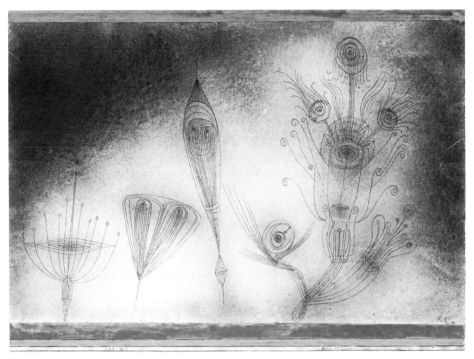

64
*Ardent Flowering* 1927  Private Collection, Canada

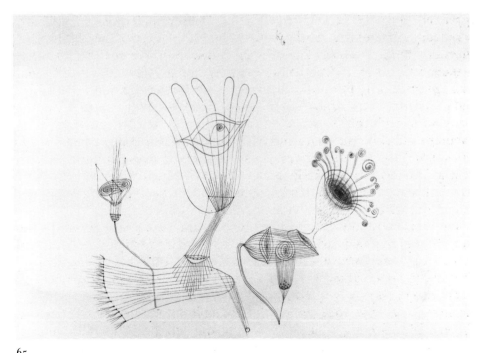

65
*Underwater* 1927  San Francisco Museum of Art

are transparent in appearance and flattened along the main body axis (or 'dorso-ventrally'). Even more importantly, *Planaria* are renowned for their remarkable powers of regeneration, with severed individuals being able to develop again into an entire animal and with portions from one animal grafted on to another resulting in just such two-headed and multi-limbed monsters as Klee here gives us (fig. 63). Notwithstanding the fanciful title of his work, then, its imagery would appear neither to derive from nor to exist in thin air but, rather, in an organism familiar to every schoolboy biologist – the indestructible and infinitely variable *Planaria*.[76]

Two closely related works of this period which descend even further down the evolutionary ladder for their subjects are the exquisite *Ardent Flowering* and *Underwater*, both of 1927 (figs. 64 & 65). Though the title of the former at least would lead one to assume that Klee was here depicting flowering plants and not animals, many of the organisms in both works are in fact closer in structure to certain of the lowest forms of animal life. The chic, tentacled blossom to the right of *Underwater*, for instance, bears a remarkable resemblance to the familiar sea anemones (fig. 66); while its lyre-like counterpart in *Ardent Flowering* is in fact most similar to a colony of those tentacled coelenterates known as *Obelia* (fig. 67). But, whatever the likely model, Klee's fertile imagination never adheres slavishly to it and remains faithful only to the essence of these primitive creatures, with their radial symmetry and frequent transparency. Artistic licence permits him, however, to combine longitudinal and radial sections in any one 'blossom', thereby providing us with a fuller account of its internal anatomy, and to introduce into *Underwater* a suspiciously cat-faced blossom, which has nothing to do with the world of lower organisms – and which belies that animal's proverbial dislike of water. Yet, however fanciful or improbable some of these creatures may seem, they could not have come into being without an acute awareness on Klee's part of the elaborate structure of certain types of coelenterates and ciliate protozoans,[77] many of which are indeed true flowers of the sea in their gaudy colours, their flamboyant, 'petalled' faces, and their sedentary ways. Fortunately, Klee's acquaintance with just such creatures as these can be securely dated to the very year which gave birth to both of these works. In the summer of 1927 the artist took a holiday on the Mediterranean island of Porquerolles. There he found himself bathing daily amidst hermit crabs, sea-carnations, charming snails and their baby snails, and 'flowers both under and on top of the water'.[78] Together they struck Klee as 'simply wonderful'; and that sense of wonder is admirably preserved in those two delicately filigreed evocations of undersea flora which resulted from these daily swims, *Ardent Flowering* and *Underwater*.

66
Beadlet Anemone (*Actina equina*)

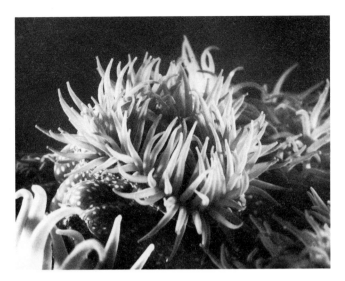

67
Various species of
*Campanulariidae* (a family of
hydroid polyps) drawn by Ernst
Haeckel

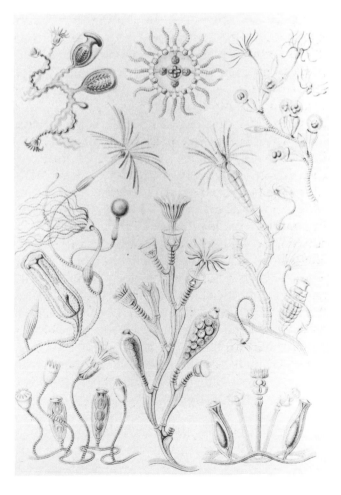

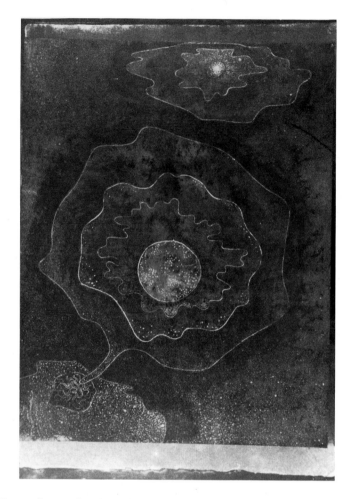

68
*Plant-like Strange* 1929
Kunstmuseum, Bern

An even more extraordinary incursion by Klee into the secretive world of microscopic nature is the 1929 painting *Plant-like Strange* (fig. 68) – 'strange', not least because the protagonist of this picture is far from convincingly plant-like. In fact, its closest analogies in nature are instead to be found among such familiar one-celled animals as *Amoeba* which, like the organism in Klee's picture, consists of a series of loosely concentric layers of protoplasm surrounding a central nucleus (fig. 69). Moreover, *Amoeba* is capable of changing shape and of sprouting precisely the kind of protruberance (or 'pseudopod') which Klee shows emerging from his creature. To be sure, such pseudopods are employed by one-celled animals not for reproductive purposes but for locomotion. In this respect Klee's organism does indeed behave more like certain types of plant cells. Tentatively putting forth a single feeler and implanting this in its desires, it here calls to mind the reproductive cells of certain fungi or liverworts (fig. 70) or even the male gametophytes of the higher plants, which produce pollen tubes to transport their sperm cells.[79] But lest one accuse the artist of merely indulging his fancy in this instance it is worth remembering that nature itself has invented beings which share the

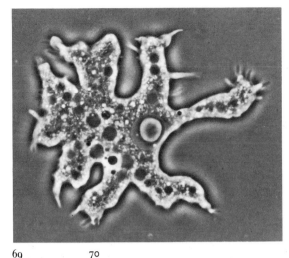
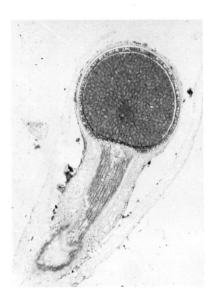

69
Soil amoeba
(*Hartmanella*)

70
*Pellia epiphylla*, a liverwort; longitudinal
section through a young sporophyte

characteristics of both animals and plants. Klee was surely aware of this; and,
in endowing the protagonist of *Plant-like Strange* with attributes of both of
these kingdoms, he tellingly made visible that fascinating limbo in nature where
nothing is quite what it seems and where animal and vegetable may come
together within the confines of a single cell.

*Plant-like Strange* is unique in Klee's career in its apparent verisimilitude.
Indeed, in a black and white reproduction at least it might almost be mistaken
for a greatly magnified photograph of some hidden secret of nature. Yet for
all its pretensions to realism, its precise subject defies identification; and the
reasons for this are not hard to find. Klee remained an artist even when he was
posing as a scientist, as he himself admitted in *On Modern Art*:[80]

> And is it not true that even the small step of a glimpse through the
> microscope reveals to us images which we should deem fantastic and over-
> imaginative if we were to see them somewhere accidentally, and lacked the
> sense to understand them? Your realist, however, coming across such an
> illustration in a sensational magazine, would exclaim in great indignation:
> 'Is that supposed to be nature? I call it bad drawing'. Does then the artist
> concern himself with microscopy? History? Palaeontology? Only for
> purposes of comparison, only in the exercise of his mobility of mind. And
> not to provide a scientific check on the truth of nature.

Thus, if it is to innumerable glimpses through the microscope that one owes
the uncanny logic of *Plant-like Strange*, it is to Klee's own 'mobility of mind'
that one owes its ultimate elusiveness.[81] Far more than in his explorations of
the animal kingdom, however, Klee found himself able to exercise this mobility
of mind in his lifelong dialogues with the world of plants. And it is to these
that we must now turn.

# 3 · The World of Plants

If Klee's earliest writings are anything to go by, his initial attraction to the world of plants was at least as intense as his interest in their higher, animal relations. Scattered throughout these may be found a series of observations on the lives and loves of the flowers and trees which reveal the young Klee's fascination with virtually all aspects of the plant kingdom and already prepare us for many of the paintings and drawings of his mature years. Indeed, by the time he had reached his early twenties Klee had alighted upon most of the major aspects of plant behaviour which would later enter his art. The emotional life of plants, their fruitfulness, their secretiveness, and their sexuality – all of these had already occupied his pen.[1] And who knows how much earlier and oftener they had also occupied his thoughts? Along with these the young artist had uncovered two other aspects of the plant world which he would later turn to creative use: namely, that the growth of plants might be compared with the growth of pictures, and that the forms and feelings of plants were not unlike those of man himself.[2] With the discovery of these two, more metaphorical levels of understanding Klee's future repertoire of plant themes and pictures was all but complete, even before he had painted a single one. Little wonder that the aspiring artist experienced such deep frustration when he found himself unable to record anything more than his sensory impressions of nature in his earliest works. Nature itself had already suggested so many more poetical ideas to him. Now if only he could find a style which would make it possible for him to give birth to these on an artistic level.

When that time – and that style – came it brought forth a body of works on botanical themes which is one of the largest in the artist's entire *œuvre*, and which is truly inexhaustible in its range of subjects and meanings. In a book which seeks to survey the broad scope of Klee's nature imagery, only the most pervasive of these may occupy us here, many of them all too briefly. Yet even from these the reader will probably deduce that, when a more detailed account of Klee's involvement with the animal and vegetable kingdoms comes to be written, the section devoted to the latter is likely to be both more substantial and more engrossing than that concerning the animals. The same could not of course be said of any other artist of recent times for whom the world of nature has provided a rich source of pictorial imagery – whether Marc, Ernst, Miró, or Masson. But in the case of Klee it is what we have come to expect. Given his lifelong search for the patterns and principles underlying all of organic existence, it is inevitable that Klee would find these most fully revealed to him by the humble plants, the begetters and supporters of all higher forms of life.

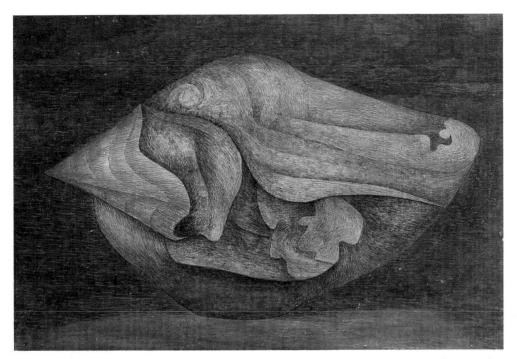

I  *Sea-Snail King*, 1933. Kunstmuseum, Bern

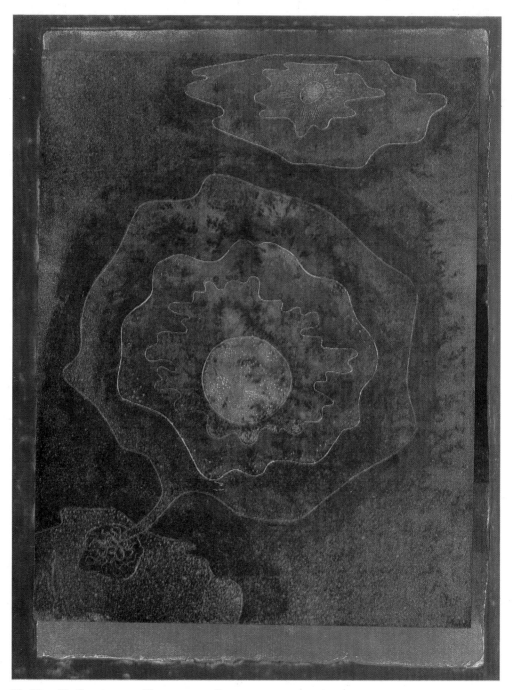

II  *Plant-like Strange*, 1929. Kunstmuseum, Bern

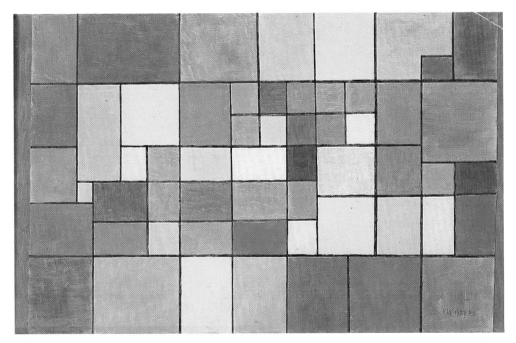

III  *Harmony of the Northern Flora*, 1927. Felix Klee, Bern

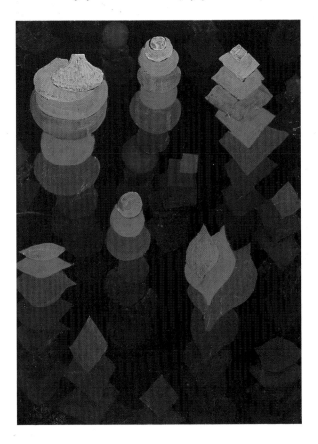

IV  *Growth of Nocturnal Plants*, 1922.
Galerie Stangl, Munich

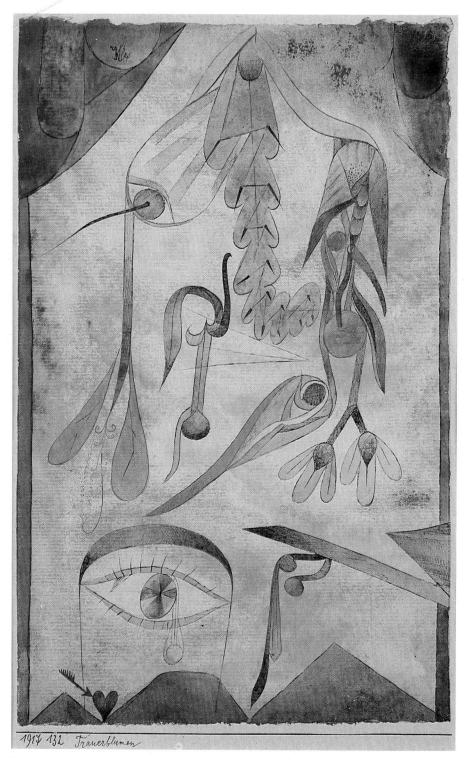

V  *Sad Flowers*, 1917. Staatsgalerie moderner Kunst, Munich

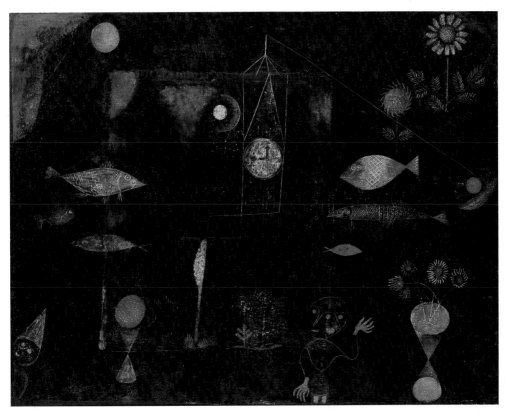

VI *Fish Magic*, 1925. Philadelphia Museum of Art, The Louise and Walter Arensberg Collection

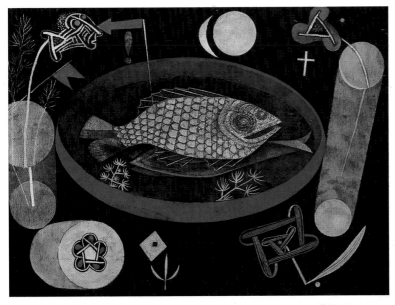

VII *Around the Fish*, 1926. Collection, The Museum of Modern Art, New York, Abby Aldrich Rockefeller Fund

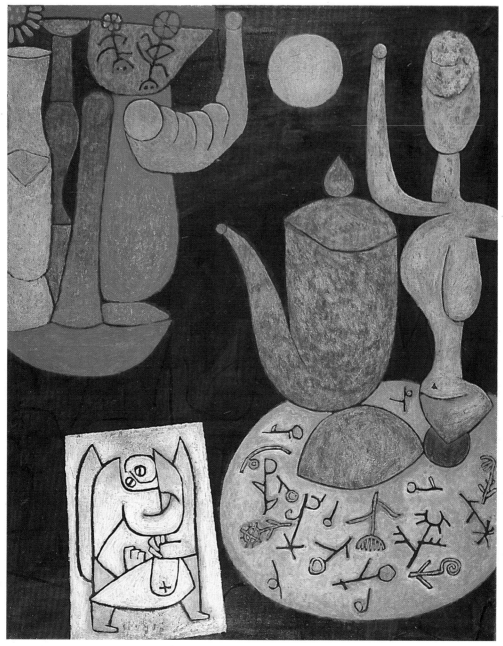

VIII  *Still-life*, 1939–40. Felix Klee, Bern

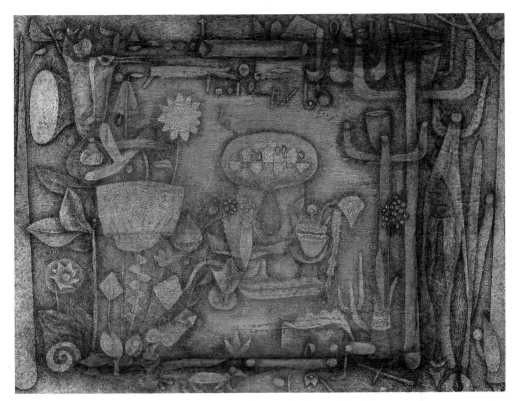

IX  *Botanical Theatre*, 1924–34. Städtische Galerie im Lenbachhaus, Munich

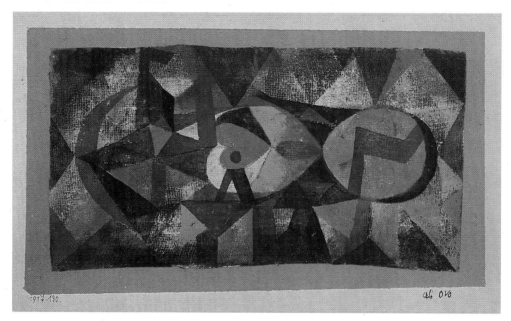

X  *ab ovo*, 1917. Kunstmuseum, Bern

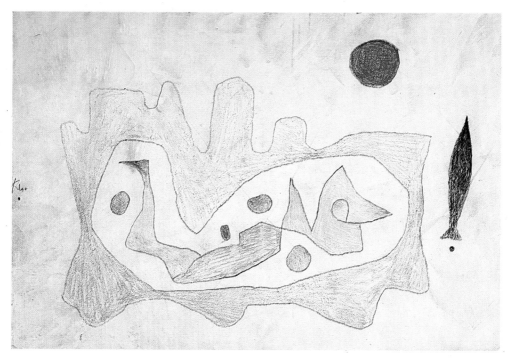

XI  *Rock Grave*, 1932. Felix Klee, Bern

Through the careful study of their birth and growth, and their leaves and flowers, the artist appears to have found himself penetrating closer than ever before to the essential secrets of life. And, accordingly, just as fishes came to represent for him the soul and centre of the animal world so too did Klee come to regard plants as the central creations of nature as a whole.

Among Klee's single groups of plant pictures the largest is probably the series devoted to parks and gardens – one which includes more than 250 works spanning his entire career and which would amply repay further study.[3] Generally speaking, however, Klee's garden pictures have less to teach the student of his nature imagery than they do one concerned with his theories of pictorial form. For parks and gardens – when seen or imagined from a distance, with their orderly divisions and their serried rows of flower beds – provided Klee with a subject which ideally combined his interest in nature with his search for a rhythmically coherent formal structure in his pictures. In short, they afforded a ready-made example of the vagaries of nature conforming to the strict and disciplined laws of the abstract art of architecture. This is apparent in any number of the titles which Klee eventually gave to such pictures, among them *Garden Rhythm*, *Garden Plan*, *Plan for a Garden Architecture*, and *Planting according to Rules*.[4]

But if this accounts for something of Klee's continuing fascination with the garden theme, it does little justice to the endless variety of gardens one encounters in his art or to his subtle delineation of their individual personalities, even when he confines himself to the pure and abstract language of his so-called 'magic square' compositions.[5] Here one has only to compare two related designs of 1927, *Harmony of the Northern Flora* and *Resonance of the Southern Flora* (figs. 71 & 72), to realize how Klee could evoke the flora of two distinct climates solely through changes in the form and colour harmony of these pictures.[6] In the northern realm tight constraints are exercised upon a group of coldly colourful blossoms, with firm black outlines containing individual areas of colour and perfectly suggesting the rigours and restraints of a habitat where there is always a slight chill in the air. But under a southern sun everything grows very differently. Klee's colours now take on a dazzling range of bold and exuberant hues; and, in keeping with this change, the artist replaces the word 'harmony' with the word 'resonance' in his title, thereby indicating a more sonorous and luxuriant realm. With this, Klee abandons the constraining black lines native to cooler climes and now permits his gaudy, tropical flora to bask uninhibitedly under a hot sun. Thus, through the mere manipulation of the basic elements of his art – line, plane, and colour – Klee here transports us to the opposite ends of the earth, revealing the essence of vegetative existence in each of these regions with the minimum of artistic means.

In his more realistic depictions of the plant world Klee predictably reveals an encyclopaedic curiosity and understanding of his subjects. As in his explorations of the animal kingdom, however, there are here too a number of evident preoccupations and equally noticeable omissions. Foremost among the latter is his general indifference to depicting particular species of plants. Unlike

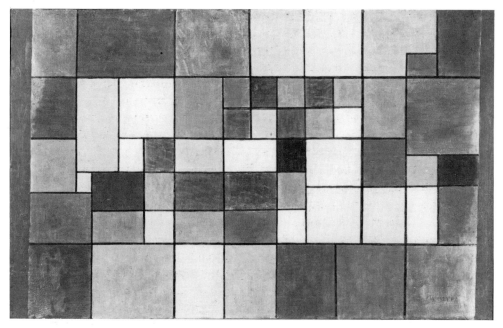

71
*Harmony of the Northern Flora* 1927 Felix Klee, Bern

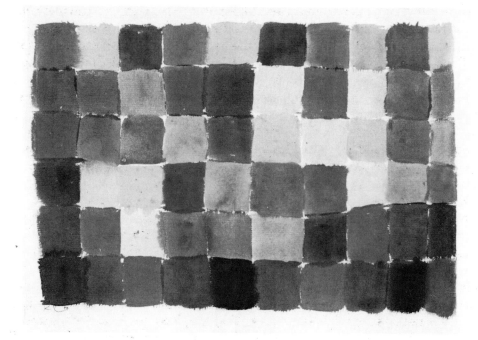

72
*Resonance of the Southern Flora* 1927 Present whereabouts unknown

his friend and contemporary, Emil Nolde, Klee was quite simply no orthodox flower painter;[7] and even on the rare occasions when he is moved to portray a recognizable species Klee avoids the flamboyant and spectacular varieties so beloved by Nolde (e.g. irises and poppies) and prefers to confine himself to the more ordinary daisies and asters. Much more often, however, Klee's search for the typical, rather than the individual, in nature leads him to reduce the multifarious plant kingdom to certain basic and recurring patterns which exemplify for him the profound inner laws which pervade it rather than the many subtle deviations from these laws visible to the naked eye. In this respect Klee's approach to the botanical world is largely generic; flowers are simply flowers in his art, and plants simply plants. Rarely does the artist show any interest in the hierarchy of organisms which make up this kingdom; and for this reason his plant pictures cannot be considered in the orderly, evolutionary progression that could be followed with the animals. Klee's art affords us with abundant evidence that he was intimately acquainted with the most diverse plant species – from the loveliest of flowers to the lowliest of fungi. But it also reveals that he uncovered more hidden similarities amongst these organisms than he did among their more strikingly differentiated animal relations. Parallels, analogies, and inner resemblances among the most diverse types readily suggested themselves to his penetrating vision, and these in turn became the true subjects of many of his plant pictures. Yet if this accounts for Klee's tendency to synthesize his impressions of plants more readily than he did of animals, it also explains the greater appeal which botanical subjects held for him. For only in his dialogues with the plant kingdom could Klee hope to approach that point in creation where all aspects of life might be seen to meet.

This is nowhere more apparent than in those rare instances when Klee purports to depict a precise species of plant, for even in these he often chooses to illustrate something much broader. This may be seen in a delicate drawing of 1927 entitled *Quadrupula gracilis* or in the 1932 painting *Young Tree (Chloranthemum)* (figs. 73 & 74). Confronted with such learned and seemingly specific Latin names, one might well suppose that Klee was here presenting us with two little-known curiosities of the plant kingdom; but, in fact, neither variety may be found in nature. Instead, *Chloranthemum* takes its name from the phenomenon of chloranthy, whereby the floral leaves of a plant revert to being ordinary green leaves – which is exactly what appears to be happening to Klee's young tree. And, as for the species *Quadrupula gracilis*, it is a pure (if beguiling) figment of Klee's imagination. As a translation of its Latin name implies, this quartet of fragile and dejected blossoms belongs to the genus 'fourfold' and the species 'graceful' – a species which owes its discovery not to Linnaeus but rather to Klee, who decked it out with a fancy Latin name which serves perfectly to characterize these wistful inventions of his drawing-board. But, however fancy its name, Klee would not have regarded this soulful species as purely fanci*ful*. Instead, as we shall see, it embodies one of his most sincerely held beliefs regarding the world of plants – namely, that it was a world permeated by the deepest feelings and emotions.

73
*Quadrupula gracilis* 1927 Staatsgalerie, Munich

Of the large number of anonymous flowers to be found in Klee's pictures the vast majority resemble the so-called 'composite' group in nature – a group which includes the daisies, asters, and sunflowers, the last of which may even be found peering over the artist's shoulder in his figurative self-portrait of 1933, *The Animals' Friend* (fig. 9). All of these varieties are marked by rayed petals arranged around a prominent, disk-like centre and, as such, they are among the simplest and most self-explanatory of flowers. They are also, however, among the most revealing; for in their basic structure may be seen that essentially radial pattern of organization which characterizes the form of the entire plant, which likewise consists of a central axis which gives rise to a series of radiating shoots. Viewed in this way they become classic examples of a well-known botanical principle which owes its discovery to Goethe: namely, that the flower is merely a repetition of the plant on a higher level.[8] Klee's intuitive awareness of this fact may well have led him to single them out in his art as his archetypal flowers – those whose structure and symmetry evoked the chief characteristics of the plant kingdom as a whole and, moreover, did so with utter clarity. With their lucid and seemingly simple organization – based, as it is, upon the repetition of like parts – and with their infinite possibilities of variation and association, these became Klee's preferred flowers; and given their general form (and the artist's own poetic turn of mind) they were occasionally enlisted to double as a sun, a star, or even a human face.[9] More often, however, as in the aforementioned *Fish Magic*, they serve simply as Klee's average flowers, here complementing and cohabiting with the fishes as representatives of the 'great middle class' of the plant kingdom.[10]

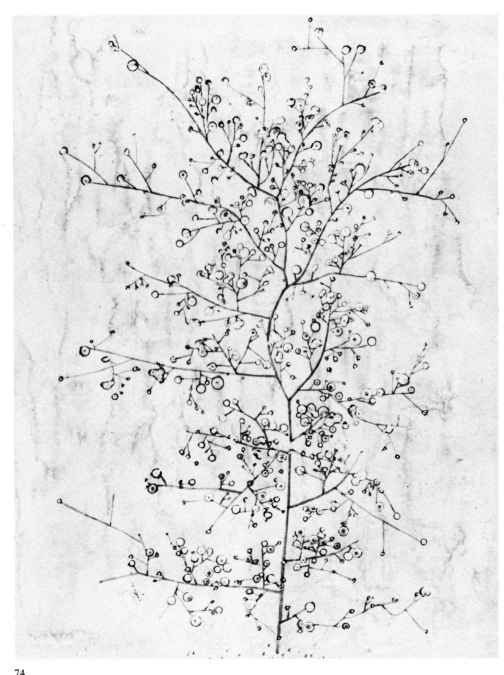

74
*Young Tree (Chloranthemum)* 1932  Private Collection, Switzerland

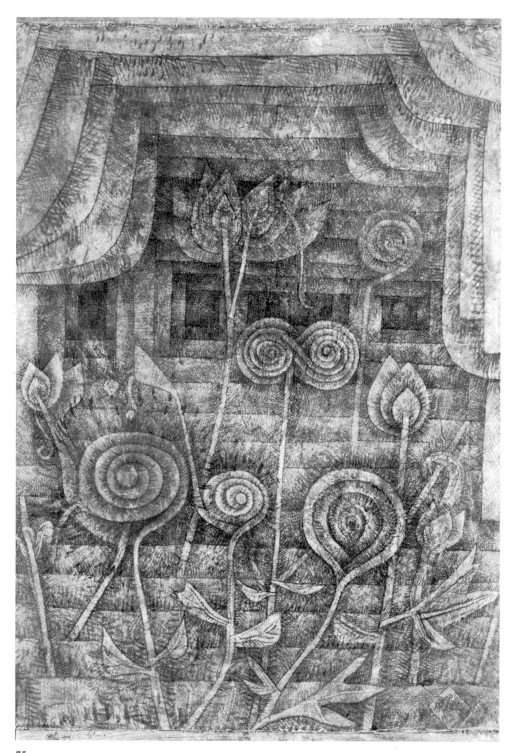

75
*Spiral Blossoms* 1926 Galerie Beyeler, Basel

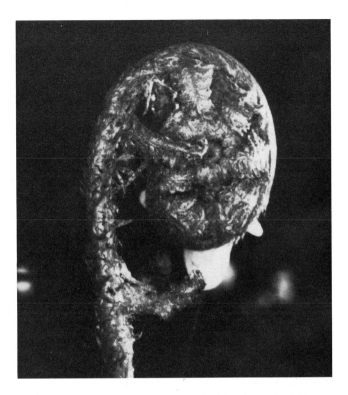

76
Young fern frond unfurling
(*Dryopteris filix-mas*)

After the composites, Klee's favourite flower type is probably the spiral blossom, a variety which gives its name to his *Spiral Blossoms* of 1926 (fig. 75) and also appears in *Portal in a Garden* of the same year.[11] Here the closest analogies to such beings in nature would appear to be in the unfurling of a young fern frond (fig. 76) or, among the higher plants, in the unfolding blossoms of the Forget-me-not family of flowers. But Klee's spiral blossoms probably owe nothing to such obscure sources as these and, instead, draw their inspiration from one of the most fundamental of all patterns governing plant development. For the spiral growth tendency may be seen to pervade much of the plant kingdom, from the arrangement of leaves around a stem to the organization of petals around the centre of a flower.[12] As such it would clearly have appealed to Klee, whose determination to lay bare the impulses common to all of botanical existence is nowhere more apparent than in his two preferred flower types. For both of these repeat in miniature two of the basic principles which pervade the form of the living plant: namely, the radial and the spiral.

Of the countless flowers which enter Klee's art the majority resemble one or another of the types already discussed and belong to no known species. Yet, if they remain ultimately unidentifiable they rarely strike one as wholly implausible. Take, for example, the weird assemblage of beings which inhabit Klee's *Cave Blossoms* of 1926 or his *Moving Blossoms* of this same year (figs. 77 & 78). Although the protagonists of both of these works defy classification, it is hard not to agree with Max Huggler's verdict on Klee's flowers when faced with either of them. Borrowing a phrase from Goethe, Huggler observed that

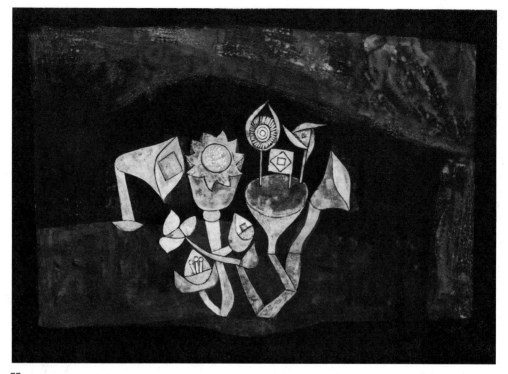

77
*Cave Blossoms* 1926  Galerie Stangl, Munich

Klee's flowers are reminiscent of nothing and of everything at the same time;[13] and, indeed, in such works as these Klee himself seems to have arrived at a point which Goethe reached in his studies of the plant kingdom in 1787. After painstakingly examining a wide variety of plants, Goethe noted that he was at last coming close to understanding the secret of the archetypal plant – that is to say, of the blueprint from which all existing plant types might be derived. 'With this model and the key to it,' Goethe continued, 'it will be possible to go on for ever inventing plants and know that their existence is logical; that is to say, if they do not actually exist, they could, for they are not the shadowy phantoms of a vain imagination, but possess an inner necessity and truth.'[14] Goethe's search for 'that which was common to all plants without distinction'[15] led him to evolve a purely mental concept of the archetypal plant – one which, when translated into art by certain of his followers, resulted in what one writer has described as a 'botanist's nightmare' consisting of all known leaves and flowers combined around a single stem.[16] But if Goethe's archetypal plant was by definition beyond visual interpretation, Klee's simple blossoms and leaves point the mind in the direction of such a non-visible archetype more readily than those of any more realistic interpreter of such subjects.

That Klee's flowers invariably possess what Goethe termed 'inner necessity' and 'truth' cannot seriously be doubted. Precisely how they succeed in doing this, however, remains one of the many mysteries of his art. Certainly it is often

86

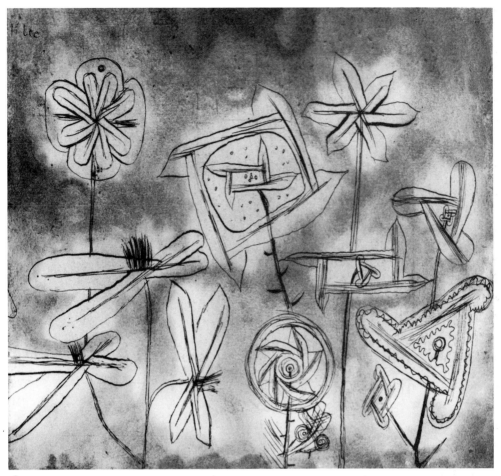

78
*Moving Blossoms* 1926  Galerie Stangl, Munich

the case that they are reduced to one of Klee's favourite '*a priori* formulas',
which typically consists of a small number of petals radiating around a square,
circular, or lozenge-shaped centre. Yet, for all their drastic simplification they
never lose their inherent naturalness or their ability to evoke the fundamental
patterns and principles which pervade the wide variety of flower types one sees
in nature. But the reasons for this are not hard to find. Comparatively early
in his explorations of the world about him Klee appears to have discovered that
nature itself is a geometrician and that, in building the lowest forms of life, it
often arranges their parts in multiples of some basic number, thereby ensuring
that they will possess both a fundamental unity and a seemingly infinite
variety.[17] In this Klee heeded nature's example and, in such works as *Moving
Blossoms* (fig. 78), he likewise confined himself to flowers which don a mere
three or four petals, or a simple multiple thereof, arranged around a variety
of simple centres. As such they not only call to mind a wide range of existing

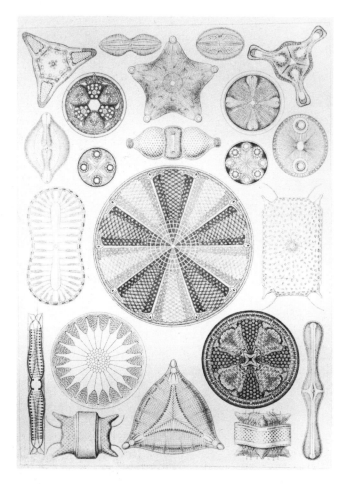

79
Various species of diatoms,
drawn by Ernst Haeckel

flower types but also remind us of the underlying clarity and economy with
which nature always creates such forms.

In addition to evoking the world of the higher plants, Klee's archetypal
flowers often recall any number of much lower organisms, both plant and
animal, and in this sense they appear to contain within them the formal
possibilities of the whole of organic creation. For instance, the aforementioned
*Cave Blossoms*, with their clean, crystalline features, are constructed in a manner
which is strikingly reminiscent of the fossilized skeletons of that group of
marine algae known as diatoms (fig. 79). Like Klee's 'blossoms' these are
characterized by a lucidly geometric plan which is subtly varied from one
organism to the next and which thereby seems to represent nature at its most
irreducible and its most endlessly inventive.

Klee's *Moving Blossoms* introduces us to yet another of his favourite flower
types which appears to have found its inspiration in the forms of a single-celled
organism, this time from the world of microscopic animal life. This drawing
is stylistically related to a group of eight other drawings of 1926 which depict
an imaginary species which Klee dubbed *Dynamoradiolaren* (fig. 80).[18] As the

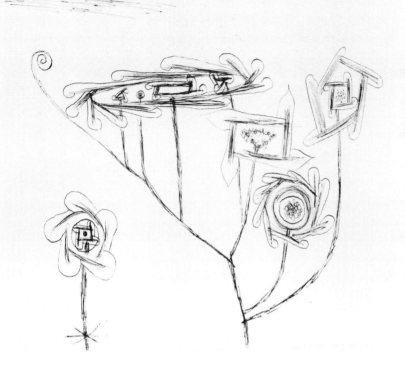

80
*Super-culture of*
*Dynamoradiolaren I* 1926
Kunstsammlung Nordrhein-
Westfalen, Düsseldorf

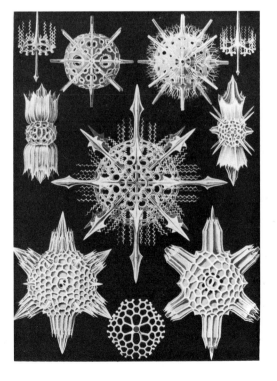

81
Various species of Radiolaria,
drawn by Ernst Haeckel

name implies, these flowers are radially organized and boast a series of mechanical petals which call to mind the rotating action of a dynamo, a pin-wheel, or (as Klee also discovered[19]) of a windmill. For all their analogies to both flower and machine parts, these simplified spoke-like blossoms may owe their inspiration to neither of these but rather to some of the most beautiful of all unicellular animals, the like-named marine protozoans of the order *Radiolaria* (fig. 81). These possess an external skeleton or shell which survives the death of the animal itself and remains a model of the basic simplicity and yet ceaseless complexity with which nature creates some of its most elementary beings. With their frequently radial symmetry, their crystalline clarity, and their infinite variety such one-celled organisms might well have appealed to Klee as diminutive prototypes of the ubiquitous flowers.

Klee could easily have been familiar with the forms of such microscopic creatures as the diatoms and radiolarians, for both figure prominently in a book that he owned[20] – Ernst Haeckel's *Art Forms in Nature*, a popular and superbly illustrated manual of nature's artistry which was published between 1899–1904 and from which two plates are reproduced here. Of the one hundred illustrations contained in this volume nearly a fifth are devoted to the diatoms, radiolarians, and related protozoans. Indeed, ten of these alone depict varieties of radiolarians, a group of organisms especially championed by Haeckel, who had devoted his first scientific treatise to them.[21] For Haeckel, the symmetry, regularity, and endless variety of these intricately designed organisms approached the basic forms of all organic existence and related these in turn to the structure of crystals.[22] Whether or not Klee was familiar with these views, his own *Dynamoradiolaren* – with their infinite diversity and exquisite clarity – tellingly evoke an even broader spectrum of creation, from crystals to single cells and thence to his own favourite composite flowers.

From the examples already considered it may be seen that Klee's ability to uncover such archetypal forms and patterns in nature owed itself not merely to his familiarity with a wide range of natural organisms but to his determination to reduce such beings to an order which remained concealed from the ordinary observer. For Klee this order and this ruthless economy of invention lay skilfully hidden by nature itself beneath a profusion of distracting shapes and appearances. In the last analysis it is Klee's ability to penetrate beneath this disguising layer and to say more about nature with fewer means that gives to so many of his creations the mysterious power of a hitherto undisclosed truth. Klee had already outlined this goal for himself as early as 1909, when he wrote: 'Nature can afford to be prodigal in everything, the artist must be frugal down to the smallest detail. Nature is garrulous to the point of confusion, let the artist be truly taciturn'.[23] What he did not add, however, is that the artist must be intelligently frugal in order to succeed in evoking nature's prodigality without describing it. But Klee himself eventually succeeded in doing just this. As a result, his disarmingly simple '*a priori*' flowers afford a tantalizing glimpse of the pattern-book of basic floral types and forms out of which nature itself has sown the gardens of this world.

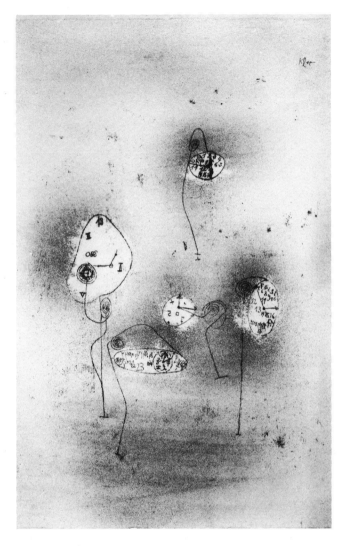

Although Klee apparently never admitted that the flowers he painted were intended to be seen as archetypal he gave ingenious expression to this intention in a little-known work of 1924 entitled *Clock Plants* (or *Uhrpflanzen*), with its quintet of radial blossoms supported by spiralling stems (fig. 82). As is often the case with the poetical Klee, the cryptic and allusive title accorded to this work may be variously interpreted; and, as is equally often the case with the scientific Klee, virtually any interpretation given to it may be found to have some basis in fact. Thus, it is widely acknowledged that plants contain a kind of time-keeping mechanism which measures the day-lengths and initiates the formation of flowers at the appropriate time of the year;[24] and, in this sense, Klee's association of clocks and plants is far from fanciful. But, in addition to this, Klee's title may also be read on a somewhat deeper level – one which paradoxically has its origins in a seemingly playful pun. 'Uhr' means clock or watch, while 'Ur' means original – or archetypal. And, although one should

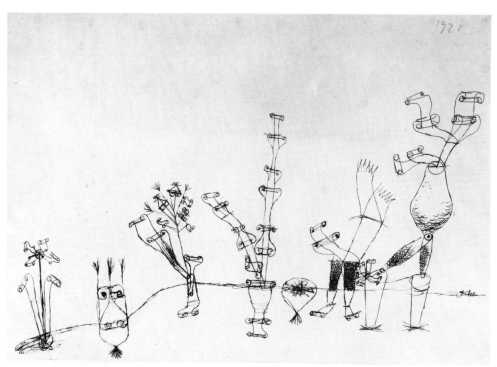

83
*Plants in a Field II* 1921  Kunstmuseum, Basel

beware of assuming that Klee was here expounding a weighty philosophical
notion in so comparatively minor a work, it is worth considering whether the
pun of his title *is* simply playful. Clocks and flowers may appear to have little
– if anything – in common beyond a very general formal similarity. But to a
poetic painter like Klee, gifted with a profound insight into the laws of both
time and nature, the analogy may well have gone further than this and reminded
him of one of the most fundamental of all laws governing the archetypal plant.
For when flowers appear on a plant its own life-cycle is nearing an end and
another generation is coming into being. In this respect the flower does indeed
function as a kind of timepiece.

   If Klee may not be said to have had a preferred plant type in the same way
as he had a favourite flower, an important group of drawings of the early 1920s
introduces us to certain features which are commonly to be found in his
imaginary plants. Chief among these is a fondness for types with thick central
stems and broad branches, which not only call to mind some of the simplest
and most primitive varieties in nature – for instance, the fungi, pitcher plants,
and cactuses – but may also be readily adapted to take on a more purely human
shape, with stems now doubling as torsos and branches as limbs.[25] Typical of
such works are Klee's two drawings *Plants in a Field* (I & II) of 1921 or his
*Drawing for 'Plants, Earth, and Kingdom of the Air'* of 1920, with its improbable
mixture of plant and animal types (figs. 83 & 84).[26] For all their self-evident

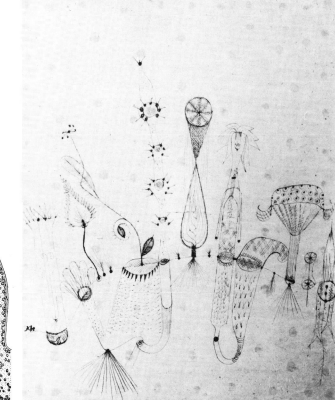

84
*Drawing for 'Plants, Earth and Kingdom of the Air'* 1920
Kunstmuseum, Bern

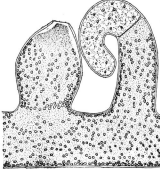

85
Development of sex organs of
*Vaucheria sessilis*

humour and inventiveness, such creations as these also reveal the extent of Klee's knowledge of the entire botanical kingdom; for, although none of these beings may be found in nature, most of the elements out of which they have been created may be discovered there. Thus, if one discounts such obviously preposterous creatures as the cat-faced 'plant' at the far left of the 1920 drawing, there is much else here to recall the world of more familiar nature. For instance, the principles according to which the tallest member of Klee's group is organized are known from a type of plant which flourished in prehistoric times and now survives only in the single genus *Equisetum*, which includes the common horsetails and scouring rushes – many of them among the bane of any gardener's existence. Like Klee's plant these are equipped with a thick underground root or 'rhizome' and prominent stems which bear minute leaves at specific junctures, or 'nodes' (fig. 86). Similarly, the lower portion of the 'body' of the plant to the right of this bears a clear resemblance to an onion seen in cross-section, while the thread-like roots which arise from this plant and from its two companions towards the far right and left recall the thread-like root system, or 'mycelium', of the fungi. Also unmistakably mushroom-like in their general form are the two beings to the immediate right of the onion-bodied plant. On closer inspection, however, the underground behaviour of these two fanciful fungi, with its frank depiction of the imminent meeting of egg and

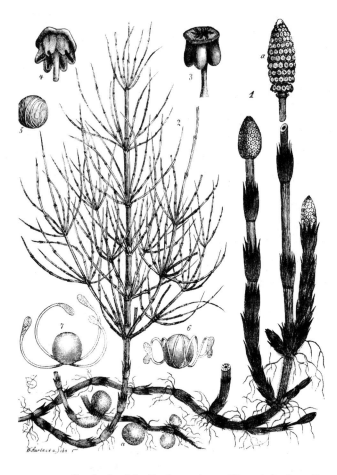

sperm cells, is decidedly less plant-like. Admittedly, analogies for it may be found in the realm of the plants – most notably in the sexual reproductive phase of the yellow-green algae *Vaucheria* (fig. 85). But a more convincing analogy is neither with the higher nor lower plants, but with humans. Viewed in this way the mushroom-like male near the far right of Klee's drawing sprouts a suspiciously phallic tuber aimed in the direction of a smug female blossom which dons a face, torso, and arms above ground, while below she surreptitiously procreates – safely out of the sight of anyone but Klee.

Much earlier, in March 1901, Klee had noted in his diaries that his friend, Jean de Castella, had 'inquired about the sexual act of plants'. 'Where did it take place,' he wondered, 'in the roots?'[27] By the time Klee came to depict it in this way he was surely aware that this was not the case. Nevertheless, Castella's intriguing suggestion may well have stayed with the artist, eventually leading him, nineteen years later, to endow plants with a capacity for sexual secrecy and discretion traditionally reserved for man.

Klee's unfailing ability in such works as this to invent a range of beings which remain suspiciously lifelike and yet truly imaginary may be judged if we compare his *Drawing for 'Plants, Earth, and Kingdom of the Air'* with a work

87
*Growth Overnight* by an
imitator of Klee
Present whereabouts unknown

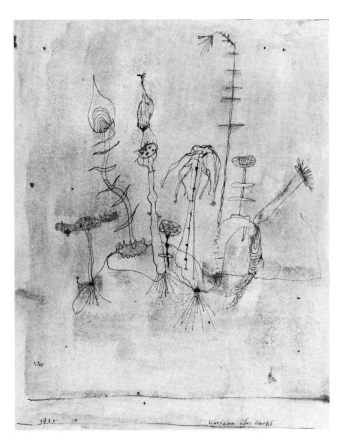

by an imitator which is clearly indebted to it (fig. 87).[28] In addition to the fact
that the latter is drawn in a flaccid and nerveless manner which lacks the
authority of Klee's tense and wiry line, the imitator's drawing is notable for
the almost pedantic way in which it unravels Klee's composite and combined
beings and unimaginatively relates them back to their apparent sources in
nature. Gone now are the faces, torsos, and phalluses of Klee's imagining; and
in their place may be found a group of plants which are no longer simply
plausible but readily identifiable – among them, the ordinary mushroom, the
horsetail, the composite flower, and the common stink-horn. That the artist of
this feeble drawing could so easily intuit the sources of many of Klee's
inventions attests to their essential truthfulness. But to this intimate
acquaintance with the vocabulary of nature Klee alone was able to add a
'mobility of mind' which here made it possible for him to evoke the whole of
nature from an ingenious recombination of its separate parts.

In a very different spirit Klee's fondness for thick, fleshy plant types, with
short leaves and tough stems, may also be found in some of his greatest
botanical paintings, among them *Spiral Blossoms*, *Cave Blossoms*, and (above
all) *Botanical Theatre* (figs. 75, 77, 177). In these works, all of which date from
the mid 1920s, the artist appears to draw his inspiration from the collection
of household cactuses he was tending during these years.[29] Like their natural

counterparts Klee's invented plants here tend to be stocky, spiny, and succulent, and to address the viewer with such a stalwart sense of presence that they appear as the sole defiant survivors of the earliest land plants, which (like them) tended to be thick-limbed and largely leafless. With their simple, radial flowers and their regular shapes, such organisms call to mind not only the primitive beginnings of the plant kingdom but those crystalline structures which Klee appears to have regarded as presiding over the very origins of life itself. But in addition to evoking the archetypal plant – the long-lost link between crystal and flower – such imaginary species also invited comparisons with much higher beings. In any number of these works the protruding limbs of Klee's primeval plants take on a decidedly human form and appear as powerful arms thrusting upwards as though in a militant salute or even a rallying call to arms. Such defences – and such postures – lend a sinister and threatening intensity to these works which Klee was only fully to exploit in his final years.[30] Already at this stage, however, the sight of such a race of humanoid plants – so strong, sturdy, and self-reliant – with their spiky, tentacled arms and their vigorous gestures unleashes a demonic element in nature which seems to lay bare those brutal instincts which ensure the survival of the species at every level, from plant to man.

For all his inventiveness before nature, and for all his concern to discover its invisible archetypes, Klee has left us with abundant evidence that he was also sensitively attuned to nature's own more specialized inventions and to its many plainly visible eccentricities. Although he never offers us a literal description of these, certain of his botanical pictures reveal such a deep understanding of the more esoteric ways of nature as to make it clear that they could only have come from the hand of an artist who was also an accomplished natural scientist. Thus, when Klee portrays a bird preparing to pollinate a blossom in his 1918 *Flower Myth* (fig. 39) he creates a blossom which is fully suited to this role – one which is sufficiently bright and pure in colour to attract its high-flying host, strong enough in structure eventually to support it, and large enough to provide it with bird-sized (rather than insect-sized) quantities of nectar. Similarly, when Klee draws his *Flowers in a Cornfield* of 1920, he offers us a collection of imaginary blooms – many of them suspiciously resembling faces, torsos, and eyes – growing amidst corn plants which themselves bear flowers of two distinct kinds (fig. 88). In one of these the separate filaments appear at regular intervals along the central axis and thereby resemble a feather, and in the other they arise from a common base, like the fingers of a hand. In this Klee is both justified and accurate. For the corn plant is among those species of higher plants in which the separate sexes are not united in a single flower but are borne instead on separate 'inflorescences' which are distinguished in nature exactly as they are in Klee, the male flower being finger-like and the female flower feather-like.

Yet another instance in Klee's art where he reveals his remarkably specialized knowledge of the characteristics of certain plants may be found in a drawing of 1920 entitled *Prehistoric Plants* (fig. 89). Although nothing in this work is

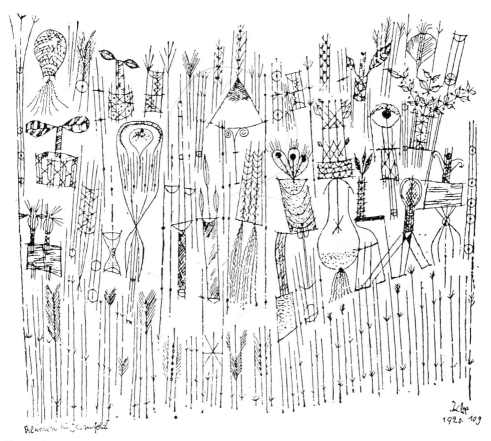

88
*Flowers in a Cornfield* 1920 Present whereabouts unknown

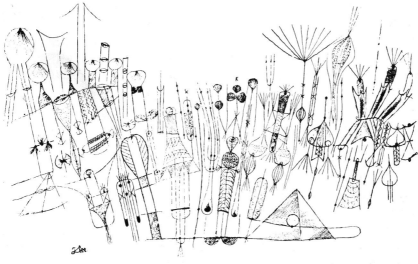

89
*Prehistoric Plants* 1920 Present whereabouts unknown

97

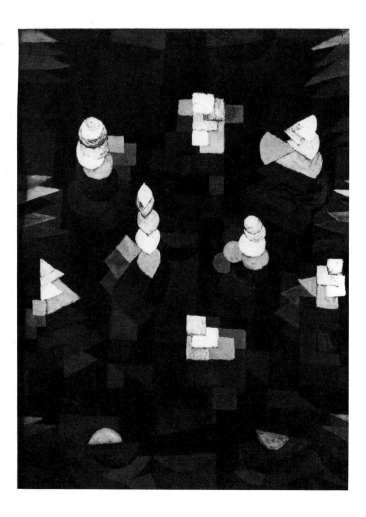

90
*Growth of Plants* 1921
Private Collection

apparently an accurate depiction of any known fossilized forms – and although
some of these 'flowers' are patently faces – the majority of them possess at least
one feature which would have made it possible for them to survive from
prehistoric times. Almost invariably they are lacking in those most delicate and
ephemeral of plant parts – the leaves – and are instead made up of wiry stems
and branches supported by fleshy underparts. This is befitting to their
prehistoric origins in at least two ways. Firstly, as we have seen, many of the
earliest land plants were distinguished by having few, if any, leaves. And,
secondly, it goes without saying that even those varieties which possessed an
abundance of foliage would most likely be preserved in fossilized form through
their more sturdy and durable veins, stems, and branches. To be sure, there
is one prominent exception to this in Klee's drawing – the readily recognizable
clover which presides over the group in the centre of the design and is marked
above with a large *K*. This reminds us at once that *Klee* means clover in
German and that a Klee of a different species presided over this invention. And
what greater poetic justice could there be than that this eternal seeker after the

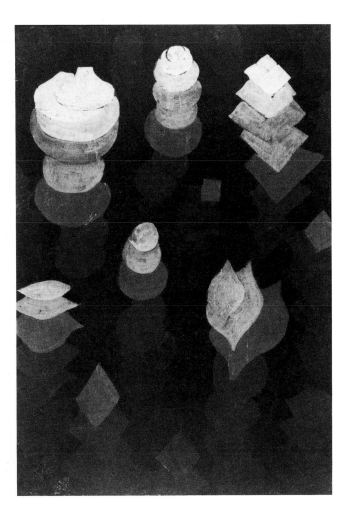

91
*Growth of Nocturnal Plants*
1922  Galerie Stangl, Munich

archetypal in nature should himself have borne the name of one of its simplest
and most endearing creations?[31]

When one moves from a consideration of Klee's favourite plants and flowers
to his interests in the behavioural patterns of the plant world a number of clear
preoccupations immediately present themselves. Predictably among these is a
fascination with the processes of germination, growth, and reproduction,
though Klee's approach to the last of these is usually so overlaid with animal
associations that it is best considered elsewhere.[32] A much more eccentric
concern, however, is with the lives led by plants during those periods when
they are normally invisible – namely, at night. Klee's diaries contain several
references to his early attraction to flowers which revealed themselves only in
the evening or at twilight;[33] and such species eventually became the subjects
of a long line of works which extends from such relatively early pictures as his
*Garden at Night* of 1918[34] to *Twilight Blossoms* of 1940.[35] Characteristically,
Klee pays little or no attention in these works to those rare varieties of plants
which are actually noted for their nocturnal habits. Instead, he invents his own

types, occasionally even going so far as to equip them with a prominent eye which may enable them to 'see' during this period of minimal light.[36] But in the majority of such works Klee also reveals a deep understanding of the essential characteristics of the nocturnal plants and flowers and invents species which are supremely well-adapted to their nonconformist ways.

Nowhere is this more apparent than in a comparison of the artist's *Growth of Plants* of 1921 and its thematic companion of the following year, *Growth of Nocturnal Plants* (figs. 90 & 91). Even from a cursory glance at these works it will become clear that Klee's night-blooming species are distinguished not only by suitably nocturnal colour harmonies but by revealing differences in physical form. For one, they are endowed with a fleshier body structure, as though to acknowledge that under low levels of light intensity most plants will tend to produce more vegetative growth. Such sluggish and broad-leaved varieties are regularly to be found among Klee's nocturnal plants, which thereby also appear unusually well-equipped to store vital nutrients during those periods when they cannot produce them. In addition, the generally lacklustre hues of these nocturnal plants recall the drab tones of any number of organisms which actually prefer shadow to sunlight, among them the largely colourless algae, bacteria, and fungi. In contrast, Klee's day-time species are leaner and more energetic in form and more widely varied in colour. Moreover, their leaves are *green* rather than grey or brown, thus reminding us that chlorophyll – that essential ingredient of life among the higher plants – can only be manufactured in the light.

Such an astute delineation by Klee of his nocturnal plants is hardly surprising, but it does not account for his interest in such curiosities of nature in the first place. Here, however, one need seek no further for an explanation than in Klee's avowed desire to make visible in his art the otherwise invisible. After all, night-blooming flowers and their close relations, the cave and forest blossoms (fig. 77), are an extreme example of nature's extravagance – and even profligacy – in their willingness to flaunt their attractions only at times (or in places) when they are normally inaccessible to the naked eye. Yet, through his art Klee could see them and render them visible as precious secrets of nature, here vouchsafed to us as though for the very first time. On this level Klee evidently relished the opportunity to spy upon the night-blooming flowers in much the same way as he did upon the private lives of birds in the air or fishes in the sea. In all three instances man's first-hand experience of nature could be enlarged beyond its traditional bounds through the limitless medium of his own art.

Much more central to Klee's achievement than his paintings of nocturnal blossoms are his many depictions of growth among plants; and in these too he ventured into territory virtually unexplored by any earlier artist. Once again, however, Klee did not do this irresponsibly; for even when creating from out of the depths of his imagination he remained sufficiently attuned to nature's ways to respect its fundamental laws. A sequence of four works spanning nearly twenty years in Klee's career may serve to illustrate this. The first of these is

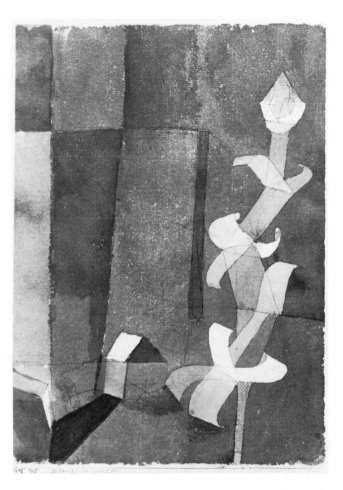

a comparatively immature watercolour of 1915 entitled *Plant in a Garden*
(fig. 92), which, with its interlocking coloured planes, still owes its formal
sources to the language of the Cubist painters. Yet one has only to consider
the rudimentary plant form that Klee creates out of these to realize that the
artist has succeeded in evoking the essence of such forms in nature. Thus, from
this deceptively simple sequence of rising, twisting, and unfurling bands of
colour there emerges an image of the three basic patterns of growth governing
the development of the higher plants – namely, the vertical, radial, and spiral
– the first two of which permit it to grow upwards and outwards and the last
of which combines these two impulses.[37]

An even more penetrating exploration of this theme appears in an iridescent
little picture of 1920 entitled *The Bud* (fig. 93), which affords us a much fuller
account of the crucial tendencies affecting the growth and differentiation of
plants. To begin with, the vertical tendency of the central stem, the radial
tendency of the leaves, and the spiralling movements of both tendrils and
subsidiary shoots (here depicted, at the bottom centre, as mere leaves) are all

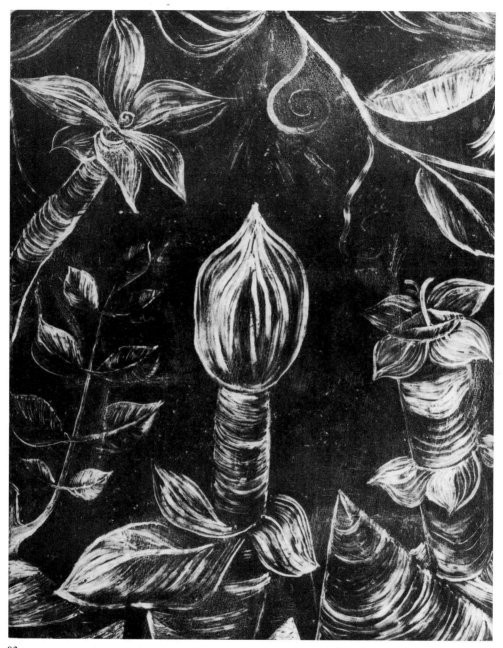

93
*The Bud* 1920 Present whereabouts unknown

vividly evoked. In addition Klee's synoptic watercolour also alludes to the
multi-layered structure of the stem and to the broad distinctions which exist
in nature between parallel and pinnately veined leaves, i.e. those in which the
veins are joined at the base of the leaf and those in which they arise from a
dominant central vein or 'midrib'. But perhaps even more remarkably Klee also

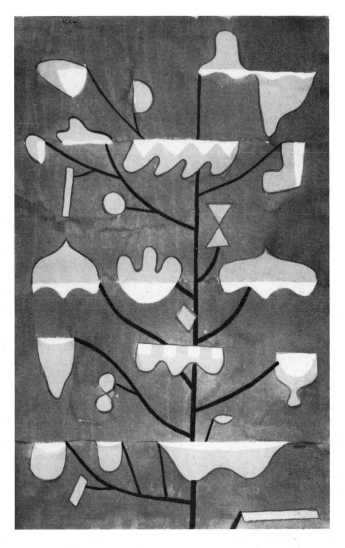

94
*The Things that Grow!* 1932
Kunstmuseum, Bern

makes reference here to the alternating processes of expansion and contraction
which mark the plant's development as it progresses from leaf to stem and then
back to leaf, or from leaf to bud and then on to flower.[38] Finally, the general
shape and the pattern of veins of the bud which forms the centre-piece of Klee's
picture immediately recall those of the surrounding leaves and remind us that
the flower ultimately arises from a transformation of the leaves of the plant.[39]
Thus, *The Bud* makes visible an encapsulated history of growth among plants
rendered in a manner which is at once so concise and so comprehensive that
it appears to contain the very blueprint of all vegetative existence.

Klee's evident wish to uncover hidden analogies between all parts of the
living plant takes on a somewhat more elaborate form in his 1932 watercolour
*The Things that Grow!* (fig. 94). In this, subtle variations in the shapes of the
forms borne by the branches of a single tree evoke the whole repertoire of such
possibilities as they may be found in nature. Leaves, flowers, fruits, berries, and

95
*Plant-like Analytical* 1932
Kunstmuseum, Basel

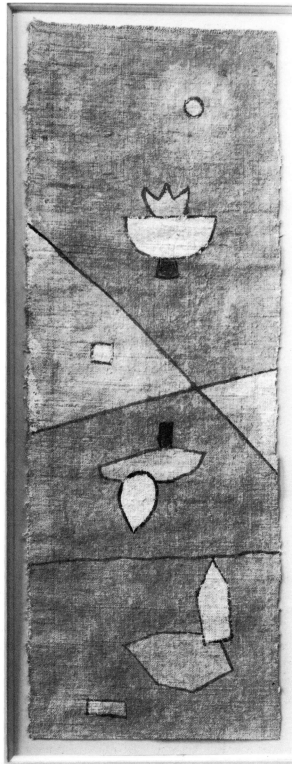

96
The Plant, pedagogical drawing
by Klee

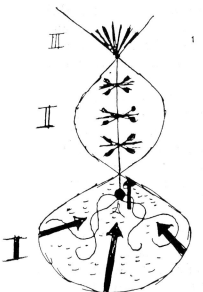

1

seeds are all called to mind by Klee's marvellously allusive language. But whatever their precise identity it is noteworthy that each of these forms is sufficiently similar in colour and configuration to make it clear that they are all products of the same parent plant. By a process akin to metamorphosis each of them tellingly declares both its individuality and its underlying affinity to the others – a phenomenon which is not of Klee's imagining but of nature's own devising, and one which was already well known two centuries before him, when Goethe discovered that all parts of the living plant were essentially modifications of one another.[40]

Finally, in a brilliantly economical painting of this same year, *Plant-like Analytical* (fig. 95), Klee succinctly outlines the impulses to plant growth from inception to fruition. Here any lingering pretence to realism has been abandoned and the forms reduced to a handful of simple and closely related motifs which are yet profoundly suggestive of plant-like existence. In fact, this sparse and powerful little picture outlines the developmental cycle of the typical plant. Under a small but luminous sun or moon floats the unmistakable form of a fully opened flower. Below it, under the earth's surface, a seed-like shape sprouts both stem and root; and below these a group of superficially similar forms come together. These last are endowed not with the rounded organic curves of the flower and seed forms but, instead, are made up of straight lines and sharp angles which seem to betray a more crystalline state. Could they be the earth's mineral resources – that is to say, those elements which, together with the sun, provide the growing plant with all that it needs to survive? One cannot be sure as Klee's formal language is here so ruthlessly abbreviated. But, for all its economies and elisions the arrangement of this handful of pregnant forms on the canvas tellingly suggests that the flower form is rising, that the seed shape is growing in both directions, and that the lowest forms are non-living and therefore stationary. Yet despite their inert appearance – and despite the rigid horizontals which separate them from Klee's organic motifs, with their livelier diagonals – these crystalline elements exert a magnetic attraction upon the germinating seed which is no less powerful than that of the sun above. As Klee had already acknowledged in his drawing of 1920 (fig. 84), both earth and air are necessary to support life in the kingdom of the plants.

Klee had already outlined the developmental cycle illustrated here in a pedagogical drawing of 1922, which shows the flowering plant divided into three broad zones: the active area of the earth, which nourishes it, the medial layer of the plant body, which converts such nourishment into form, and the passive layer of the flower, which results from these impulses (fig. 96).[41] In addition to recalling Klee's comparison between the tree and the artist in *On Modern Art*,[42] this classroom diagram reveals the gulf between even his most imaginative teaching and his own creative art. Thus, while the pedagogical example still relies upon an essentially visual understanding of the impetus to plant growth, *Plant-like Analytical* presents us with a more cosmic interpretation of this theme. The separate phases of germination, growth, and flowering are now brought together, and the ineluctable progress from the

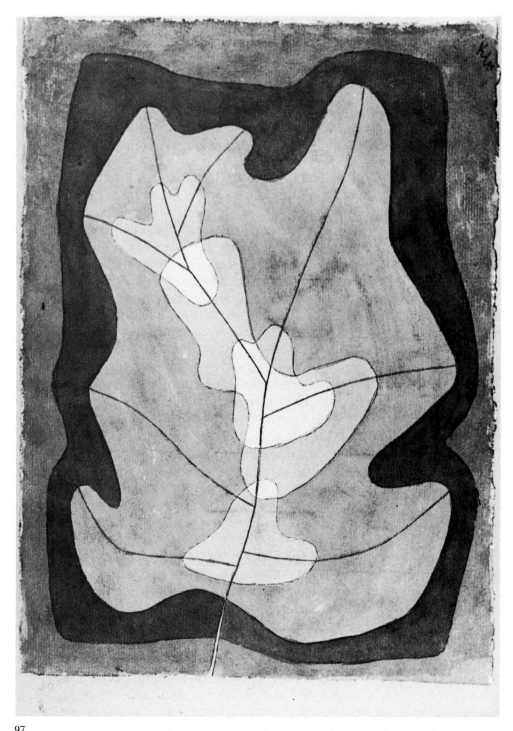

97
*Illuminated Leaf* 1929  Kunstmuseum, Bern

imprisoning earth to the liberating heavens is graphically charted for us through a gradual metamorphosis of the germinal elements of the picture itself. For if we cast our eyes back to the simple shapes which make up Klee's picture we will notice that these develop from lines to curves, from curves to semi-circles, and from semi-circles to the full circle of the sun as one progresses ever upwards. In this sense they may be seen to recapitulate on a formal level that steady progression from aspiration to fulfilment which also marks the life history of the typical plant.

Closely related to Klee's interest in the general phenomena of birth and growth in plants is his concern with the individual participants in these processes and especially with leaves, seeds, and fruits. In his numerous depictions of all three of these the artist often created some of his most powerful images of the procreative instincts of nature. That Klee should have reserved such statements for depictions of what he himself called mere 'organs' of the living plant is wholly characteristic. The reader of his diaries will readily recall his own early admonitions to himself to seek to penetrate to nature's deepest mysteries through concentrating upon its smallest motifs. 'Our initial perplexity before nature,' observed Klee in 1903, 'is explained by our seeing at first the small outer branches and not penetrating to the main branches or the trunk. But once this is realized, one will perceive a repetition of the whole law even in the outermost leaf and turn it to good use.'[43]

Twenty-six years after writing these words Klee gave creative expression to them in his well known watercolour of 1929, *Illuminated Leaf* (fig. 97). By the time he painted it the example of the individual leaf had already served him in his classroom discussions both as an object worthy of the closest scrutiny in its own right[44] and as a convenient introduction to the more complicated laws of structure and articulation in an entire tree.[45] Thus, just as the crown of the tree unfolds around a central axis, so too do the leaf's veins derive from a central stem, branching off from their own main axis at points marked by a greater concentration of energy. In Klee's transparent, 'polyphonic' style of 1929–30[46] these centres of growth could be rendered in a series of overlapping planes, with those areas of the leaf containing the largest inflow of sap – and therefore the greatest growth potential – painted in the lightest and most energetic tones, while areas of less vascular activity are rendered in duller mauves and grey-greens. The result – as Klee had demonstrated to his students in 1923 – reveals relations 'that reflect on a small scale the articulation of the whole'.[47]

Klee's recognition of the essential similarities between the structure of a leaf and a tree was not his own discovery; for already in the seventeenth century it was acknowledged that some leaves resembled in miniature a whole branching system and, by implication, an entire plant.[48] Yet if Klee's awareness of this fact was not new his introduction of it into the world of creative art surely was. And just how creative his *Illuminated Leaf* is may be seen by comparing it with any of his pedagogical drawings of this same subject (fig. 98). In all of these the artist remains content to present his students with diagrammatic renderings

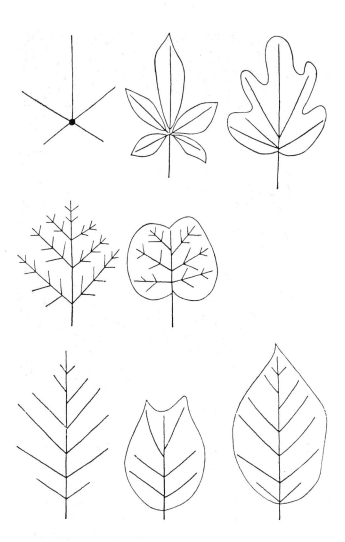

of the leaf form, carefully drawing attention to the basic symmetry and regularity which pervade such creations in nature. Having imbibed these lessons through the classroom study of the 'typical' leaf, however, Klee then instructed his students to go home and invent 'imaginary leaves on the basis of the foregoing basic rules';[49] and his own watercolour of six years later may best be seen as Klee's own belated contribution to this assignment in truly creative homework.

Although it would be tempting to try to discover the prototype of Klee's *Illuminated Leaf* in nature – and although it bears a certain resemblance to the leaf of an oak – all such efforts are bound to end in failure. The 'basic rules', to be sure, are applied. The form of the leaf is determined by the network of its veins, with those areas of maximum growth potential producing corresponding expansions to the contour of the leaf. But if such features vividly call to mind the factors which determine leaf growth and form, Klee is yet careful to keep his painted leaf wholly within the bounds of the imaginary. Thus

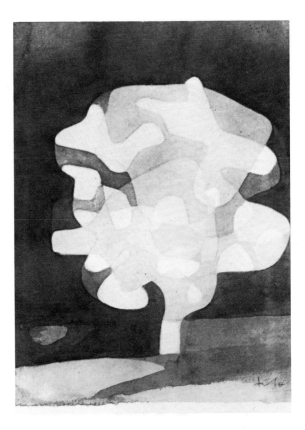

99
*Fig Tree* 1929
Private Collection, New York

his favourite combination of 'essence' and 'appearance' is made plainly visible
to us in a way that nature itself never permits; we see the fully-formed leaf
and the generative impulses – here rendered in lines, overlapping planes, and
colours – which have brought it into being. Moreover, on an even more basic
level Klee's leaf is unlikely ever to have existed in nature, where the vast
majority of such forms are at least broadly symmetrical in shape and veination
and are arranged along a true centre line, as Klee himself had demonstrated
in his classroom examples. Accordingly, his own *Illuminated Leaf* emerges not
as a leaf from the visible world but as an invention parallel to those which nature
creates. Precisely because it reproduces no known form it succeeds in evoking
the principles according to which a whole category of elements of the living
plant have come into being, together with the endless variations which nature
itself has woven around these principles.

Although the 1929 watercolour remains a depiction of a leaf, its simplicity
and monumentality already point our way towards the image of an entire tree.[50]
In Klee's late art these two creations of nature often become interchangeable,
with the simple, forked pattern of a leaf's veins now doubling as a tree and
with whole trees themselves being reduced to the relatively simple shapes of
mere leaves.[51] Even within the same year as he painted *Illuminated Leaf* Klee
created the stylistically related *Fig Tree*, a work which already prompts one to
make this comparison (fig. 99). Only the greater intricacy of the overlapping

planes in the latter picture departs noticeably from the principles governing the structure of Klee's *Leaf*. But the reasons for this can be discovered in nature itself. However much a leaf may be seen as a tree writ small, there is one essential difference between them. Whereas the branching system of a tree develops around a central axis, that of a leaf remains tied to a single plane. Hence Klee accords to his *Fig Tree* a density and three-dimensionality denied to his solitary leaf.

There is, perhaps, another noticeable difference between these two paintings of 1929. For all their obvious analogies Klee's rendering of a single leaf strikes one as probing more deeply to the very heart of nature – a heart which is inevitably obscured when one is confronted with the wayward and entangled form of an entire tree. As we have seen, this desire to lay bare the complex and elusive workings of the macrocosm through the careful study of an element of the microcosm was Klee's preferred approach to nature throughout his career and explains why his depictions of a solitary leaf, fruit, or flower so often appear to contain his profoundest thoughts on the workings of nature. It may also explain why the majority of such works date from his later years. Having already immersed himself in the study of entire trees, plants, and gardens, Klee could at last turn his eye to uncovering the patterns which pervaded them on the most elementary level. Once again, however, this goal was already deeply ingrained in Klee's attitude towards nature from his earliest years. 'Why should you concern yourself with the being of God,' the young artist asked himself in 1908, 'look at one of his flower beds, that is sufficient.'[52] And it was by repeatedly looking at such flower beds that Klee attained that state of inner illumination before nature which eventually made it possible for him to reveal the full mystery and majesty of creation even when confronting a single leaf.

Immediately after Klee's lecture on articulation and development in the individual leaf the artist devoted two sessions to the corresponding processes in the seed and fruit.[53] In addition to the obvious botanical link between these elements, the seed, leaf, and fruit also exemplified for him the active, medial, and passive forces in nature generally. Thus, if the seed initiates growth, the leaf realizes it, and the fruit results from it. But, although these distinctions imply a hierarchy of energies and impulses all three of them are of course necessary for the successful development of the mature plant.

In Klee's own art depictions of seeds alone are a rarity; though, characteristically, when he does choose to paint or draw them he tends to overlay them with a series of concentric rings as though to emphasize the potential energy and growth they harbour (fig. 100). With this, the artist shows a certain fondness for consigning his seeds to the currents of the air,[54] where they join the privileged birds as beings capable of truly dynamic, anti-gravitational movement – a movement which seems to have symbolized for Klee his own search to free both himself and his art from the fetters of the earthly. As the wind and air remain the most capricious and irresponsible of all seed distributors such works may also be seen as sad reminders to us of the important role played by chance in the birth of any of nature's creations.

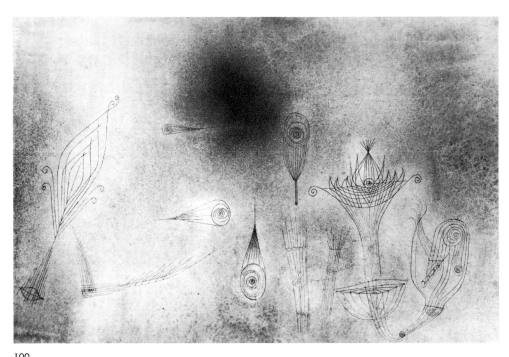

100
*Plant Seeds* 1927 The Galka Scheyer Blue Four Collection, Norton Simon Museum, Pasadena

Much more often, however, the seed figures among Klee's broader concerns with the processes of germination in both nature and art. 'Despite its primitive smallness,' noted the artist, 'a seed is an energy centre charged to the highest degree.'[55] As such the seed served Klee as a natural parallel to his own creative endeavours; for just as the seed was a charged point equipped to give birth to a line (i.e. the first shoot or the seedling) so too was the point of the artist's pen stimulated by his own form-creating energies to give birth to its lines. Thus, if one could come closer to understanding the impulses acting upon the germinating seed, the 'irritated point in nature', one could proceed 'under nature's guidance,' observed Klee, 'to recognize our own creativity'. In both cases Klee noted that the process of 'form-giving' was 'a way of life developing from a mysterious motivation towards purposive action'.[56] And in both cases too he noted that the end was predetermined from the start, with the seed destined to give rise to a particular species of plant and acting as a 'talisman for the regeneration of that species' and with the work of art already conditioned 'by some inner or outer necessity' in its human creator to assume a certain, finished character. While the broader significance of the parallels Klee here draws between creation in art and nature are best discussed elsewhere,[57] his explorations of this 'mysterious motivation' in nature itself may concern us here. Nowhere does his profound understanding of this phenomenon find more eloquent expression than in such late drawings as *Germinating* of 1937 (fig. 101), with its poignant depiction of a solitary seedling bristling with energy waves

101
*Germinating* 1937 Present whereabouts unknown

as it slowly gropes its way upwards, towards the light. With the mind of a scientist and the heart of a poet, Klee here gives truly creative expression to the fact that this seedling is a 'talisman' for the regeneration of its species by already investing it with a vision of its future self. For if we look again at Klee's drawing we will see that, with miraculous economy and suggestiveness, the artist endows its embryonic stages beneath the earth's surface with a general configuration which may also be read as the form of one of its eventual leaves.

Klee's *Germinating* may serve to introduce us to a whole group of his last works which concern themselves with this general theme. Indeed, it is impossible to contemplate this phase of Klee's career without calling to mind his many depictions of birth, growth – and often overgrowth – among the plants.[58] In this rests one of the most consoling paradoxes of his development – one which shows the late Klee preparing for his own death as much with symbols redolent of life (and especially of new life) as with those signalling death. Seen in this way, such works become a clear expression of the artist's firm belief in the ever-renewing powers of nature. It is not hard to imagine that the very process of giving birth to them may even have afforded him with a kind of refuge from death.

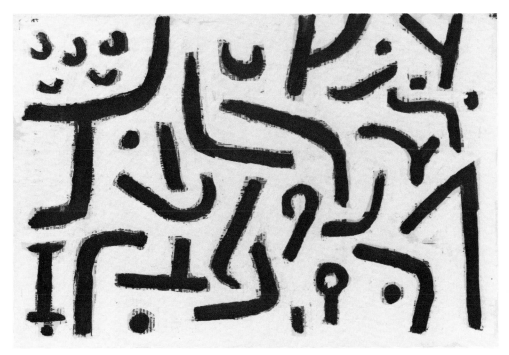

102
*Growth Stirs* 1938  Felix Klee, Bern

Closer consideration of Klee's many late works in this vein forces one to admit, however, that their message is decidedly ambivalent. Though their apparent theme is normally one of burgeoning life, often these final renderings of birth and growth among plants take a decidedly tragic turn, with the broken and fragmented forms of sprouting seeds or blossoming flowers reminding one more of thwarted growth than of anything else. Admittedly, this interpretation assumes that one is entitled to attach a symbolic significance to the fractured and disjointed formal language of the late Klee, whereas, as we have seen, that language was necessitated by his declining physical powers. Questions of style apart, however, it is undeniable that many such pictures were accorded titles which refer more to potential growth than to actual growth. *Signs of Growth*, *New Growth*, *Awakening Things*, and *Growth Stirs* (fig. 102) are typical of these.[59] Furthermore, poignantly embedded in any number of these paintings of burgeoning nature are unmistakable human heads[60] – evidence, it would seem, that Klee accepted the fact that new life could only come into being through the sacrifice of old life.

Where the life of plants is concerned Klee pursues this idea to its remorseless conclusion in his many late renderings of fruits – another theme which, although not confined to his last years, was undeniably one of his final obsessions. Generally speaking fruits held a fascination for Klee as visible proof not only of the fecundity of nature but of its artistry. After all, for a plant to

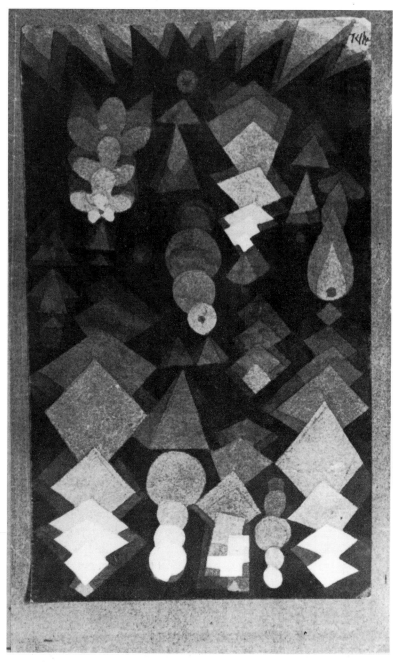

103
*Hanging Fruit* 1921 Present whereabouts unknown

produce such a growth testified to its complete success at all previous stages
of its development, a creative achievement which Klee regularly likened to those
of his own life. Perhaps this explains the inordinate interest the artist showed

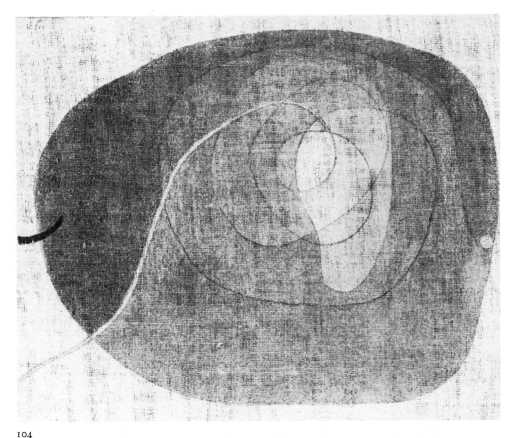

104
*The Fruit* 1932 Present whereabouts unknown

in fruit subjects at the end of his career, when his own art had itself come to fruition – and when its creator had now only to follow the course of the fruit.

Among Klee's earliest depictions of fruits is one of his so-called 'fugal' pictures, *Hanging Fruit* of 1921 (fig. 103).[61] In this a series of gravid and weighty fruit-like forms are shown inexorably ripening, cutting their connections with the parent tree and falling to earth to recommence the life cycle. An analysis of the structure of individual fruits is also introduced into Klee's teachings of the early 1920s, from which it is clear that their appeal for him was not only as symbols of fertility but as key examples of the phenomenon of spiral development around a centre (in this case, the seed) in nature.[62] This aspect of fruit anatomy, which we have already encountered in our discussions of the snail-shell, was subsequently introduced into Klee's art in a series of drawings of 1926–7, all executed in a pleated linear style and often combining fruits with flowers, or even with eyes.[63] Whatever else such works may mean on a metaphysical level, their formal language, with its concentric layers of flesh expanding around a central kernel, is profoundly evocative of the impulse to growth in nature.

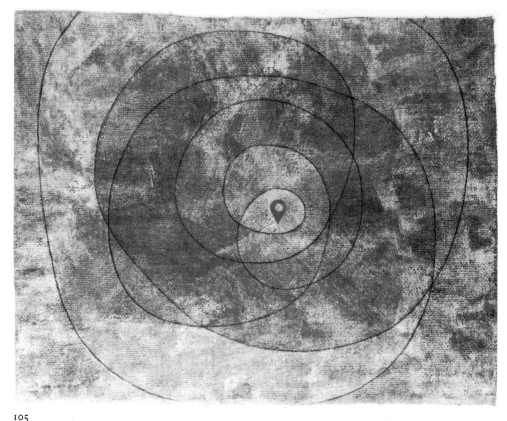

105
*Around the Seed* 1935 Present whereabouts unknown

By the 1930s Klee had moved from these delicate linear depictions of fruit to portray them in a series of awesome images in which one or two fruits typically fill the picture field as potent reminders of the generative forces in nature. To this group belongs one of the artist's most unforgettable renderings of this subject, *The Fruit* of 1932 (fig. 104), wherein the fleshy inner rings of a pear-like fruit double as an umbilical cord, growing whiter as they approach the fruit's energy centre – the seed – as though to indicate the inspiration to the formation of so lavish a creation in the first place. Once again, of course, Klee employs artistic licence by combining animal and vegetable motifs within the same being. But, on a poetical level at least, this is justifiable; for, as we have already seen, although a fruit does not actually possess an umbilical cord, it does provide a kind of womb or life-line for the seed. In like manner Klee's *Around the Seed* of 1935 (fig. 105) focuses even more closely upon the layers of nutrient flesh which protect the seed – promise of a new generation – and in literally gorging the picture space with this image the artist creates one of his most overpowering evocations of the inexhaustible bounty of nature.[64] Luxuriantly protected by layers of succulent growth Klee's seed here becomes

116

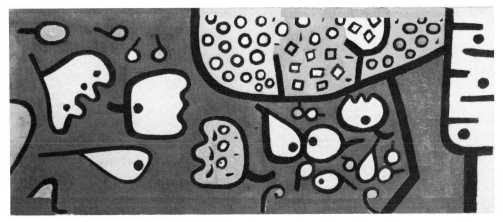

106
*Fruit on Blue* 1938 Kunstmuseum, Bern

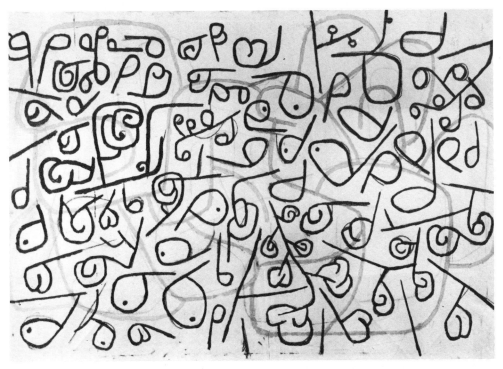

107
*Composition with Fruits* 1940 Felix Klee, Bern

a symbol of the untrammelled procreative instincts which pervade the whole of organic life.

During Klee's last five years fruits provide the subjects of an ever-increasing number of major works, among them *Fruitfulness*, *Coelin Fruit*, *Fruit on Blue*, (fig. 106), *Voluptuous Fruit*, and the large untitled *Composition with Fruits*, which was apparently one of the artist's very last works (fig. 107).[65] In all of these pictures fruit-like forms are rendered as though imprisoned in the paint surface, sometimes accompanied by vestiges of their preceding stages, the leaves and seeds. Rarely, however, are they shown still attached to their life-supporting branches. Instead Klee prefers to present them to us strewn against a coloured background, their prominent black calyxes (i.e. the remains of the flower) often doubling as eyes, or even seeds, and poignantly reminding us that out of these images of completed life will come forth new existences. In the prevailing colours of many of these works, too, Klee succeeds in endowing them with a universal significance. Thus, several of the most important of them are dominated by pasty, even petrified blues of a decidedly cold and deathly cast. Far from calling to mind the fruits of nature such inert and lifeless hues speak to us instead of the realms of the eternal and the infernal in nature. Once again, the dangers of over-interpreting these pictures are all too evident – and must be resisted. But one cannot deny that such images are a preoccupation of the late Klee or that they are treated in a manner which is curiously double-edged. Nothing proclaims the fecundity and regenerative capacities of nature more than the fruit; and yet its very appearance signals the end of the plant's life-cycle and the beginning of that of another. In Klee's obsessive concern with this theme during his final years a similar message appears concealed. For never were his own creative powers so fruitful – or his own physical powers so atrophying.

# 4 · The Two Realms Meet

Two years after painting *The Fruit*, in 1934, Klee completed a number of further works on this theme, among them *Suffering Fruit* and *Heavily Fructifying* (figs. 108 & 109). In addition to attesting to his growing interest in this subject – and to preparing us for the gravely monumental art of his last years – these two works exemplify a central aspect of Klee's attitude towards nature: namely, his belief in the essential interrelatedness of its many diverse beings and processes. In *Suffering Fruit* a large and unidentifiable fruit ominously fills the picture space in a manner which anticipates Magritte's handling of similar subjects in the 1950s.[1] Though its stem and calyx suggest that it is a kind of dessert fruit its lumpy, irregular shape more closely resembles that of an ordinary potato; and, as if this were not humiliation enough, its skin bears all the marks of an insidious and disfiguring blight. In the centre of its body a large, downcast eyelid poignantly conveys both its pain and its shame, and (like the lone eye of the Cyclops) redoubles our pity through its pathetic singleness. In *Heavily Fructifying*, on the other hand, a gravid female figure supported by stem-like legs is rendered in a series of concentric layers of flesh resembling the growth rings of a tree or of Klee's own *The Fruit*. She sustains a different kind of humiliation – that of growing and reproducing in a wholly vegetative manner. Thus, while the theme of fruit and fruitfulness is common to both works the ideas underlying them are directly opposed; for, in *Suffering Fruit* Klee's fruit behaves like a human and in *Heavily Fructifying* his human behaves like a fruit. And, if the former elicits pity and compassion in us, the latter at least elicits tacit recognition. There are, after all, some human activities which are most aptly characterized with reference to the sub-human.

Such analogies between the actions or emotions of man and those of the lower organisms are not unique to Klee's art at this time but are a constant concern of his work from the start. Indeed, their beginnings may be traced to those early satirical etchings already discussed, wherein the substitution of man by beast so often serves the artist in describing, and then deriding, mankind's more bestial instincts.[2] With the formation of Klee's mature style, however, the range of analogies drawn between man and the animals, the animals and plants, and the living and non-living worlds is greatly extended to form a large body of works which many will regard as the very quintessence of Klee. Of these, a significant proportion bear witness to the artist's ingenuity and endless powers of invention – and to the essentially poetical nature of his gifts – but do not necessarily go beyond this. However, an equally large number penetrate much deeper and clearly belong to the so-called 'inner circle' of Klee's inspiration.

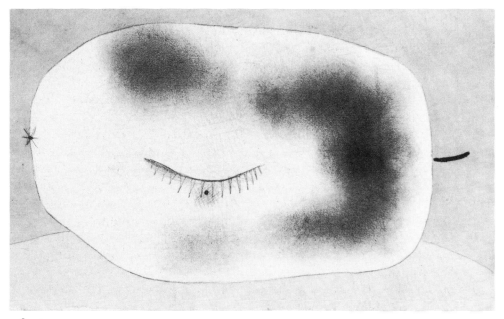

108
*Suffering Fruit* 1934
Felix Klee, Bern

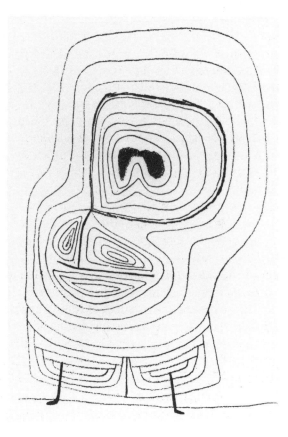

109
*Heavily Fructifying* 1934
Present whereabouts unknown

120

And although the precise meaning or symbolism of many of these works remains uncertain, there can be little doubt that they have their origins in a profoundly mystical view of nature – one which regards all of creation as subject to certain pervasive laws and rhythms and which seeks to understand and explain any one facet of nature with reference to any number of others.

In Klee's mature art this attitude is most immediately apparent on the level of pure formal analogy. This may conveniently be demonstrated by returning to three of the lower animals and three of the plant motifs already considered: namely, the snail, louse, and snake, and the fruit, leaf, and seed. We have seen how, at several points in his classroom teachings, Klee encouraged his students to study the form of a snail in conjunction with that of an apple and reminded them that, for all their obvious differences in appearance, the essence of both of these forms could be reduced to a spiralling line radiating outwards from a central kernel.[3] For Klee the discovery of such similarities revealed 'the secret of the creative will to form'[4] in both organisms and made visible a basic and recurring formal principle to be found in nature – one which, in certain circumstances may lead to the creation of a snail and, in others, to that of an apple.

Similarly the louse and leaf would seem to have little to do with one another except in so far as they may function as predator and prey, a relationship with which Klee was well familiar.[5] Considered from the purely formal point of view, however, they bear much more in common; for, as Klee's own art demonstrates, both may be reduced to a central 'spine' or vein from which arise a series of limbs or subsidiary veins. Seen in this way both lice and leaves appear essentially pinnate in form – a similarity which, in Klee's late art, occasionally made them virtually interchangeable.[6] Finally, the snake and the germinating seed would appear to have even less in common than those pairs already discussed. Yet they too exemplified for Klee a basic organizational impulse in nature – that of the charged point which is capable of developing into a line. We have already seen how this aspect of the germinating seed served Klee as a convenient model in nature for that ineluctable progress from point to line which was necessary for the growth of a picture. In this respect the example of the snake was also relevant; for more than any other organism in nature the snake may be viewed as a walking line, with its entire body acting as what Klee called a 'giant foot'.[7] When one remembers the journey that Klee himself undertook with a walking line in his *Creative Credo*,[8] it is little wonder that this aspect of the snake form particularly appealed to him.

In all three instances, then, Klee has penetrated beneath the very dissimilar exteriors of these organisms to uncover telling analogies in their underlying construction. In so doing he has reminded us of two of his most fervently held beliefs regarding the forms of this world: firstly, that their essence is more important than their appearance and, secondly, that the processes which give rise to a form are more important than the finished form itself.[9] The first of these is readily demonstrated by the fact that, in ignoring the outer appearance of these organisms and probing to their essence, Klee has revealed to us those deep and invisible truths about them which link them with other living beings and which approach nature's most universal forms of expression. Where the second of these is concerned it is worth noting that the finished forms of all six of the organisms considered appear (at least) to reveal a good deal about the processes of their formation. In one way or another all are made up of a series of rhythmically repeated units – whether coiled (in the snail and apple), forked (the louse and leaf), or segmented (the snake and germinating seed) – which make it seemingly easy to retrace the course of their development. When one combines these two phenomena one arrives at the true goal of Klee's explorations of the living world – namely, to discover the basic patterns according to which nature creates its forms and the means by which it proceeds to build them. The resulting motifs of the spiral, the forked shape, and the extended line might be seen as a kind of alphabet of formative patterns which Klee discovered among the most diverse living beings and out of which he forged a pictorial vocabulary which mirrored nature's own underlying harmony, economy, and consistency.

Even from these three examples it will be evident that Klee was especially attracted to those creations of nature which readily invited such formal comparisons; and, indeed, this preference must be seen as one of the most distinctive features of his art. For all its wealth of themes and pictures Klee's output remains remarkably economical in its repertoire of basic shapes and images, consistently avoiding those organisms which are in any way out of the ordinary – for example, orchids, butterflies, or birds-of-paradise find no place in his art – and confining itself instead to those more run-of-the-mill creatures which reveal nature at its most constant, and even conventional. Nature's constancy in building its own forms leads him to reveal to us a series of hidden analogies between the most disparate beings which together create the impression of having reduced a bewilderingly complex world to a semblance of order. At this level, the forms of cactuses and humans may be seen to meet; the secret shapes of crystals, diatoms, protozoans, and radial blossoms all reveal their hidden kinship; and the skeleton of a lowly leaf may be metamorphosed into a louse, a flatworm, or even a fish. It is doubtless this ability to uncover unexpected links between dissimilar things which partly accounts for the popular image of Klee as a 'poetical' painter. Although it would be foolish to deny that a streak of poetry – indeed often of sheer magic – informs many of the analogies to be found in his art, an equally large number of them derive instead from a rational pursuit of those elementary forms and forces which pervade all of existence. Whatever one chooses to call this pursuit it clearly proceeded under what Klee himself saw as 'nature's guidance' and its apparent aim was to discover and lay bare that grand master-plan out of which all of life had been born – or at least to come a step or two closer to discovering that plan.

In Klee's laconic late style the basic repertoire of formal patterns which he had slowly pried loose from nature's creations increasingly becomes the very substance of his art, with those simple forks and spirals now serving in themselves to evoke a multitude of beings. Here again both poetry and reason may be seen to mould his images, with one or the other occasionally gaining the upper hand. Witness Klee's two paintings of 1938 entitled *Timid Brute* and *Heroic Roses* (figs. 110 & 111), which bear consecutive numbers in his *œuvre* catalogue and which are clearly concerned with the same general formal motif. The form in question is, of course, that which Klee had already discovered beneath the exteriors of the snail and the fruit. Now, however, the coiled spiralling energies of nature are revealed to have two further and very different applications: firstly, to depict the latent strength of a cowardly, bell-bedecked figure who retreats in the opposite direction to Klee's arrow; and, secondly, to describe a group of unfolding roses gifted with almost demonic powers of self-assertion. While the latter has its foundations in the essence of the flowering principle in nature, only Klee's poetic bent – together with his deep understanding of human nature – could have led him to adopt a similar formal conceit for his *Timid Brute*, whose spiral presumably uncoils to assert his brutality and recoils to disclose his timidity.

Finally, in a brush drawing of 1937 entitled *Snail Paths* (fig. 112) Klee brings all three of these formal motifs together on the same sheet, with the spiral, the forked shape, and the moving line now evoking a myriad of possibilities as they exist in nature – from snail to whirling heavens, from serpent to growing stalk, and from louse to entire tree. In such a work as this the aged artist appears to have pared his art down to a point towards which it had been inexorably moving all along – towards that magical moment when nature's depths had at last been plumbed and its most closely guarded creative secrets could finally be laid bare.

Hand in hand with Klee's search for nature's germinal formal elements went his explorations of a wide range of more specific analogies between various members of the plant and animal kingdoms. Although many of these likewise rely upon the discovery of hidden formal resemblances among the most disparate creatures, the majority are devoted instead to exploring the fundamental unity of life itself and typically take as their theme those currents of emotion or instinct which run through all of creation. In such works Klee often appears to us to be at his most enchantingly poetical, if not purely fanciful. Nevertheless, the undoubted profundity with which he imbues many of his creations in this vein and the consistency with which he explores certain favourite themes suggest that such pictures warrant more serious consideration. Far from being products of mere ingenuity a number of them at least reveal a coherent and deeply pondered view of life and provide us with a moving reminder that its passions, its processes, and its pathos are as real and as complex among the humblest beings as they are among the noblest. Only man's own egocentricity, Klee seems to suggest, prevents him from seeing this. And only Klee's crystalline detachment (one is tempted to add) makes it possible for him to do so for us.

Appropriately enough, Klee's earliest depictions of this invisible face of nature date from the years 1914–17, when they serve as conclusive (and quite

110
*Timid Brute* 1938
Private Collection, New York

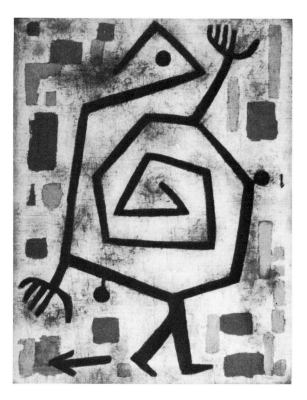

111
*Heroic Roses* 1938
Kunstsammlung Nordrhein-
Westfalen, Düsseldorf

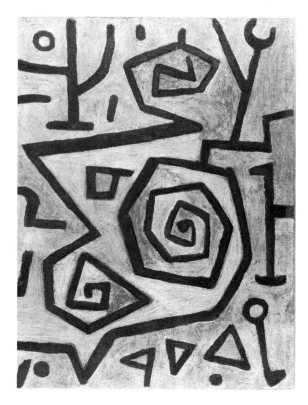

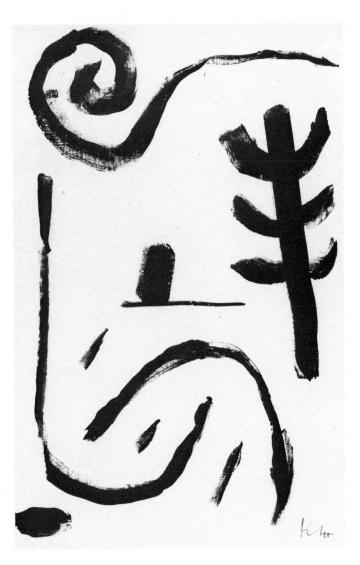

literal) proof of his new-found ability to join nature and poetry in his art. In
more than a dozen works of these years Klee begins his creative investigations
of what was to become the most familiar of all such comparisons in his art –
that between the lives of the plants and those of man. By the time he had turned
to exploring these relations on an artistic level Klee had already made many
such comparisons in his early writings. Though these alone cannot account for
his lifelong fascination with this theme they do at least anticipate certain of his
favourite later subjects. Thus, already in his youth the artist had discovered
that the actions and emotions of plants paralleled those of man; that their
upright 'limbed' bodies likewise invited such comparisons; and, conversely,
that his own moods and emotions – not to mention his own artistic 'fruits' –
had clear counterparts in the domain of the plants.[10] In addition to these it
is worth remembering that the young Klee's deepest thoughts on the harmony

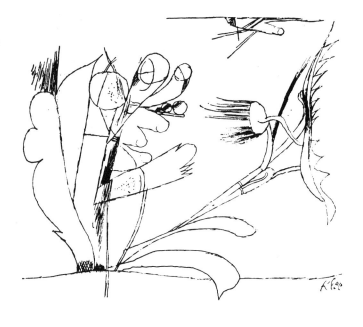

113
*Passionate Plants* 1914
Present whereabouts unknown

1914.200. leidenschaftl. Pflanzen

and economy of nature were largely inspired by his dialogues with the plant kingdom. And, finally, at least one other explanation may be put forward for Klee's preference for this broad analogy over the many others available to him. In choosing to explore the inner kinship between man and the plants rather than between the plants and lower animals Klee not only created an art of greater relevance to his own species but he also encompassed the totality of creation, from top to bottom, and thereby permitted himself to explore the most universal facets of life.

In what would appear to be Klee's first essay on this theme – the 1914 drawing *Passionate Plants* (fig. 113) – he already outlines one of his favourite of all such comparisons: namely, that between the courting behaviour of man and that of plants. In this instance a lusty male 'blossom' gazes leeringly in the direction of a prospective partner, his arm, nose, and bulging eyes already betraying his phallic intentions. Urging him on is an alluringly eye-lashed female blossom which serves as a kind of smokescreen suddenly thrown up to conceal an even lovelier prize – a fully-faced flower which turns hastily away, as though preparing to make a quick getaway. While the outcome of this encounter may still be in some doubt, the relationship as Klee outlines it is one all too familiar in life itself. Uncannily, the artist suggests to us here that the svelte female blossom is a practised coquette, more given to teasing than to pleasing, and that her portly pursuer is likewise an old hand at his game.

This distinction between a thrusting male blossom and a labile female one is subsequently employed by Klee in any number of later depictions of the sexual life of plants. It already reappears in two works of 1915, *The Flower as*

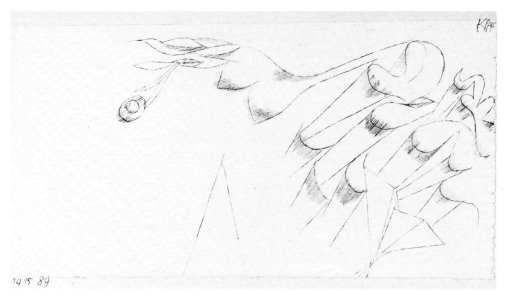

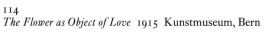

114
*The Flower as Object of Love* 1915 Kunstmuseum, Bern

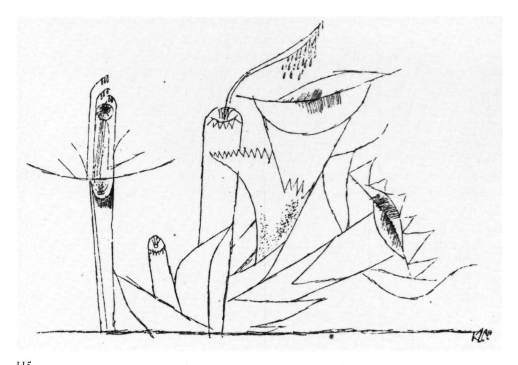

115
*Hermaphroditic and Unisexual Plants* 1915 Present whereabouts unknown

*Object of Love* and *Hermaphroditic and Unisexual Plants* (figs. 114 & 115). In the former Klee's 'flower' – with its seductive swaying motions and sinuous curves – is unmistakably female. With her ample and available breasts and her 'come-hither' gaze she here waves a single, irresistible eye towards any comers. Nor do her efforts appear to be in vain, for already emerging from the base of Klee's drawing is an aggressively phallic triangle tellingly aimed at the juncture between her pendulous breasts. In the latter work Klee turns from so overtly human a view of plant courtship to consider the differences between those flowers which are self-pollinating and those in which the sexes remain separate. To the left of Klee's drawing an hermaphroditic plant bearing a single arm-like stamen appears poised to drop pollen grains into the female part of its own anatomy (the 'pistil'); while in the two blossoms at the right Klee fancifully creates a phallic-like male flower whose stamen now reaches out to deposit its pollen into the swelling receptacle of an adjacent female flower apparently borne on the same plant. Although Klee's treatment of both of these phenomena is decidedly free it is worth noting that both means of fertilization are known in nature and that the male and female parts of the flower are broadly distinguished there as they are in Klee, the former being lean and upright and the latter gravid and fleshy.

Two further works in this series celebrate successful partnerships between plants which are in one case wholly imaginary and in the other surprisingly realistic. In the former – a drawing of 1915 entitled *Mutual Relations among the Plants* (fig. 116) – Klee depicts a moment of intimacy between male- and female-faced blossoms, their petal-like lips meeting to exchange a kiss or a fondling caress, she gazing adoringly up at him and he suddenly gazing inwards, as though already weighing the consequences of this first embrace. In the latter – a drawing of 1916 called *Milkwort and Pansy* (fig. 117) – the artist presents us with a rare depiction among his mature works of two distinct varieties of plants. Although a courtship or union between these two blossoms would thereby appear to be out of the question, as Klee renders them one senses a deep bond between this virile Milkwort and its endearingly nubile partner. Admittedly, the straightforward title and the apparent realism of this drawing, which looks suspiciously like a study from nature, would appear to discourage any such fanciful interpretation of its theme. But here the points of contact between Klee's two blossoms say more than any poetical title might have done, with the strong and protective gesture of the male petal meeting with a light, grazing response from its chosen mate. For all its seeming fantasy, however, even this partnership has some basis in theory; for as long ago as Linnaeus the pansy was characterized as a flower which was unashamedly female in its feminine parts.[11] Whether or not Klee was aware of this description he here creates an unmistakably female pansy, as though paying heed to the German name for this flower (*Stiefmütterchen*), which, when translated, means 'little stepmother'. Along with this Klee also reminds us that, although the majority of flowers are both male and female, the form and structure of certain of them often seem more befitting to one sex or the other. Even in his purely imaginary

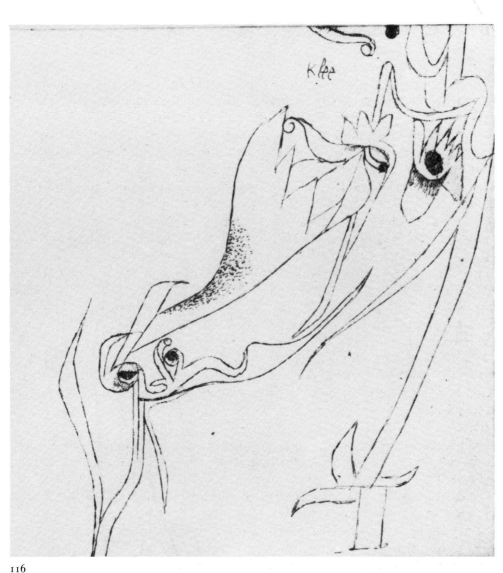

116
*Mutual Relations among the Plants* 1915 Present whereabouts unknown

blossoms Klee adopts these general sexual characteristics as he apparently sensed them in nature so that they might be made to mirror those of mankind itself. Thus his male flowers tend to be straight and strong and his female ones soft and pendulous; or, to put it more frankly, the former tend to be unashamedly phallic and the latter alluringly frilly.

In a number of other works of these years Klee confines himself to a single plant-like being seen from a variety of emotional points of view. Two consecutive works of 1915, for instance, depict *Plant Love* and *Plant Wisdom*; and in both of these the artist presents us with flowers which double as faces and thereby transgress the bounds of the purely vegetative. In *Plant Love* (fig. 118) Klee's flower has sprouted a long, prehensile proboscis. At the end

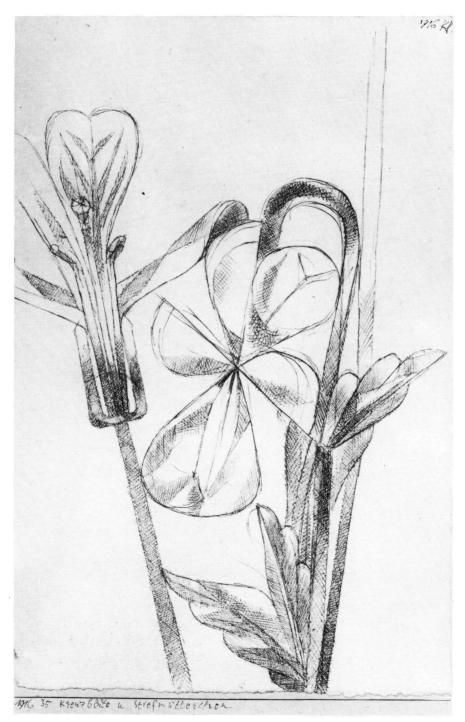

1916 35 kreuzblue u Stiefmütterchen

117
*Milkwort and Pansy* 1916 Kupferstichkabinett, Kunstmuseum, Basel

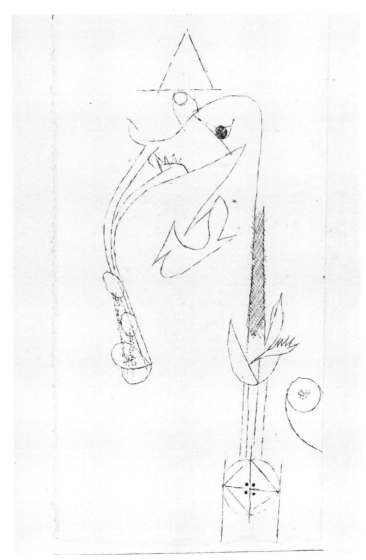

118
*Plant Love* 1915 Felix Klee, Bern

of this appendage a pair of dripping pollen grains attest to the amorousness of
this blossom, while a bulging eye reaching out from its head to establish contact
with a triangle floating overhead seems to symbolize a state of blissful and
perfect union with another.[12]

Finally, in two further drawings of 1915 – *The Blossom* and *Lonely Plant*
(figs. 119 & 120) – Klee evokes our sympathy for those precocious plants which
aspire too high in life. *The Blossom*, for instance, may purport to depict no more
than its non-committal title suggests. Yet nestled within it is a protoplasmic
creature which bears a superficial similarity to a group of free-swimming
protozoans of the genus *Klebsiella* (fig. 121), which are themselves half-plant

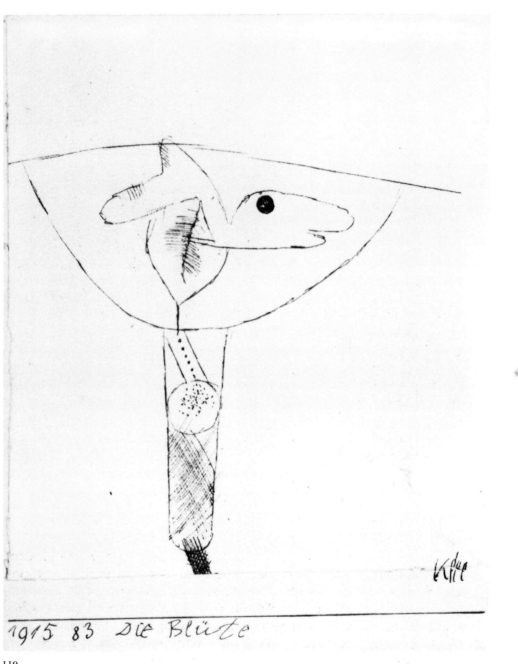

119
*The Blossom* 1915 Kunstmuseum, Bern

120
*Lonely Plant* 1915
Present whereabouts unknown

121
*Klebsiella alligata*

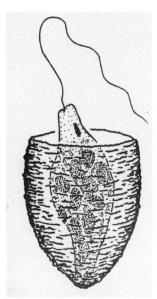

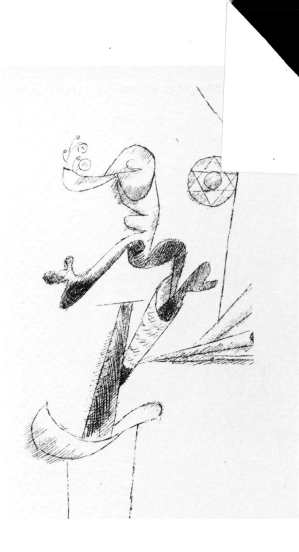

and half-animal. Equipped with an eye, head, mouth, and body, Klee's blossom yet remains seemingly dependent upon the stem of its parent plant; and herein perhaps lies its undoing. For, while the anatomy of this creature strikes one as more convincingly animal than plant-like – and while its plaintive expression suggests that it is clearly striving to become something more – it remains ultimately ensnared to a vegetative existence, as though a freak creation of nature destined for an early extinction. Only slightly more successful, however, is Klee's *Lonely Plant*, wherein a strangely humanoid blossom steps out from its vegetative base wearing a smugly solemn expression and sporting a florid nose which it waves unrequitedly at some unseen partner. But, having so radically transgressed the bounds of the vegetative, this ultimate creation of the plant's ingenuity appears fated to remain unique and thereby alone, as Klee's title indicates. Is it too far-fetched to suggest that the artist might also have subtitled this drawing 'What Price such Freedom!' or 'such Progress!'?

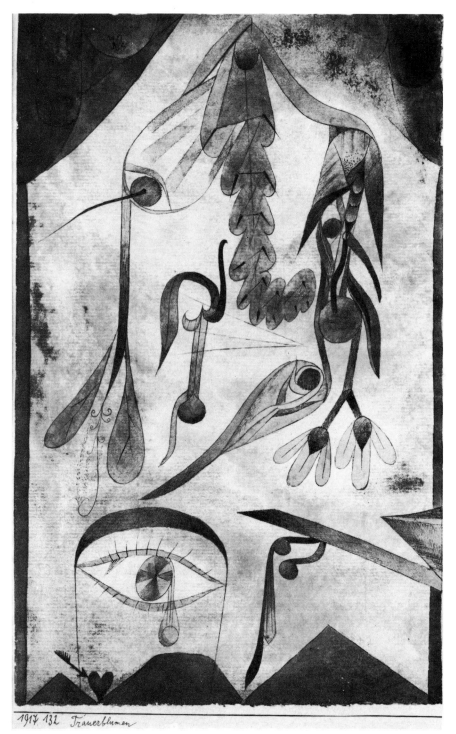

*Sad Flowers* 1917 Staatsgalerie moderner Kunst, Munich

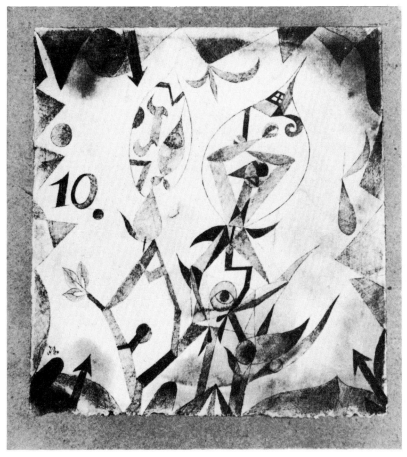

123
*10 (Twin Plants)* 1917 Private Collection, USA

Klee's early explorations of the emotional lives of the plants culminate in two closely contemporary watercolours of 1917 entitled *Sad Flowers* and *10 (Twin Plants)* (figs. 122 & 123). Of these the latter would appear to be the less puzzling. Whatever the precise nature of their relationship the two plants of Klee's picture here enjoy a rare degree of compatibility. Springing from common roots and blossoming in unison they may be seen as a twin brother and sister or even as an ideal match. With arrows converging upon them from three sides of the sheet Klee's tapered and sperm-like male blossom and his swellingly egg-like female one here seem made for one another. Perhaps this accounts for the ecstatic dance being performed by the human figure concealed within the right-hand blossom. With its wanton sexuality and its audaciously choreographed pose this figure already appears to exult at the prospect of a happy and fruitful union.

In *Sad Flowers*, on the other hand, Klee creates one of his earliest and most heart-rending evocations of the darker side of plant emotions. In this, one of his first botanical stage landscapes, the artist raises the curtain on a series of mountain peaks above which float the flowers of his title. Although none of these flowers is identifiable their general derivation from the world of plants is familiar enough – and even more familiar are their emotions. Dominating the scene is a sprig of downcast blossoms and leaves, one of which (at the left) assumes the form of an eye seen in cross-section from whence individual petals fall like tears. At the right a similar motif, while expressing the same emotion, assumes the shape of a winged seed about to float free from its parent plant. Finally, at the lower left of the design Klee clinches this analogy between the emotions of plants and man with a monumental head bearing a single tearful eye and a heart about to be pierced by an arrow. Regardless of precisely how one wishes to interpret this scene – and too precise an interpretation would obviously deprive it of much of its poetry – there can be little doubt that it is a highly imaginative rendering of recognizably human emotions affecting the plants. And given the tears, the stricken heart, and the apparently feminine and masculine nature of the upper and lower organisms respectively, it is not inconceivable that the picture's sorrow is the sorrow of unrequited love. Moreover, whether it is plants or man who are subject to this emotion is probably less important than the emotion itself as Klee senses it behind all of nature. Thus, the eyes and tears – borrowed from the world of human form and feeling – visibly convey their sorrow in a manner impossible among the plants. Complementing these, the drooping and dejected blossoms – familiar enough from any number of well-known flowers (e.g. the so-called 'Bleeding Hearts') – physically express this emotion in a way much rarer among humans. When combined these two motifs permit Klee to create a poignant image of universal sorrow – of a sorrow which is as real and as intense at the bottom of the hierarchy of life as it is at the top.

Although Klee's initial explorations of the human side of plants are in many respects quite unassuming works they already introduce us to those three major analogies between man and plants which the artist was to pursue in his many later creations in this vein. Broadly speaking these analogies may be classed as ones of form, function, or feeling – or, to give them their fancier names, of morphology, physiology, or psychology. As in the early paintings and drawings of 1914–17 Klee's later treatments of this theme frequently combine more than one of these comparisons in a single work. But beyond this it is difficult to generalize about such works except to note that they are a special preoccupation of the artist during the early 1920s and late 1930s and that, in keeping with the broader evolution of Klee's art, they progress from being ingenious (and often very witty) reminders of the fundamental sameness of existence in his early years to becoming deeply disturbing reminders of its underlying seriousness in the very last works – though obviously there are exceptions to this in either case.

Where formal analogies between man and plants are concerned Klee's ingenuity literally knows no bounds. At any point in his career – but especially in the early 1920s – plants may be made to sprout breasts, arms, legs, or pudenda and thereby to approach the human. Conversely, humans may themselves don flowery faces and leafy limbs and forsake the drab hues of their

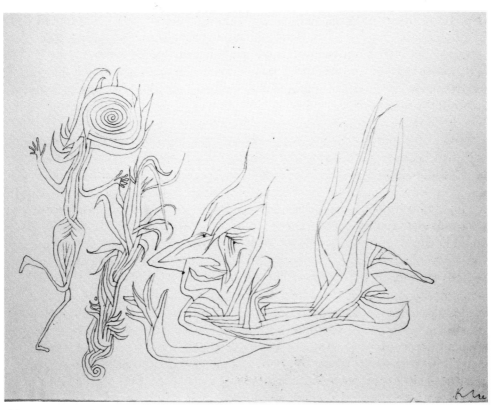

124
*Vegetal Evil* 1927 Private Collection, USA

own world for the gorgeous colours of the floral kingdom. In either case the
result is often similar, with each realm giving to the other what it most needs,
the human world contributing movement and expression to the still and silent
plants and the latter in turn bestowing their florid forms and variegated hues
upon the monochromatic human race. Although the images thus created may
strike one as pure fantasy they also afford us a welcome insight into the
characteristics and limitations of the two kingdoms. One is reminded of how
the unobtrusive movements of plants often seem to reveal their own inner states
of being or feeling and of how the clothing and finery which adorn so much
of humanity serve to provide it with a beauty and allure which nature has
lavished upon the lowly plants but largely denied to man. Klee's drawing of
1927, *Vegetal Evil* (fig. 124), here presents us with the best (or should one say
the worst?) of both worlds: a group of hybrid hags whose disguises are
borrowed from the pleated and wrinkled forms of leaves and flowers and who
work their evil with the aid of those pointedly hooked noses and chins which
are among nature's more malevolent bequests to humanity.

On a more esoteric level Klee's drawing of 1934, *Calix Abdominis* (fig. 14),
reveals to us a hidden formal analogy between these two realms – that between
the convoluted form of an unopened flower contained within its protective outer
covering (or calyx) and the comparably tangled intricacies of the human

abdomen. Moreover, as the 'stem' which supports this blossom here doubles as an umbilical cord the blossom itself may be read as a human embryo nestling within its mother's womb and drawing sustenance from her in a manner similar to that by which the flower derives nourishment from its supporting stem and parent plant. Nor may the analogy which Klee draws here be interpreted in purely formal terms; for, as we have already seen, both the flower and the foetus bring with them the promise of a new generation.[13]

But by far the most frequent formal analogy of this kind to be found in Klee's art is that between the flower and the human face – a theme which qualifies as a near obsession in the early 1920s and which may often be found both before and after this time. In drawing this analogy Klee is, admittedly, far from original, for leaf- and flower-faces are familiar from many other periods in the history of art, from the leaf-men of Gothic art to the even more fantastic creations of an Arcimboldo, a Grandville, or a Redon.[14] But, while Klee was doubtless aware of many of these prototypes his interest in this theme cannot be accounted for on these grounds alone; and, in any case, he was to turn it to quite different creative ends. For unlike his predecessors in this vein Klee seems to have been attracted to such subjects neither as exercises in pure fantasy nor as merely ingenious visual puns; and still less did he employ them in a conventionally symbolic manner. Instead they enter Klee's art as yet another manifestation of his steadfast belief that, for all its apparent diversity, nature was essentially all of a piece.

Paradoxically, the most unforgettable flower-face to be found in Klee's art is one which would not appear to belong to this category at all. This is the famous and oft-reproduced painting of 1922, *Senecio* (fig. 125). Confronted with this soulful rendering of childhood sorrow one is hardly led to immediate thoughts of the flowers. Yet the somewhat cryptic title of Klee's picture is in fact borrowed from that world, where it gives its name to a genus of composite flowers which includes a number of familiar wild and garden varieties (fig. 126). In common with the protagonist of Klee's picture many of these are predominantly yellow in colour; and, as composite blossoms, all are essentially rayed in construction, with their petals rotating around prominent centres in much the same way as the eyes, eyebrows, and nose of Klee's head appear to be preparing to do. In the case of the latter this slight misalignment of the features poignantly suggests a state of dawning inner unrest; but this does not explain why Klee was led to make the comparison with flowers in the first place. In themselves the regularity, the prevailing colour, and the rayed construction of this head may have suggested the comparison to him. But in so mysterious and knowledgeable an artist it is also possible that the connection went much deeper than this. After all, if the flower is the 'face' of the plant so too is the face the 'flower' of the human body. Both tend to be the most colourful, animated, and decorated parts of their respective organisms; to be the seat of their feelings and emotions; and, most importantly of all, to be their initial object of attraction or repulsion. Such analogies of form and strategy on nature's part would not have been lost on Klee when it came to naming this woeful

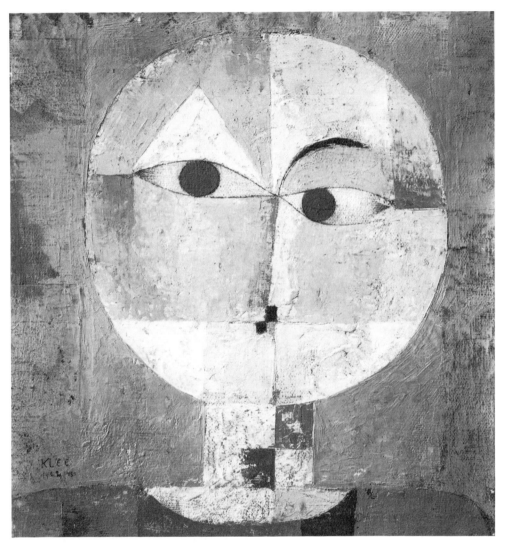

125
*Senecio* 1922
Kunstmuseum, Basel

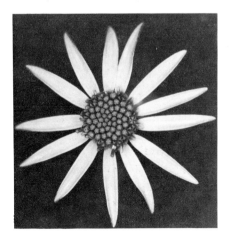

126
*Senecio jacobaea* (Common
Ragwort)

127
*Plant-like Physiognomic* 1922
Kunstmuseum, Bern

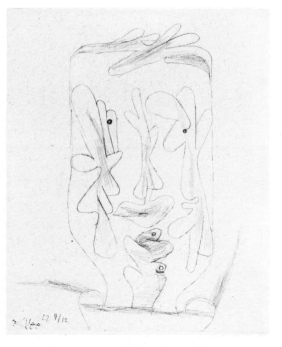

129
*Flower Face* 1922
Private Collection, New York

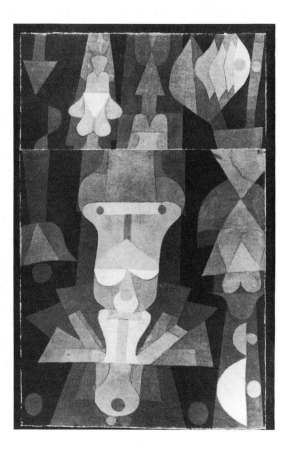

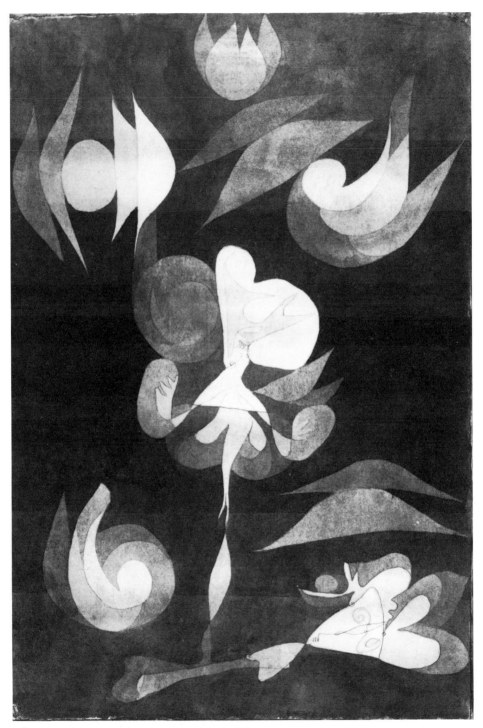

128
*Dying Plants* 1922 Collection, The Museum of Modern Art, New York, The Philip L. Goodwin
Collection

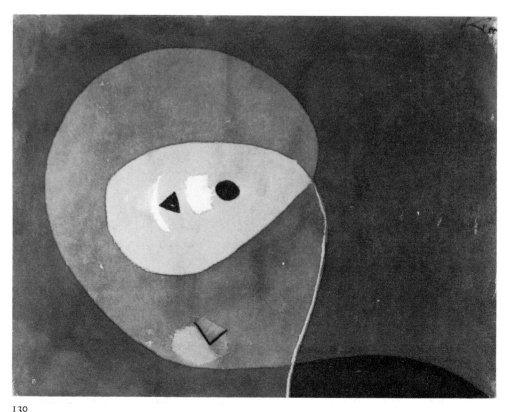

130
*A new Face* 1932 Private Collection

countenance, which already appears old before its time. Burdened with
thoughts of its own destiny Klee's *Senecio* reminds us of yet another similarity
which it shares with the flowers. Since their appearance marks the end of the
plant's life-cycle they too may be seen as messengers of their own destiny.

Not all of Klee's leaf and flower-faces immediately speak to us on so solemn
a level as *Senecio*. Some – for instance, *Plant-like Physiognomic* of 1922 (fig.
127) or *Bud of a Smile* of the preceding year[15] – seem more purely comical
than anything else. But, contemporary with them Klee created such works as
*Dying Plants, Flower Face*, and *Physiognomy of a Flower* (figs. 128 & 129);[16]
and with these one enters a different world. Petal-like or not the faces of the
last two of these pictures are suffused with sorrow; and, in the case of the last
– where the blossom in question seems so childlike – with an early sorrow which
recalls that of *Senecio* and already seems to prefigure the plant's end. Nowhere,
however, does Klee explore this analogy between the appearance of the flower
and the imminent death of its plant more touchingly than in *Dying Plants*. In
this a bewitchingly feminine flower – magnificently florid and almost
unbearably fragile – dances her last dance, a dance of death, against a sombre
background, watched over by suns and moons but otherwise pathetically alone.

Beneath the earth's surface her roots merge with the reclining form of an already deceased plant whose flower is even more recognizably face-like and bears all the marks of having suffered a painful death.

Finally, when his theme demanded it, Klee could also adapt this analogy to uncover more appropriate botanical equivalents for certain types of human physiognomy. Thus in a 1926 drawing, *Old Woman*,[17] the face depicted resembles not a flower but a withered leaf whose network of parallel veins here serves to describe the dried and wrinkled skin of its aged human subject. And, at the opposite end of the life-cycle, in *A new Face* of 1932 (fig. 130), Klee's analogy is between the birth of a new face and the unfolding spiral of a germinating plant.[18] Yet so subtle and flexible are his means of expression here that the lines described also evoke another symbol of birth and growth in nature, this time from the world of the mammals – namely, the umbilical cord. In this respect *A new Face* reminds one of *The Fruit*, which was painted shortly after it in 1932.

Moving from formal analogies between man and the plants to those of a more functional nature Klee's predominant interest is undoubtedly in the theme of sexual reproduction, as was already apparent in his works of the period 1914–17. In contrast to his many flower-faces, which would appear to contain at least as much human as botanical significance, Klee's erotic plants seem preeminently concerned with revealing the animal nature of plant-like sexuality rather than the vegetative nature of human reproduction. Precisely why the artist should have devoted so many works to this general theme remains one of the mysteries of his art. For, at least after the satirical etchings of his early career, Klee's art distinguishes itself from that of any number of his contemporaries through the surprising lack of interest it shows in eroticism or sexuality, whether human or otherwise. The principal exceptions to this, however, are his many incursions into the sexual lives and habits of plants. While the artist's writings on nature reveal an occasional interest in such matters the most likely explanation for his inordinate creative fascination with this theme may once again lie with the fact that the sex life of the plant is unique among virtually all other organisms through its very secretiveness. As an aspect of nature which remains largely undisclosed to the human eye it might well have appealed to Klee's fondness for revealing such hidden secrets of nature in his art. To do so, however, the artist had inevitably to rely upon comparisons with more plainly visible modes of sexual reproduction, principally among the higher animals. In the process he created a race of mixed beings – part-plant and part-animal – which may be seen as symbolic of the procreative instincts which pervade the entire organic world.

Klee's art of the early 1920s is especially rich in such images, among them a drawing of 1921 entitled *A Table set with strange Flowers* (fig. 131). Bearing blossoms and leaves on the appropriate parts of their bodies this quartet of erotic plants then proceeds to violate the norms of vegetative existence by sprouting breasts and pudenda where one would expect to find roots. The result – as Christian Geelhaar has observed[19] – is that Klee here converts a seemingly

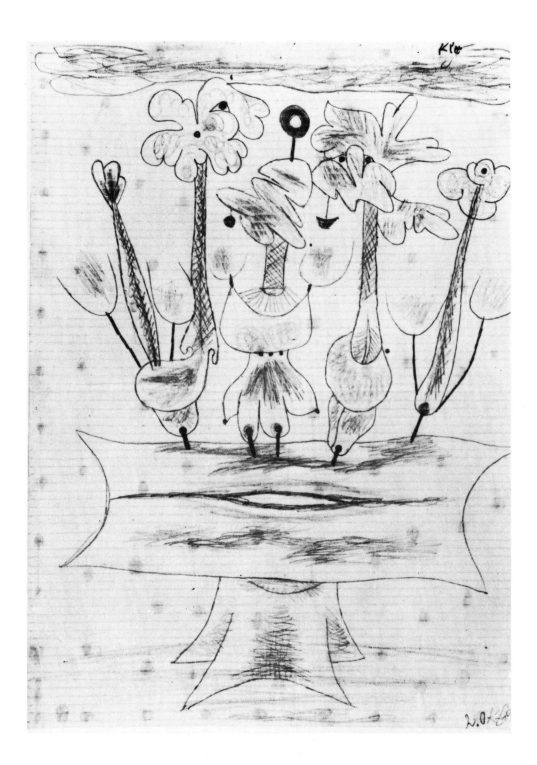

131
*A Table set with strange Flowers* 1921  Present whereabouts unknown

144

132
*Erotic Super-plant* 1923
Kunstmuseum, Bern

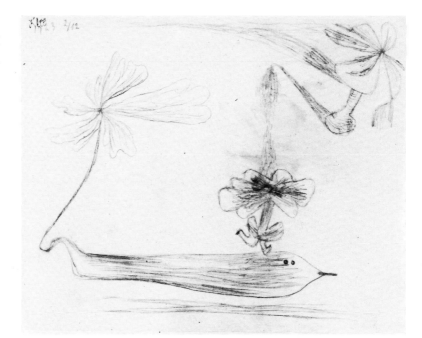

133
*The Plant as Sower* 1921
Present whereabouts unknown

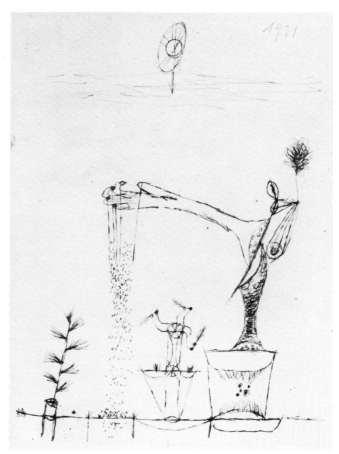

145

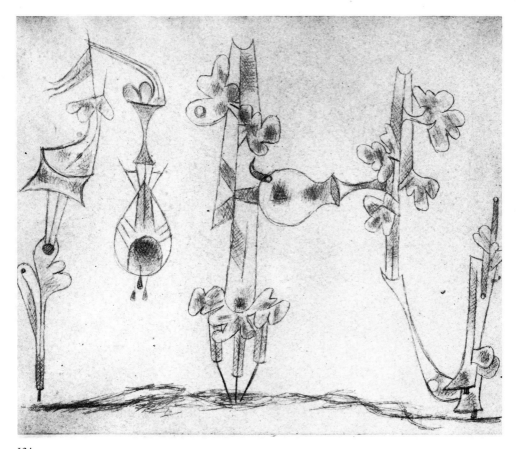

134
*Strange Plants* 1921 Kunstsammlung Nordrhein-Westfalen, Düsseldorf

innocent scene into 'an altar to nature and fertility'. Similarly, Klee's *Erotic Super-plant* of two years later (fig. 132) is little more than a lusty, torpedo-shaped phallus which blasts its way through the air and carries with it an opened flower whose stem turns into a pair of legs and who willingly receives a shower of pollen from an air-borne blossom no less male – and no less over-sexed – than her priapic transporter. In yet another work of these years, *The Plant as Sower* of 1921 (fig. 133), a large and humanoid plant, equipped with eyes and a torso-like stem, dons an arm and hand which reach over a neighbouring plant to scatter seeds upon an empty garden plot. How much more efficiently a plant could distribute its seeds, Klee seems to say here, if it only had the wherewithal of the human sower! Finally, in *Strange Plants* of the same year (fig. 134), the artist presents us with a trio of plants, two of which reach out to establish contact, presumably as a prelude to mating. But the third is ignored; and, as in the human world, it reacts with sadness. Its large heavy blossom becomes a single eye which hangs dejectedly downwards prefaced by a constricted heart

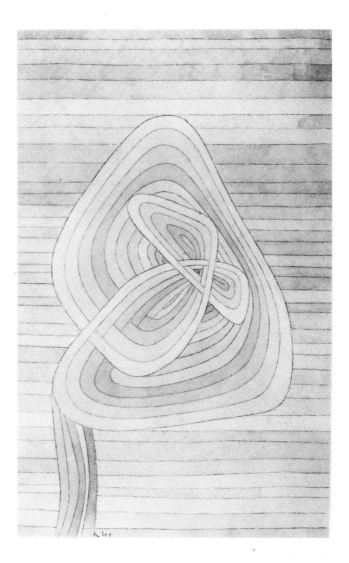

135
*Lonely Flower* 1934
Private Collection, USA

and emitting three soulful tears. Who is to say, after all, that plants don't shed their own kind of tears when disappointed in love?

*Strange Plants* recalls *Sad Flowers* in its concern with the essentially human aspects of plant emotions; and although this was an analogy which Klee appears to have pursued only occasionally his interest in it was far from negligible. Two emotions in particular seemed to him relevant to plants – loneliness and sadness. The latter is perhaps most movingly depicted in the 1917 watercolour already discussed (fig. 122) and in the many downhearted blossoms which follow it in Klee's career. But the notion of lonely plants moves far beyond the somewhat bizarre drawing of 1915 which bears this title (fig. 120) and finds its most eloquent expression in a delicate watercolour of 1934 entitled *Lonely Flower* (fig. 135). Here an intricately plaited, orange-pink blossom, rendered in Klee's familiar parallel style of this period, fills the picture space against a

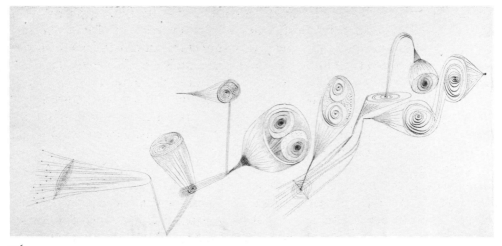

136
*Blossoms bending* 1927 Collection, University Art Museum, University of California, Berkeley

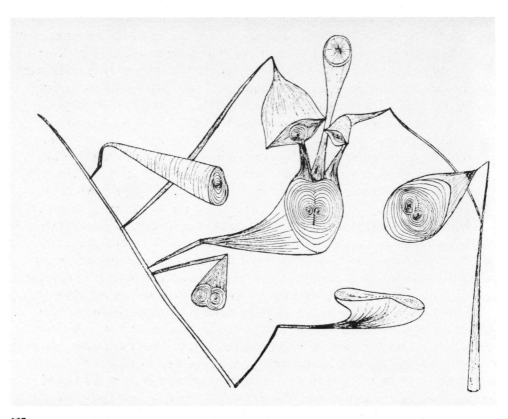

137
*Family Matters* 1927 Present whereabouts unknown

148

similarly striated background. But, if both flower and surroundings share something of the same structure Klee nevertheless evokes a sense of loneliness both through the decidedly unvegetative nature of his background and through a slight but agonized twist in the form of his solitary flower. Moreover, one's sorrow for this blossom is redoubled by its frail and ephemeral beauty and by the obvious pains nature has taken in creating it. For if flowers are nature's ultimate extravagance – deliberately created to draw attention to themselves and thereby to ensure its continuity – then a lonely flower must be seen not only as an object of pity but as a tragic waste.

Although less specific in their emotional overtones a handful of Klee's other works suggest that he was also a firm believer in the humane social instincts of the plants. Among the most memorable of these are two drawings of 1927 entitled *Blossoms bending* and *Family Matters* (figs. 136 & 137). In both of these the artist presents us with a closely-knit community of blossoms, many of which assume the form of an eye – a device which obviously affords Klee the maximum expression of emotion. As they bend and turn towards one another the actions of these 'seeing' blossoms recall the familiar tropisms of plants – that is to say, those impulses which lead them to turn automatically towards a source of light or gravity in nature. But such purely mechanical responses could hardly be further from the thoughts of Klee's blossoms, which now turn instead to see, feel, and care for one another. Indeed, in *Family Matters* they would appear to go even further than this as they cluster around a large central blossom which appears to be receiving a kind of emotional transfusion from two members of its 'family'. However one wishes to interpret the remedy being administered to this ailing patriarchal blossom there can be little doubt that Klee is here crediting the plants with profoundly compassionate feelings towards their fellow beings. Indeed, as the artist presents this action to us it is invested with a pathos sufficient to call to mind not merely the succouring instincts of the supposedly lower organisms but the devotion and tenderness one associates with depictions of such themes as the Seven Acts of Mercy.

In addition to exploring a wide range of individual analogies between the actions and emotions of man and plants Klee devoted a small group of major works of the 1920s to landscape or garden scenes of an unparalleled richness in which may be found the hidden forms of plants, animals, and (above all) man. In Klee's own career such pictures would seem to have their origins in a series of drawings and etchings of 1913–14, such as *Garden of Passion*, which typically depict densely populated garden settings in which the forms of men and beasts may be deciphered amidst a profusion of vegetative growth, with leaves suddenly doubling as limbs and blossoms as heads, in Klee's familiar metaphoric manner.[20] Where the works of the 1920s differ from these, however, is both in the greater range of their imagery and in their increased technical complexity. At their most elaborate such pictures consist of a kaleidoscopic range of carefully drawn forms embroidered with intricate hatchings and cross-hatchings and overlaid with a sequence of rainbow hues which often change colour independently of whatever is beneath them. The result is a

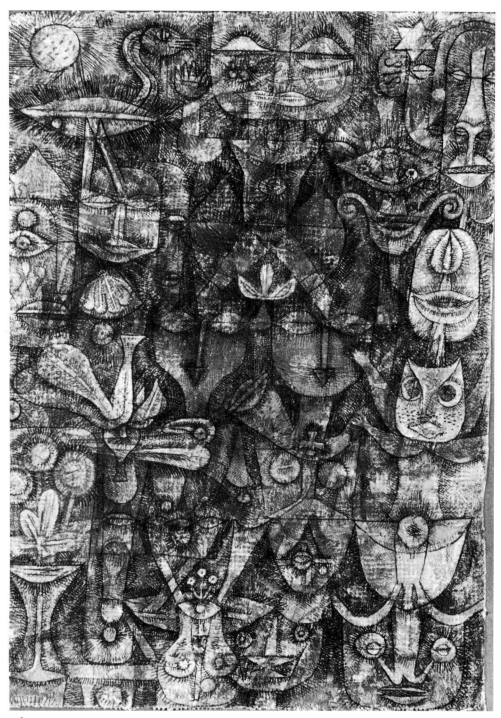

138
*Strange Garden* 1923  Present whereabouts unknown

phantasmagoria of barely distinguishable shapes and beings rendered in a manner which is at once so dense and so delicate that it conveys the impression of a primeval world in which nature is still shaping itself – in short, of a kind of *Urlandschaft* (or archetypal landscape) which contains within it the germinal elements for all of future creation. One of the finest of these pictures is the 1923 *Strange Garden* (fig. 138), which harbours within its maze-like surface of interwoven lines and colours the forms of cats and birds, men and plants, many of them overlapping and interpenetrating to create a translucent web of dimly nascent forms. Of these the majority are human and animal heads which vary in expression from the deeply meditative to the anxious, or even startled. A number of others call to mind instead the reproductive organs of the higher animals and thereby enhance the generative theme which seems so implicit throughout this picture. Most evocative of all, however, are the countless visual puns and metamorphic shapes with which Klee fills his scene – leaves which double as eyes, eyes which serve as flowers, bodies which become faces, and faces and pudenda which may also be read as plants. In their richness and resourcefulness these constant transformations from one motif in nature to another afford us a vivid demonstration of Klee's ability to uncover secret links between the most diverse facets of creation.

Stylistically related to *Strange Garden* are two pictures which no longer concern themselves with the menagerie of birds and beasts of that work but solely with the image of man gleaned through the landscape of nature. These are *Landscapely Physiognomic* of 1923 and *March Flora* of 1926 (figs. 139 & 140). Plainly decipherable through the exquisitely hatched surfaces of both of these are mysterious human heads which add a solemn and portentous meaning to the scene. In *March Flora* a single face and torso confronts us with an expression of anxiety – if not of pure anguish – as it greets the change of seasons and thereby the passage of time, a bell-like flower emerging from its left shoulder as though literally tolling these changes. In *Landscapely Physiognomic* Klee presents us with two heads, one of which (at the bottom left) resembles a tribal mask intended to convey a mood of diabolical frenzy or even of sheer psychic distress. In contrast the larger head in the centre of the design wears a withdrawn and all-knowing expression and emerges, appropriately, out of a sequence of cool, crystalline shapes. To the reader of Klee's diaries both works will immediately call to mind the youthful artist's many comparisons between his own states of mind or being and those of his natural surroundings;[21] and such comparisons probably provide the most helpful clues to the interpretation of these pictures. Despite the mystical aura which emanates from both of these scenes it is hard to see them in any more conventionally religious way. This is not the visage of the divine glimpsed through the landscape of Genesis, or (to borrow Klee's own turn of phrase) the image of God appearing in one of his flower beds.[22] Rather it would seem to be simply a vision of ordinary man united with the rhythms of the cosmos, his destiny controlled by its superintending laws and both his beginning and his end shaped by nature. The only choice remaining to him is how he comes to terms with this fate; and here

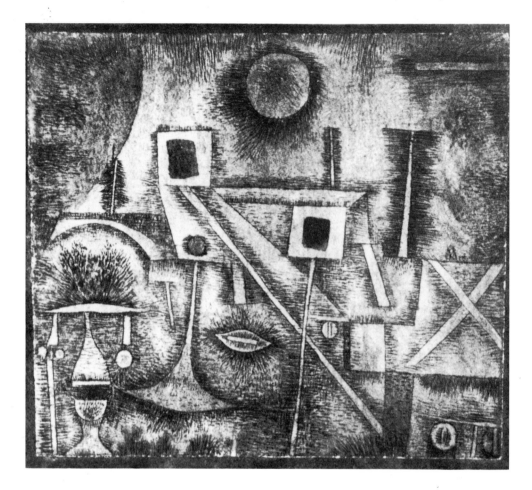

139
*Landscapely Physiognomic*
1923
Private Collection, Switzerland

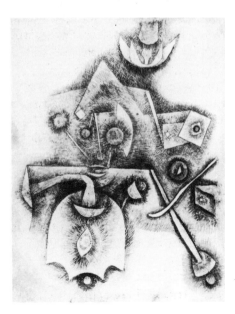

140
*March Flora* 1926
Fuji International Gallery,
Tokyo

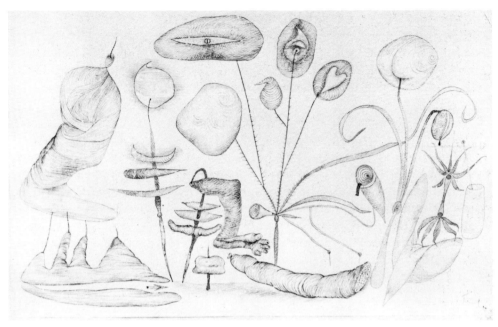

141
*Menu without Appetite* 1934  Private Collection, Canada

the two heads in *Landscapely Physiognomic* seem to present us with the
alternatives – either abortive emotional outrage or serene acceptance. There can
be no doubt as to which of these Klee himself chose.

In the seriousness of their themes and images both of these physiognomic
landscapes anticipate Klee's handling of such subjects in his later years.
Although many of the general analogies between man and vegetative nature
which had concerned him in the 1920s may also be found in works of the last
decade the prevailing mood of these is inevitably very different. To begin with
it is much less playful, with Klee largely forsaking those humorous comparisons
between human and plant behaviour with which his earlier works abound and
even abandoning his interest in the sexual lives of plants to concern himself
instead with the regenerative capacities of nature in the deepest sense. In
addition, the later works in this vein no longer depend upon ingenious visual
puns between the anatomy of man and the plants and rarely resort to the
creation of those composite beings – part-plant and part-animal – which had
so intrigued Klee in earlier years. In place of such mixed and hybrid forms the
artist now presents us with a race of metamorphic creatures which combine the
general characteristics of plants and animals in a new and disturbing way.
Ultimately unidentifiable with any known forms of life, these new creations of
Klee's imagination yet remain profoundly evocative of life itself – but of a life
which is no longer subject to nature's apparent order and reason but obeys
instead its own wild and irrational laws.

One of the first works in which Klee presents us with this alarming new
vision of nature is a pen drawing of 1934 entitled *Menu without Appetite*, which

remains one of his most unnerving – and even repellent – images (fig. 141). Perhaps prompted by the fact that his own brand of fantasy was coming to be admired and exhibited with that of the Surrealists during the early 1930s Klee here creates what is probably his most truly surrealist work. Although its design recalls those drawings of the previous decade showing a community of plants growing in a row (figs. 83 & 84), nothing could be further from the innocent and engaging inhabitants of such earlier works than this loathsome collection of ulcerated flowers and dismembered limbs impaled on skewer-like stems. For all their vigour and realism these creatures call to mind no known forms of life but instead suggest those nauseous substances – half-bone and half-raw meat – of such true Surrealists as Miró, Dali, and Tanguy.[23] But whatever the chosen comparison the protagonists of this scene constitute a unique work in Klee's career in the sheer perversity with which they transgress the norms of vegetative existence. This is apparent if one compares them with the inhabitants of *Botanical Theatre* (fig. 177), which was completed in the same year and likewise depicts a community of unidentifiable plant and animal types of imposing authority. For all their elusiveness the forms in the latter picture still speak to us of the generative forces in nature, while those in this drawing appear instead as diseased and denatured mutations of life itself. Less nascent than noxious in character, they ultimately call to mind only rotting flesh.

However singular Klee's *Menu without Appetite* may be it does herald certain general tendencies in the artist's late treatment of organic forms. These may conveniently be approached through such characteristic works of the final years as the 1939 drawing *Attempt to become a Plant* or the 1940 painting *Giant Plants* (figs. 142 & 143). Although both of these works avoid the painstaking surface realism which renders Klee's *Menu* so repulsive they do evoke a race of biomorphic monsters which likewise seem to represent a deformation of all known life and yet remain obscenely redolent of life itself. In *Attempt to become a Plant* Klee presents us with one of those familiar images of species reversal already encountered in the 1920s – in short, of a human seeking planthood. But whereas such earlier works had enlisted the aid of a variety of human and floral motifs to effect such a transformation, this late drawing offers us a humanoid plant which seems moulded out of a neutral substance somewhere between flesh and foliage. Similarly, Klee's *Giant Plants* take on the characteristics of both realms, reclining like the ponderous torsos of a race of lethargic giants and yet burgeoning with new life like the plants. In both instances the forms have been reduced to simple, swelling shapes of an indeterminate consistency which slowly and ominously wrap themselves around one another. This tendency to reduce all of organic life to a common substance which seems to hold within it the ethos of both the plant and animal kingdoms is one of the most distinctive features of Klee's late art. Although it would be tempting to see such a development as merely a logical conclusion to the artist's lifelong search for archetypal forms in nature, so pedantic an explanation will not do when confronted with the cumbersome and prodigious beings of so many of Klee's late pictures. A more convincing explanation is in the ageing artist's

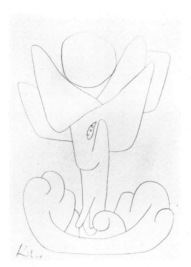

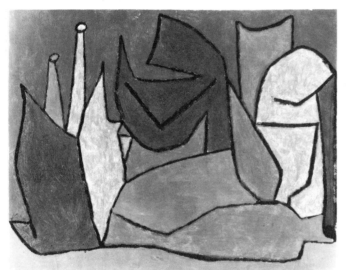

acknowledgement of the fact that nature is ultimately subject to forces beyond human comprehension and that these forces are not only eternally mysterious but utterly remorseless. Far from being archetypal images of organic life Klee's monstrous late plants and beasts seem to have swallowed up all of ordinary nature in their wake; and in this respect they remind us not only of the cruel and awesome powers of nature itself but of the deepest fears of their creator.

Klee's fullest exploration of this theme of the perils and evils of monstrous nature during his late years may be found in a sequence of sixteen drawings of 1939 which all bear the preface *The Infernal Park* and are clearly intended to be seen as a group.[24] In these the artist appears to chart a journey made by man through a garden of the nether-regions – one which Jürgen Glaesemer has astutely compared to the Stations of the Cross.[25] Although Klee's narrative is much more difficult to unfold than its biblical counterpart the comparison

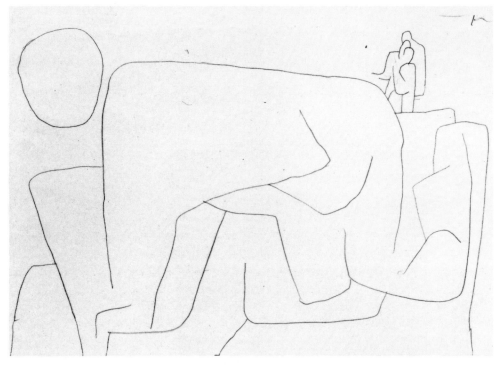

144
*The Infernal Park: 'entrance'* 1939  Kunstmuseum, Bern

is apt in that this series of images appears to describe a kind of obstacle course
of trials, temptations, and sufferings set in a wildly overgrown landscape in
which all inhabitants of the scene – trees, clouds, suns, and rocks – are rendered
as overblown and torturously convoluted shapes. Recumbent limbs and torsos,
many of them recalling the forms of long extinct creatures, here cohabit with
pendulous trees, voluptuous fruits, and entangled thickets – all of them
seemingly lying in wait to engulf their next victim. Though it would be idle
to point to precise sources for any of the imagery which fills these sheets, the
abnormally bloated protruberances which make up so many of these infernal
beings – and indeed so much else in Klee's late art – probably have their closest
analogies in nature in the hard, tumescent forms of malignant tumours.
Unpleasant though such a comparison may be it is not entirely inappropriate
coming from an artist whose own flesh and muscle were hardening and
degenerating under his very eyes.

The way-stations which chart one's progress through Klee's infernal park
concern themselves with many of the central experiences of human life. In the
first drawing two intertwined figures (Klee's own Dante and Virgil?) stand at
the entrance to this inferno, its configuration suspiciously resembling that of
a giant crawling on its hands and knees (fig. 144). Having gained entrance one
is afforded a glimpse of the terrain, with its primordial plants and trees basking

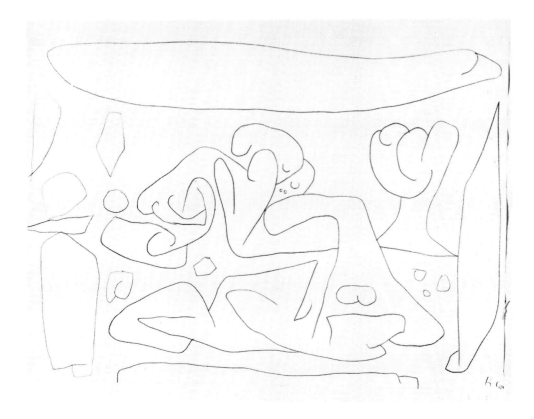

145
*The Infernal Park: 'the region of repentance'* 1939
Kunstmuseum, Bern

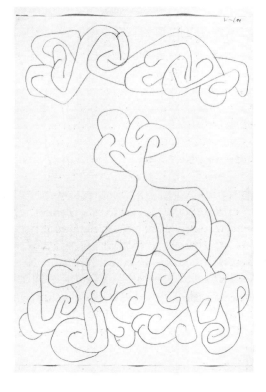

146
*The Infernal Park: 'Vase N'*
1939  Kunstmuseum, Bern

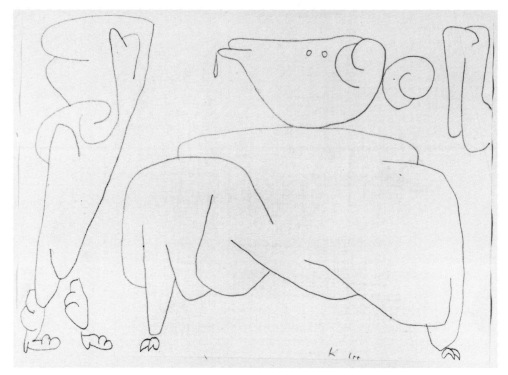

147
*The Infernal Park: 'Scene towards the end'* 1939 Kunstmuseum, Bern

in the sun. Awe-struck, one takes a premature rest and then embarks upon an arduous journey through a region of labyrinthine voluptuousness. A perilous bridge is crossed, followed by a moment of repentance, which depicts the broken and inconsolable form of a human traveller merging with its overgrown surroundings (fig. 145). Two terrifying and decidedly unnatural obstacles then present themselves – a huge and threatening flower and a living vase, its body riddled with tumorous swellings (fig. 146). The next five drawings return to more universal themes: the anguish of motherhood, strife, chance, a fruitless turning-back, and the scene of a murder. The series concludes with a scene of *Haste without Rest* and with a *Ship of doubtful Salvation*, which is presumably intended to ferry the travellers out of this living hell. Just how doubtful that salvation is may be seen in the final drawing, entitled *Scene towards the End* (fig. 147), where two monstrous forms fill the page, their mouths frothing and their bodies now hideously deformed. At the end of this journey through nature's inferno they have become infernal themselves. Like the more orthodox travellers of an ordinary human life their trials and sufferings on earth have served only to prepare them for those of the underworld.

Quite apart from his broad views of nature, Klee's obsession with its looming and threatening power during his late years is also evident on those occasions

148
*Pansy* 1939
Kunstmuseum, Bern

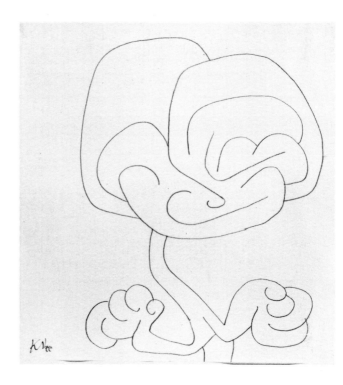

149
*Rose* 1939
Kunstmuseum, Bern

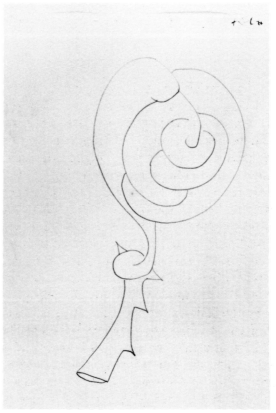

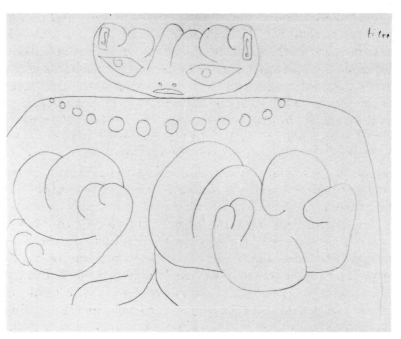

150
*Buys the last giant Blossoms!* 1938  Kunstmuseum, Bern

151
*Buys giant Fruits!* 1939  Kunstmuseum, Bern

when he chooses to focus upon an individual motif – or even a recognizable species – from the world of nature. Thus, in two closely contemporary drawings of 1939 (figs. 148 & 149) he transforms the harmless pansy into a belligerent figure with clenched fists and a knotted brow and reduces the form of a rose to a spiralling hammerhead borne on a viciously spiky handle – in short, to an object of torture rather than of delight. In two other thematically connected works entitled *Buys the last giant Blossoms!* and *Buys giant Fruits!* (figs. 150 & 151) Klee presents us with two female shoppers who have just bought two of his favourite things – in the one case composite flowers and in the other fleshy fruits. Suddenly overpowered by these seemingly innocuous purchases Klee's figures now wear expressions which mix terror with demonry as they sprout arms, hands, and heads which come to resemble those selfsame flowers and fruits. It is as though Nature has cast an evil and transforming spell over them. Having dared to clutch her, they are now in her clutches, doomed to become one of those mutant species with which she is inexorably destroying all of normal existence. As so often in late Klee one turns away from such images hoping for a miracle. Only an exorcism, it seems, would succeed in ridding these innocent victims of their demonic captors.

That such a miracle will not occur is apparent in Klee's many other late drawings of fructifying humanity – a subject which must be seen as one of the most overtly autobiographical of all from this period. In these the artist presents us with human figures which are slowly metamorphosing into the inert and gravid forms of fruits. The flowering period of their lives now over, they have only to ripen and die. However distressing are Klee's depictions of single human beings in this guise, the most moving of all such works are inevitably his renderings of fructifying couples. Thus, in two drawings of 1939 entitled *At the Sign of Fruitfulness* and *Maturing Separation* (figs. 152 & 153) the artist presents us with two such partnerships which, figuratively speaking at least, must be seen as representing Klee and Lily. In both cases these faithful companions have sprouted protruberances which have become encumbrances. In the former drawing a monstrous finger poised between their two heads signals to us that the time has come. Accepting their fate, the two turn away from one another in *Maturing Separation* and mournfully prepare to fall from the tree of life.

Their destination forms the subject of a final group of late works by Klee which bring the animal and plant worlds together. These consist of a series of images of the human form embedded in a natural setting in a manner reminiscent of the physiognomic landscapes of the mid 1920s. Now, however, the metaphysical detachment of those earlier works is abandoned in favour of a more emotional – and clearly more personal – approach to this theme, with the artist converting such images into potent reminders of the inevitability of death. Thus, if the works of the preceding decade explored the theme of the life of man seen through the life of nature those of the last years dwell instead upon the continuing life of nature even after the life of man. In a series of paintings and drawings of 1937 – among them *Blooming, Figure in a Garden,*

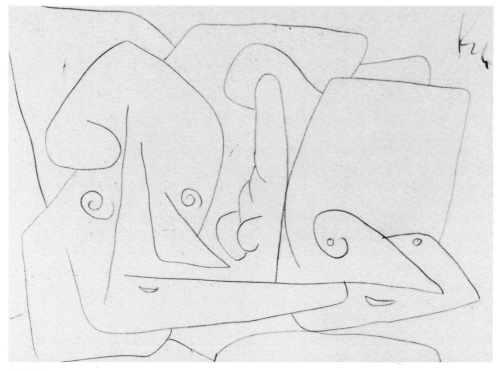

152
*At the Sign of Fruitfulness* 1939 Kunstmuseum, Bern

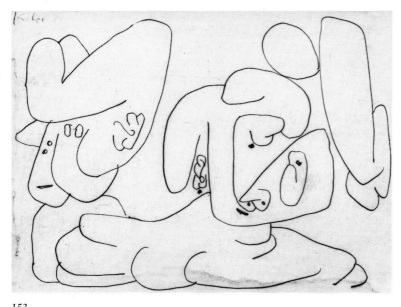

153
*Maturing Separation* 1939 Felix Klee, Bern

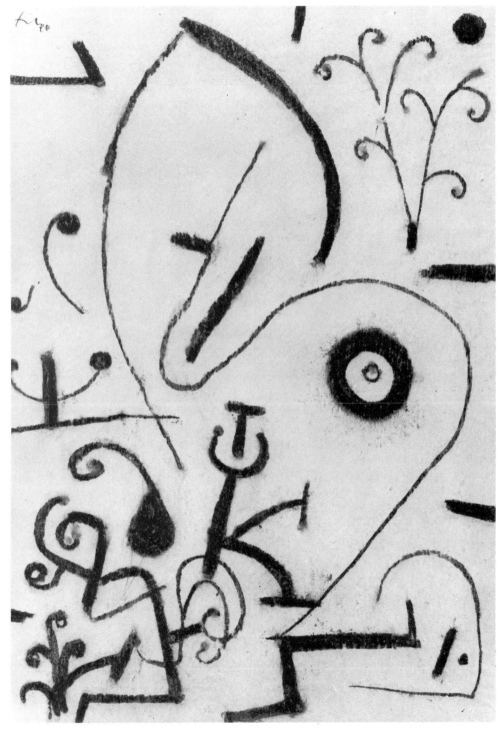

154
*Blooming* 1937 Kunstsammlung Nordrhein-Westfalen, Düsseldorf

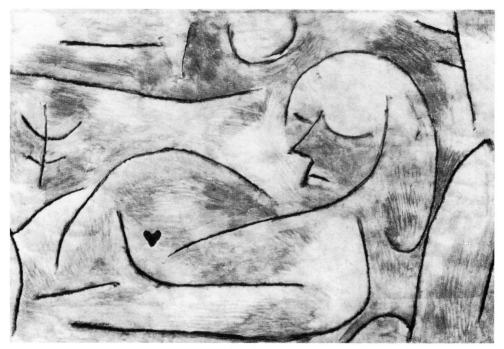

155
*Hibernating* 1937 Private Collection

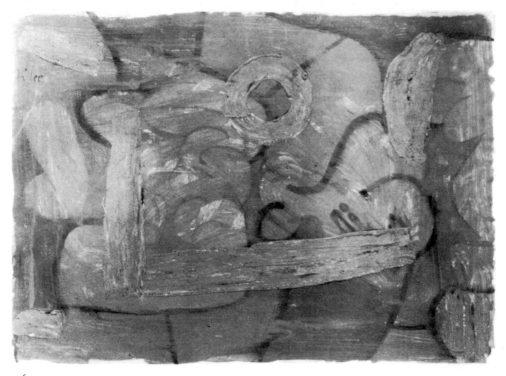

156
*Spring is coming* 1939 Present whereabouts unknown

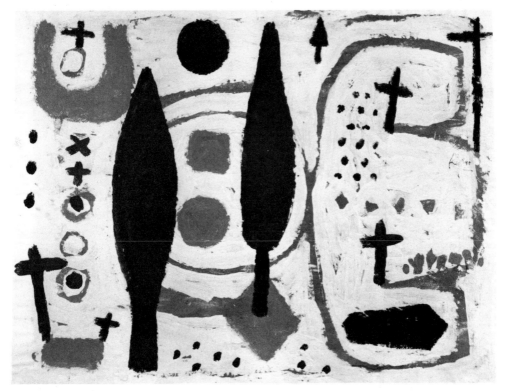

157
*Graveyard* 1939 Kunstmuseum, Bern

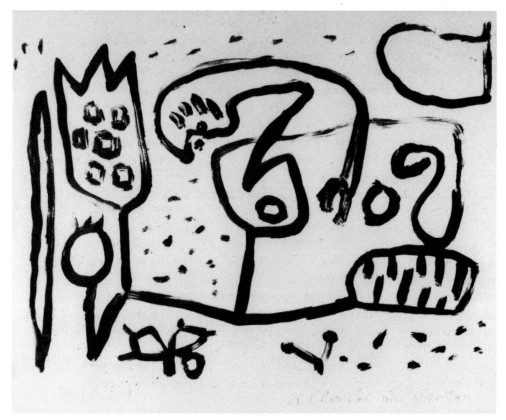

158
*All Kinds of Things in the Garden* 1940 Present whereabouts unknown

and *Hibernating* (figs. 154 & 155)[26] – human figures which respectively appear anguished, broken, and slumbering may be deciphered through the forms of their landscape settings, as though indissolubly linked with the rhythms of nature. In the last of these, *Hibernating*, a recumbent female figure, her red heart trustingly beating, sleeps beneath the snow as though awaiting the return of spring to recommence a more active life. Such an image cannot help but recall the youthful Klee's own desire 'to lie down for a long sleep, to wake up only on the return of spring';[27] and as such it may be seen as another of those distant memories of his youth which returned to haunt the dying artist.

But what if spring returns without the expected awakening? This, it seems, is the subject of *Spring is coming* of 1939 (fig. 156), wherein a struggling human figure, engulfed in an inferno of red death, wrestles to release itself from under the green and hopeful signs of an awakening year. So jarring are the colour contrasts here and so desperate are the figure's efforts that one cannot help but feel that its only hope of rebirth will be in the inevitable way of thrifty nature: namely, as a support for other life. And such becomes the theme of what is perhaps Klee's single most disturbing treatment of this theme, the 1939 *Graveyard* (fig. 157), which harbours within it the truncated torso of a youth[28] – the spirit and substance of the dead from whence there comes forth new life, a contrast poignantly suggested by Klee through the visual similarities between the crosses which adorn its grave and the cypresses which draw life from it. Finally, in 1940, Klee gives us *All Kinds of Things in the Garden* (fig. 158) – a work which could equally have borne the title of an earlier picture of 1919, *Legend of Death in a Garden*;[29] for prominent among the 'all kinds of things' in this garden is the devouring presence of death itself. Thus the tomb of man merges inevitably with the seedbed of nature. And far from offering us a tantalizing glimpse of the divine creator seen through one of his flower beds, Klee here concerns himself with a different, but no less consoling, vision. From one life will come others, albeit in a different form. In short, the springtime into which the twenty-year-old Klee wished to awaken and wander now becomes the bitter-sweet springtime of nature's own unalterable plan and purpose – the ineluctable springtime of life gained through life lost.[30]

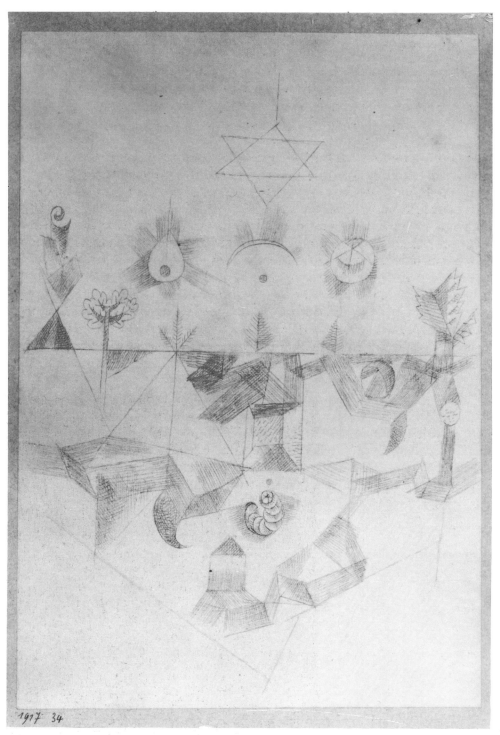

1917 34

159
*Mystical Landscape with a Worm in the Ground* 1917 Present whereabouts unknown

# 5 · Cosmic Compositions

From time to time one comes upon a work by Klee which seems to penetrate to the very heart of things. In the years before 1920 such works are often landscapes – drawings like his *Mystical Landscape with a Worm in the Ground* of 1917 or paintings such as *Cosmic Composition* of 1919 (figs. 159 & 160). In both of these the separate realms of heaven and earth meet. A sky spangled with suns, moons, and stars floats above a terrain whose trees, plants, and houses mirror the forms of these celestial bodies. Indeed, in Klee's *Mystical Landscape* even the humble earthworm, tunnelling deep below the surface of the earth, echoes the shape and size of the planets above and appears to safeguard the secret of the drawing's mystery. As a creature whose meandering movements seemed to Klee to defy gravity it here seems to symbolize those broad and invisible bonds which unite heaven and earth and which express

160
*Cosmic Composition* 1919
Kunstsammlung Nordrhein-
Westfalen, Düsseldorf

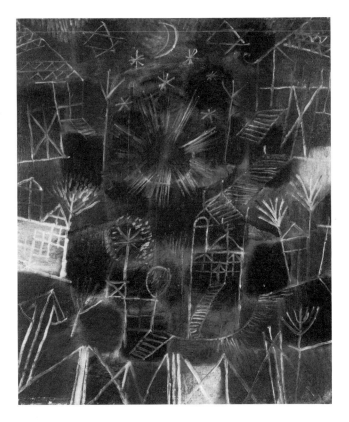

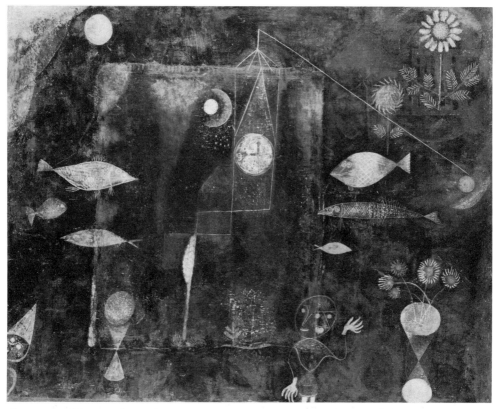

*Fish Magic* 1925 Philadelphia Museum of Art, The Louise and Walter Arensberg Collection

Nature's dominion over all her creations, from the giant sun to the tiny worm.[1]
In his *Cosmic Composition* Klee carries this theme even further and now permits
the separate domains of heaven and earth to overlap. Trees and houses reach
upwards to touch the stars, pathways ascend to heaven and, in the middle of
the design, a large, omnipotent sun descends like a benediction upon the
rainbow hues of the landscape. Directly above it hovers a single, omniscient
eye – the eye, it would seem, of the creator of all of these things. Like Klee's
own omniscient eye it affords us a vision of the unity and harmony of all of
creation, or – as the artist here demonstrates to us – of those hidden bonds
which link the shimmering stars with the shimmering trees. For all their
beguiling simplicity and undeniable enchantment, such works as these
ultimately speak to us of the deepest mysteries of existence and take as their
true subject the awesome and unalterable face of nature. In this sense they are
all 'cosmic compositions'.

   In the following decade Klee created a group of equally mysterious works
which move beyond this general theme to concern themselves with the
unending cycles of life which unfold against this cosmic setting. In these the
destiny of the individual becomes his chief interest. Fishes and flowers, plants

and planets, figures and crystals – all of them among Klee's favourite things of this world – now float weightlessly against a portentous black void, like stars against a midnight sky. In themselves such forms are readily identifiable, and one can easily relate them to those in any number of much less mysterious works by the artist. But the strange combinations in which they are now conjured forth on to Klee's easel or drawing-board defy so rational an explanation and force one to seek another. Assisting us along the way are the pictures themselves. In their sombre and illimitable backgrounds one confronts both death and infinity; while in their iridescently painted fishes and flowers one is reminded of those myriad existences which play themselves out against the boundless backdrop of time. Such pictures might be grouped together as a series of mystical equations in which the inhabitants of earth and sky are strewn against the void of eternity like so many hapless hostages of Fortune.

This small but momentous group of works, which lies at the heart of Klee's creative achievement, may best be approached through one of the artist's greatest masterpieces, *Fish Magic* of 1925 (fig. 161).[2] Both in its content and its physical construction this picture remains one of the most complex of Klee's entire career; and, as it happens, these two aspects of it may be even more intimately related. Even in reproduction it is clear that *Fish Magic* – which was also Klee's largest picture to date – consists of a rectangular piece of canvas to the middle of which a smaller and nearly square piece has been added.[3] Although it was not unusual for Klee to build up his pictures in so piecemeal a fashion, rarely in his work did he employ additional canvas or paper to overlay (rather than simply to enlarge) a picture. Whatever may have been Klee's reasons for making this addition it is immediately apparent that the boundaries defined by these two pieces of canvas have been respected by certain of the inhabitants of the scene and that, in this sense, Klee would appear to be introducing us to two different worlds.

*Fish Magic* belongs to a series of stage landscapes which Klee created from 1917 onwards and which includes some of his most important works. In the majority of these the curtain rises upon an enchanted vision of earth and sky. But, in contrast, *Fish Magic* introduces us to an indeterminate space and realm where fishes swim and plants grow in the company of people and planets. Only the curtain and clown which frame the scene at the upper and lower left appear not to belong to this reality. Instead, they reveal it to us; for in the midst of this crystalline world, the face of the clown, peering around the edge of the picture, acts as a call to attention.

Of the remaining inhabitants of Klee's scene, most are easily identifiable. At its heart beats a clock on a church steeple. This in turn is suspended in a wire trap supported by a lengthy rod and 'worked' by one of Klee's familiar radial flowers of this period. Above this mechanism sits a vigorous blue daisy and below it swim three fish. In the lower right corner stands an hour-glass vase of daisies; and to the left of this a gesticulating figure with two profiles gazes to both sides of the picture. Continuing around one comes upon a sapling conifer, a tall scape to which the wire trap appears attached, an hour-glass

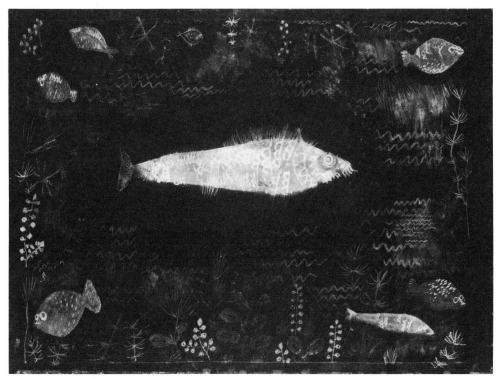

162
*The Goldfish* 1925 Formerly Kunsthalle, Hamburg

supporting a glowing red disk and, above this, three more fish. Finally, a celestial body hovers near the curtain edge and, to the upper left of the church steeple, a bright yellow circle floats nestled in a powdery blue crescent.

Of these objects only the fishes which provided Klee with his title appear to ignore the boundary between the two portions of canvas and swim freely into and out of the added central patch. Otherwise the wire trap appears suspended within this patch, while its supporting rod rests upon its edge. Moreover, plants grow from the base of this central area, the curtain edge is reflected in its upper left corner, and the hour-glass overlaps the two zones in such a way as to suggest that its upper half is really only a mirror image of its cone-like base. But most noticeably of all, the seam between the two pieces of fabric bisects the head of the gesticulating figure through a common eye, once again suggesting a reflected image. Now, however, the two profiles do not merely mirror one another but present us instead with two sharply contrasting emotions.

Superficially at least Klee has raised the *Fish Magic* curtain up on an underwater landscape; and, with this in mind, it is worth noting that this picture appears immediately before another such scene – the *Goldfish* formerly in Hamburg (fig. 162) – in his catalogue of works. Like *Fish Magic* the latter

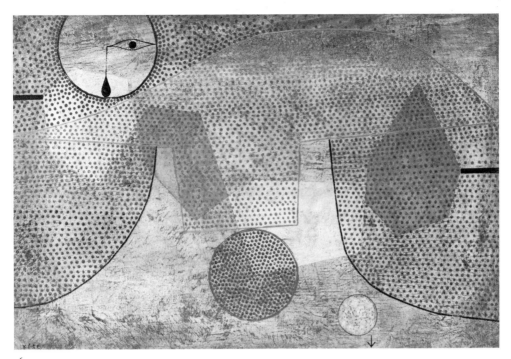

163
*Sunset* 1930 Collection of the Art Institute of Chicago

reveals to us a ghostly nocturnal setting – the hidden depths of the sea-bed –
against which a group of iridescent fishes glimmer like jewels. One of these,
in the centre, appears motionless and, with its timeless glow, addresses us with
all the magic and mystery of an ancient rune. Gaunt, scaly, and spiny, this fish
appears like a lone survivor from another age when compared with its darting
companions and readily casts our minds forward to those primitive and
seemingly fossilized species one encounters in Klee's late art.[4] It is as though
the artist is here affording us with a vision of the original fish – of the distant
archetype from whence all others derived. In this respect even so seemingly
uncomplicated a picture as this may be seen to possess a symbolic dimension
and a more universal meaning which prefigures that of the more mystifying *Fish
Magic*.

*Fish Magic* differs from all of Klee's other fish pictures of the mid 1920s
through the inclusion of elements which are not normally found underwater:
above all, the double-profiled figure, the planetary bodies, and the church
steeple. Although it has for this reason become customary to dismiss this work
simply as a 'dream picture',[5] closer acquaintance with it encourages one to
embark in search of a fuller explanation; and here the church steeple itself
provides us with an important clue. Nestled in the centre of the work the yellow

164
*Church, the clock with contrived
numbers* 1883/4
Kunstmuseum, Bern

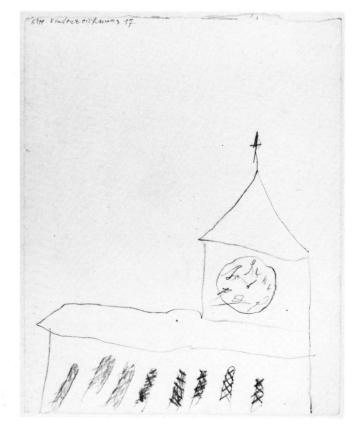

disk of the clock-face provides a clear compositional focus for Klee's picture
and stands out as the largest and most regular of the many rhyming circular
forms which pervade and unify this entire design. Moreover, a comparison of
this clock-face with the celestial bodies which float to its immediate left readily
calls to mind one of Klee's favourite themes: namely, that of the difference
between cosmic and earthly time, or infinite and finite time. Such a comparison
also appears in the artist's first great 'divisionist' picture, *Sunset* of 1930
(fig. 163), wherein the unending cycles of night and day are witnessed by a
sorrowful human presence, whose otherwise featureless face wears an eye and
a tear like the hands of a clock. Although this poignant combination of images
is absent from *Fish Magic*, its meaning is not. Four of the clock's numerals are
painted red and glow within the white and yellow face of the whole. These are
not, as one would expect, 3, 6, 9, and 12 but rather 1, 2, 5, and 9. Rearranged,
they record the picture's date – 1925. And beyond this they were, of course,
when the picture was completed, Klee's own moment in time.

This is not the first such cryptic clock that one encounters in Klee's art.
Already in 1883–4, when he was only four or five years old, the fledgling painter
made a drawing of a *Church, the clock with contrived numbers* (fig. 164), which
may have been inspired by that most famous of all landmarks in his native city
of Bern, the clock-tower on the Kramgasse. Even at this early age, however,

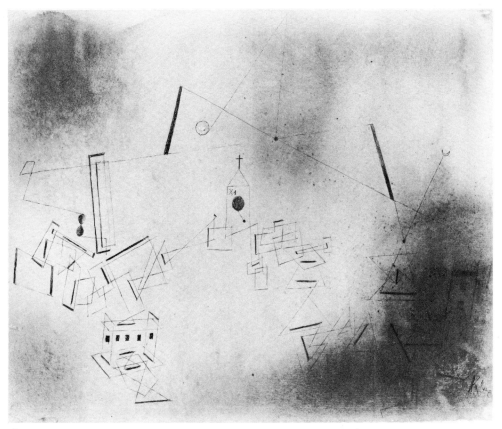

165
*Heavenly and Earthly Time* 1927  Philadelphia Museum of Art, The Louise and Walter Arensberg
Collection

Klee appears to have sought to conceal a secret message within the clock-face.
In this childhood drawing his message remains indecipherable. But to the
viewer aware of the decidedly personal message of the *Fish Magic* clock it makes
one important disclosure. More than forty years before creating that
masterpiece Klee had discovered that, through the medium of art, a clock might
be made to tell something more than the time of day.

Deeply rooted, this image remained with Klee; and in a 1927 watercolour,
*Heavenly and Earthly Time* (fig. 165), he presents us with one of his most bitter-
sweet restatements of it. As in *Fish Magic* the design of this work centres around
a church, clock, and steeple; while to either side of these floats the fragile
armature of a townscape, in itself scarcely less intricate than clockwork. Gently
suspended from a single wire of heaven, the entire construction appears
delicately balanced by the complementary motions of two pendulums, one
earthly and the other heavenly. The former, which is dark, solid, small, and
affixed to the clock, measures and records time elapsed. But the latter, which
is larger and yet lighter, appears to swing forever and records nothing.

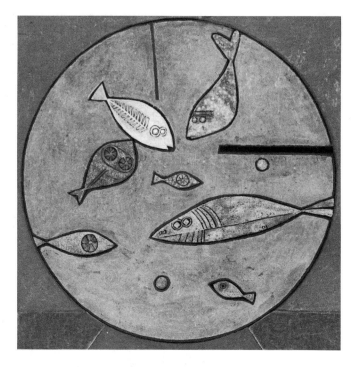

The message of the clock-face in *Fish Magic* may also help to explain the wire trap in which it is contained. Although this has been described as a 'fishing-net whose threads form the outline of a belfry'[6] – and although the clock has been seen as simply indicating the time remaining before the fishes are caught – on a deeper interpretive level the improbable motif of a captive church steeple may be seen to belong not to the reality of the undersea habitat of Klee's picture but, rather, to that of its cosmic theme: namely, the subjection of all life to the rule of time. In contrast to the freely floating planetary bodies, symbolic of the ceaseless rhythms of the universe, stand the imprisoned clock and steeple – made and obeyed by man.

When one moves from the clock-face to the gregarious fishes which are the apparent protagonists of Klee's picture one comes upon one of the artist's favourite motifs of the 1920s, when they form the subject of more than a dozen major works.[7] Like so many other companions of Klee's daily life, however, fishes enter his art on many different levels. In certain instances – for example, the 1926 *Fish in Circle* (fig. 166) – they would appear to remain content to swim smugly in their small bowls and to represent no more than meets the eye. But in such works as *Fish Magic* they would seem almost inadvertently to have acquired a more symbolic meaning for the artist in the course of creating his picture. That Klee himself was perhaps not always aware of this sudden shift of emphasis is suggested both by the unusual physical make-up of this picture, which may indicate a major change of mind in the course of painting it, and by the equally unusual fact that the artist gave this work two titles: *Fish Magic* (on the stretcher) and *Large Fish Picture* (in his catalogue of works). As the

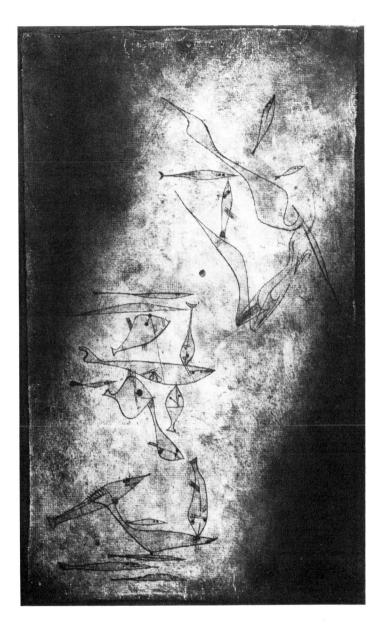

167
*Fish Picture* 1925
Present whereabouts
unknown

latter of these makes clear, Klee originally conceived of it as a sequel to his smaller *Fish Picture* of the same year, which is a straightforward underwater scene (fig. 167). Upon completing it, he appears to have entered this earlier title in his catalogue and signed and dated the canvas below the hour-glass at the lower left. Only then does Klee seem to have realized that the rather colourless title he had given to this work did little justice to the mysterious creation into which his *Large Fish Picture* had grown. At this point he apparently turned it over and re-christened it *Fish Magic*, as though in acknowledgement of the fact that, although it may have begun life as just another fish picture, it had become something more. It was now one of those 'ultimate things' towards which his art unwittingly strove.

As we have seen, both the fishes and composite flowers which inhabit this bewitching scene were beings whose form and behaviour had come to symbolize for Klee average nature.[8] In their general patterns of organization both appeared to him to be reducible to a series of like parts – whether scales, fins, or petals – and, in this sense, they represented nature's most characteristic way of building its forms. But it was not only in this respect that Klee came to regard them as representing the great middle class of their respective kingdoms. In their actions and aspirations, too, they appeared to stand half-way up the hierarchy of beings, aiming neither too high nor too low. Thus, as the artist presents them to us in *Fish Magic* they sway unconcernedly in their vases, revolve mechanically, or swim aimlessly across his picture – in all cases oblivious to the presence of such 'higher' inhabitants of the scene as the church steeple, the clown, and the gesticulating figure.

Of these the most enigmatic is undoubtedly the last. Although double faced or interwoven figures are not uncommon in Klee's art,[9] the double-profiled figure is much rarer. Whatever may have been the artist's intentions in creating this figure it is noteworthy that the edge of the patch of canvas which bisects it has afforded him with the opportunity to combine two different moods and expressions within the confines of a single human frame. Gazing outwards – towards the charmed world of the fishes and flowers – Klee's figure waves its arm about and wears a welcoming smile on a sensuous, heart-shaped mouth. But gazing into the picture, towards the grim reality of the clock on the church steeple, this figure drops its hand solemnly to its side and assumes an altogether more thoughtful character. It is as though Klee is here seeking to distinguish between man and the rest of living nature. While fishes and flowers do not differentiate the finite life of the individual from the continuing life of the species – and thereby inhabit the worlds of both finite and infinite time – man remains unique among God's creatures in being burdened with the knowledge of his own mortality. In him there is 'one eye which sees, another which feels', as Klee noted in his diaries as early as 1914[10] in a passage which itself seems burdened with a premonition of the Janus-headed figure in *Fish Magic*. Perhaps it is more than mere coincidence that Klee followed this remark in his diaries with an entry which seems to summarize (and indeed prefigure) the essential theme of the whole of this great picture: 'Man-animal, clock made out of blood'.[11]

Thus, if the whole of *Fish Magic* is given over to a poetical evocation of the unending cycles of Nature, there is embedded within it a stark reminder of the cruel laws according to which she functions. This reminder coincides with the boundaries of the patch of fabric glued – untidily and unashamedly – to the centre of the picture. That Klee came to regard this as defining a distinct area within the whole is further confirmed by the appearance of a dim reflection of the red curtain edge in the upper left-hand corner of this patch. In contrast to the mirror-image reflections of the hour-glass or the double-profiled figure, this is a true, cast reflection. It serves to frame a picture within a picture. Though plants and fishes may indiscriminately inhabit both realms, to man their difference is clear and their meaning distinct. Seen in this way the ultimate irony of *Fish Magic* also becomes clear to us. Man – and not the fishes – remains the true victim of the trap of time set in the middle of Klee's picture. For, figuratively speaking at least, this trap catches man in a way that it could never catch fish.

Klee was surely aware of the underlying theme of this important picture and more than once in his life he gave poignant personal expression to the heavy burden which the trap of time had placed upon the life of man. Indeed, only a year before painting *Fish Magic*, in 1924, he wrote:[12]

One speaks especially of tragedy when there is an especially large disproportion between the advantages of spiritual freedom and the disadvantages of physical dependency. The spiritual plus is then experienced as misfortune; one feels the dichotomy, and a certain envy takes hold when one contemplates the undivided lower creatures in their wholeness, in their restriction to a harmony of body and spirit. The secret admiration for animals begins at this point.

Few works by Klee attest more fully to this 'secret admiration' or to that 'certain envy' which accompanies it than does *Fish Magic*. For if one looks again at Klee's picture one notes that both the wholeness of the lower creatures and the dividedness of man are made plainly visible within it. In the former, symmetry – and thereby wholeness – abounds in radial daisies and spoon-shaped fishes. Indeed, two of the fishes at the left are bisected by the seam in Klee's canvas in such a way as to remind us of the most rudimentary of all features of the fish form: namely, that minus its tail its front half is essentially a mirror image of its rear. But not so Klee's human figure, whose divided profile reveals to us precisely that greater complexity – and tragic dichotomy – of which the artist wrote. As a creature gifted with a measure of 'spiritual freedom' man may don the pensive and inward-looking profile of Klee's picture and thereby inhabit a realm of mind and spirit superior to that of the flowers and fishes. But in the end he remains physically dependent upon those selfsame forces which have shaped their modest lives. On this level he must turn his back upon the tolling clock-face and don a different profile – one which accepts its fundamental oneness with the rest of sentient creation, and one which must resign itself simply to flowing with the tide.

With his customary wit and wisdom Klee encapsulates this last point into one ultimate visual pun between the form of his human figure and that of the neighbouring vase of daisies in *Fish Magic* (fig. 168). As kindred creations of nature both appear clad in hour-glass bodies, their days literally numbered in grains of sand. From this vantage point the two engage in a playful dialogue, with Klee's spray of wavering pink and blue daisies mimicking the forms and motions of his flower-faced figure, with its pink and blue eyes and waving,

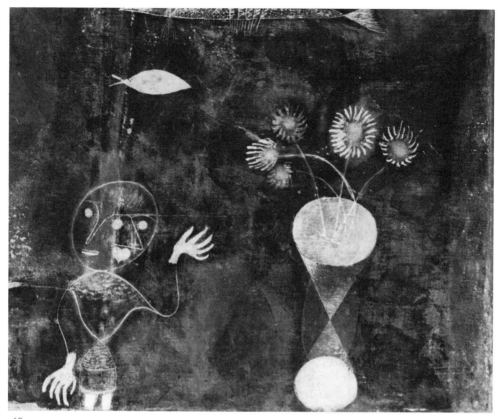

168
Detail from *Fish Magic*

daisy-petal fingers. Like the lowly (if lovely) daisies Klee's figure here declares its indissoluble union with the rest of creation. But, unlike them, he remains fated to build his view of the world by gazing both without and within – by reacting and reflecting, like the visibly divided figure of Klee's picture. A creature of the earth, he is forever beckoned by the stars, as Klee himself had acknowledged as early as a diary entry of 1905, when he wrote: 'O keep the infinite spark from being stifled by the measure of law. Beware! But do not quite leave this world behind, either!'[13]

*Fish Magic* may not have resolved the dilemma Klee here outlines between the 'infinite spark' and the stifling 'measure of law'. But the very creation of this wonderful picture at least forged a new and consoling link between its creator and these two opposing forces. Whether one chooses to regard this picture as an enchanted deep seascape, a dream-like phantasmagoria, or a mystical equation of man, time, and nature, its very existence sharply refutes its gloomy message. For although time must move and man must go, art remains capable of catching the instant and of holding it fast.

Although the precise theme of Klee's next great work in this vein, the 1926

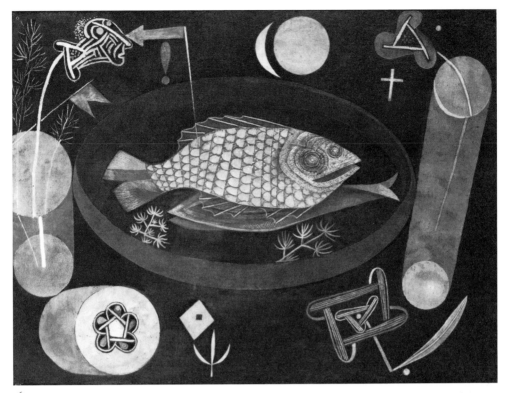

169
*Around the Fish* 1926 Collection, The Museum of Modern Art, New York, Abby Aldrich Rockefeller Fund

*Around the Fish* (fig. 169), would appear to be somewhat different – and although it certainly has been interpreted very differently[14] – this picture is sufficiently similar in content to *Fish Magic* to suggest that their underlying themes may also be related. As in its great predecessor Klee here summons forth a range of elements representative of the whole of natural creation and casts them adrift against an impenetrable black void. As in *Fish Magic*, too, the artist draws his imagery from three distinct points in the hierarchy of beings – from the highest point on the evolutionary scale (i.e. man), a middle point (fishes), and a low point (plants), with the last of these now represented not only by his familiar radial flowers of this period but by the crystalline forms of their even lower relations, the diatoms, which also appear in Klee's *Cave Blossoms* of this same year (fig. 77). Finally, as in *Fish Magic*, pride of place is accorded to the second of these creatures – the fish – and in this case to an horrifically dead carp offered up on a serving dish as a sacrificial victim in the centre of Klee's picture. In this form the fish is most readily exploited by man – a fact which may account for the vigorous arrow which Klee here depicts linking the two. The fish is also, of course, a traditional symbol of Christ; and this may explain the cross hovering to the upper right of it in Klee's picture. But, if one passes beyond the apparent Christian symbolism of this work – that is, beyond the very un-Klee-like theme of mankind living through Christ's sacrifice – a number of other interpretations suggest themselves.

One of the most striking features of *Around the Fish* is the clear visual analogy Klee draws here (as in *Fish Magic*) between man and the plants. Thus, just as the human figure is about to benefit from the sacrifice of the fish he is himself demoted to the status of a flower in a vase. His head now appears at the end of a long stem-like body which echoes that of the flower at the far right of the scene; his neck and shoulders assume the shape of a radial daisy; and his face bears a similar pattern of veins to that of the leaf and flower forms throughout the picture. The cycle, then, is complete. The fish, which has nourished itself on plants – those selfsame plants which ironically now adorn its carcass – in turn nourishes man. But man himself returns to the status of a plant as Klee depicts him and thereby recommences this continuing cycle of life and death in nature.

That Klee's picture is concerned with a cycle of some kind cannot be denied. The orbital arrangement of the forms around the central fish argues strongly in favour of such an interpretation. What is more, for the viewer familiar with the textbook diagrams of the biologists, the picture immediately calls to mind a typical food chain in nature – that is to say, a schematic representation of the dependence of any one species upon another (fig. 170). In such diagrams plants are typically shown supporting life among such lower creatures as fishes, while the latter in turn support that of man himself – all in the way of economical nature. But Klee's *Around the Fish* takes us a step further than this. Now, through man's own demise and decay he is unwittingly returned to the soil, from which he will eventually provide fodder for the lowly plants. And presiding over the whole of this merciless chain in nature (as in Klee's picture) are the sun and moon, which seemingly know nothing of the hierarchic organization of life on earth.

Lest this interpretation of *Around the Fish* be rejected on the grounds that it humbles man to an unacceptable degree, there is evidence elsewhere in Klee's art that he was not averse to doing just this. Witness his comparatively minor but easily fathomable drawing of 1920, *Man-Fish-Man-Eater* (fig. 171), where man devours fish and fish in turn devours man while, at the bottom of the sheet, the sum total of this chain of carnage is disgustingly reduced to excreta. Although it may seem perverse to summon so relatively slight a drawing as this in support of an interpretation of a major masterpiece like *Around the Fish*, this is precisely the way in which so much of Klee's symbolism was nurtured, first finding expression in a witty and readily intelligible manner and then in a more sublimated and infinitely more mysterious fashion. Yet another instance of this in Klee's career where the general theme of *Around the Fish* is concerned may be found in his watercolours of fishing subjects of 1901, which, as we have seen, likewise contain oblique references to the interdependence of the species.[15]

At its profoundest level, then, *Around the Fish* may be interpreted as an astute and yet deeply imaginative evocation of the natural order as seen in microcosm.

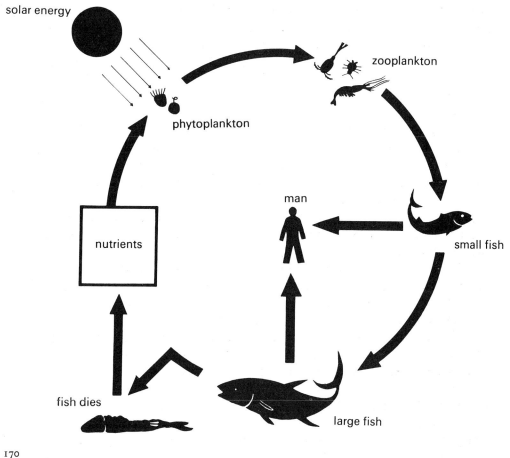

170
Marine Food Chain

Man – the greatest of all predators – exploits a chain of existence which moves down through the fishes and higher plants to the humble diatoms. But eventually man is himself destined to replenish the life upon which he has subsisted and thereby to repay his debt to nature. It is at this point that Klee's picture departs from those conventional biological diagrams which may have provided its unconscious inspiration. For whereas such diagrams usually depict a pyramid of beings in which man is shown as the ultimate beneficiary of all of the efforts of nature, Klee presents us not with a pyramid but with a continuous cycle. Here there are no ultimate victors but only stages – and stations – leading unremittingly unto the next. Yet however humbling man's final place in this scheme may be, it must be admitted that it is Klee – rather than the scientists – who affords us with a more truthful portrayal of the ever-renewing powers of nature. Moreover, it is also a deeply consoling vision – no less consoling than an uncannily similar one experienced by Govinda at the end of Hermann Hesse's tale *Siddhartha* of 1922:[16]

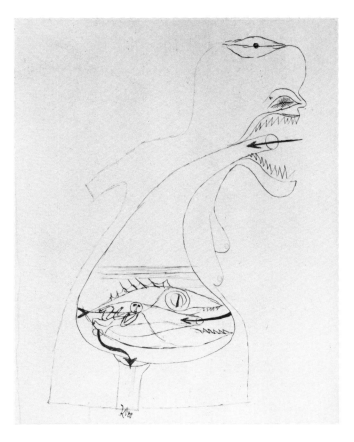

He saw the face of a fish, of a carp, with tremendous, painfully opened mouth, a dying fish with dimmed eyes. He saw the face of a newly born child, red and full of wrinkles, ready to cry. . . . He saw corpses stretched out, still, cold, empty. . . . He saw all these forms and faces in a thousand relationships to each other, all helping each other, loving, hating and destroying each other and becoming newly born. Each one was mortal, a passionate, painful example of all that is transitory. Yet none of them died, they only changed, were always reborn, continually had a new face: only time stood between one face and another. And all these forms and faces rested, flowed, reproduced, swam past and merged into each other . . .

One year after completing *Around the Fish*, in 1927, Klee returned to this general theme in his *Time of the Plants* and *Plant and Window – Still-life* (figs. 172 & 173). Both of these works may be seen as modern equivalents to the traditional *vanitas* still-lifes of the old Dutch masters in their clear concern with the ceaseless rule of time. In the former a handful of blossoms lie strewn across a table watched over by a clock-faced object from which a pendulum swings, mercilessly marking time. Though the protagonists of this scene are self-evidently seen by the artist as blossoms, certain of them are also highly

184

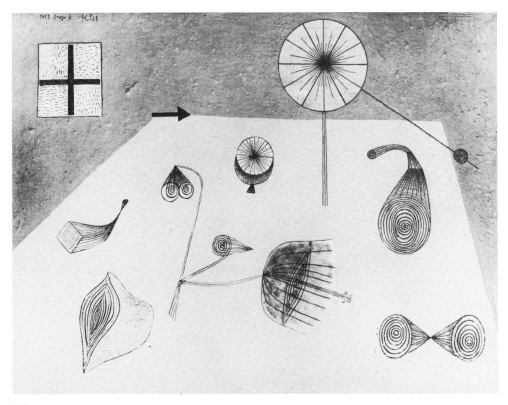

172
*Time of the Plants* 1927 Private Collection, Rome

evocative of other forms. Two or three at least might double as seeds or fruits
and thereby look forward to the advent of a new generation. And at the bottom
right one of Klee's 'blossoms' reclines and, in so doing, assumes the form both
of an hour-glass and of a pair of eyes. When taken together with the general
theme of this picture such motifs firmly proclaim the temporal nature of all
of creation – an idea rendered even more explicit by the striking visual
similarities Klee uncovers here between the separate forms of pendulum,
blossom, seed, eye, and hour-glass. In all of these the artist finds a common
denominator: namely that each in its way resembles a kind of timepiece. And,
as if this were not enough to make his message clear, Klee has distributed all
of these elements upon a bare table-top, as though on an altar – a motif which
not only emphasizes the symbolic nature of his subject but reinforces the
sacrificial undertones of his theme. In this respect all of the objects in the
picture may be seen as representative of the various stages of the plant life-cycle
– from seed to blossom and fruit – each of them leading inexorably to the next.

Despite its non-committal title the same basic theme would appear to
pervade Klee's *Plant and Window – Still-life*. Here, however, the imagery is
at once both less specific and more universal, with its inclusion of the cosmic

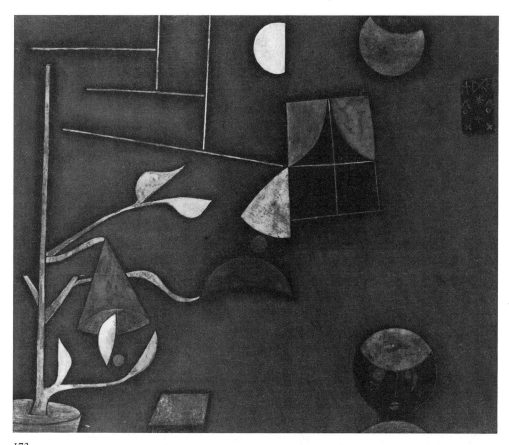

¹73
*Plant and Window – Still-life* 1927 Private Collection, Switzerland

symbols above the window and of the human figure below it. Although (as is usual with Klee) a dogmatic interpretation of this enigmatic little picture is probably unwise, its temporal concerns are implicit both in the forms of the sun and moon and in the pendulum-like motions of its plants. More puzzling is the inclusion of the black human head, which is presumably that of a child, one of whose eyes assumes the form of a sun and crescent moon while also doubling as a tear. The sad child is, of course, a familiar theme in Klee's art;[17] and in the case of this picture the cause of such sadness is not hard to find. Though still youthful, this figure is already a prisoner of time, which is impersonally marked and measured by the motions of plants and planets but is most deeply felt by him. Moreover, with the inclusion of what appears to be a tally-board above this figure Klee seems to indicate that his fate is already sealed. No less than the humble plants and flowers he is merely a pawn in nature's grand design. Such an interpretation becomes even more likely when one recognizes the obvious affinities between this soulful figure and his similarly burdened counterpart in *Fish Magic*.

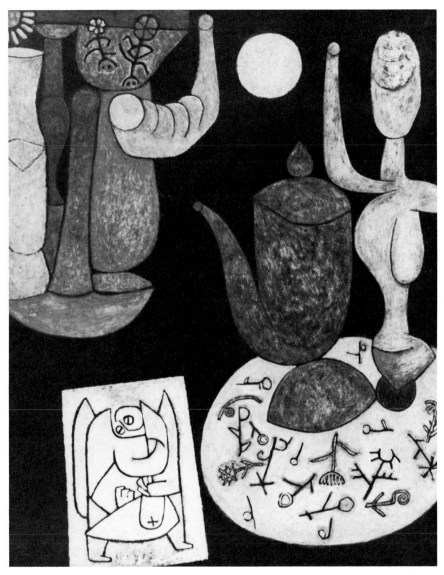

174
*Still-life* 1939–40 Felix Klee, Bern

Although Klee's concern with the cycles of nature persisted throughout the final decade of his career – most notably in the physiognomic landscapes discussed at the end of the previous chapter – only one of his late pictures presents us with so richly symbolic a treatment of this theme as the great masterpieces of the mid 1920s. This is the late untitled *Still-life* of 1939–40 (fig. 174), a large and ambitious work which is the only one of Klee's last pictures to recall the style of *Fish Magic* or *Around the Fish* in its boldly cut and coloured forms which loom into view from out of nowhere and strike us with all the force of a sudden revelation. With its basic repertoire of figures,

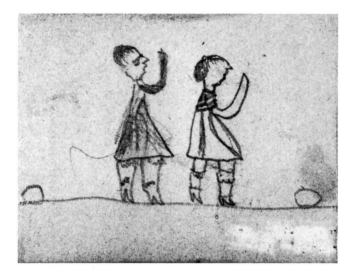

flowers, and planets, this mysterious canvas immediately announces to us that
we are confronting the dying artist's final thoughts on the order and balance
of nature. By any reading of this picture these thoughts would appear to be
deeply distressing and profoundly pessimistic. Although the art of Klee's last
years is replete with references to the fecundity of nature, it is impossible not
to see this valedictory canvas as casting some doubt even upon these. Such,
at least, is the message inherent in this picture's symbolism, especially when
it is considered in relation to certain other works of these years.

Most striking about the late *Still-life* is its perverse overturning of the
apparent natural order. Now the living things of this world – in this case, plants
and flowers – are depicted as dead or thwarted in their attempts to beget new
life. Thus, the broken forms of Klee's blossoms here languish on a table-top
as though scattered over a gravestone or swim in their vases as though more
drowning than drinking.[18] Indeed, when viewed upside down the cut flowers
in the vase at the upper left of this picture become acrobatic schoolgirls
pedalling on a unicycle underwater and thereby literally drowning. In contrast
to all of this, however, the creations of inanimate nature here appear endowed
with almost obscene powers of growth, procreation, and self-assertion. Jugs and
pitchers sprout arms, breasts, faces and phalluses, and suddenly stake a claim
for themselves among the most vigorous and dynamic creations of nature. In
such a guise they also become amongst the most threatening and perverted,
especially when one recalls that their thrusting and saluting gestures are a
recurring motif in works from the opposite end of Klee's own life-cycle –
namely, the dozen or so drawings which survive from his childhood (fig. 175).[19]
In these works such poses are invariably assumed by human figures, and usually
by children themselves, where they speak to us of the power, promise, and
optimism of youth. But how is one to interpret such gestures when they are
donned by the mechanized creations of Klee's last years? Can it have escaped
the dying artist's notice that such aggressive salutes were also a hall-mark of

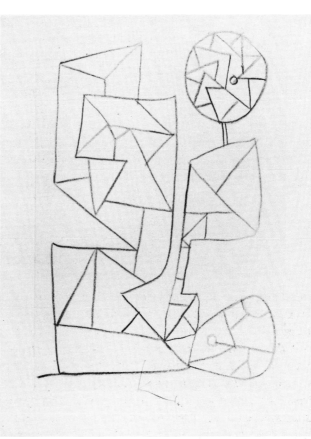

176
*Armed Plant* 1940
Kunstmuseum, Bern

the militant youth of the 1930s? Now, however, they would bring in their wake not the promise of burgeoning life but only the certainty of mass death.

So topsy-turvy a view of the natural order is not confined to this one great work among Klee's late pictures. In the well known *Revolt of the Viaduct* of 1937, too, man-made objects clad in menacing, flourescent hues suddenly acquire life, break ranks, and run amok, marching threateningly out against their very makers.[20] Conversely, in *Armed Plant* of 1940 (fig. 176) Klee seems to concede that, with the approach of war – and of his own death – there would appear to be no better defence for his beloved plants than that of donning armour and disguising themselves as impervious and mechanized creations capable of withstanding the onslaughts of an insane and irrational world. No less than that of Klee's late *Rose* and *Pansy* (figs. 148 & 149) the only hope of survival for this *Armed Plant* is by becoming a weapon or a fist. Time and again in Klee's late art so sombre a view of the order of existence prevails. Living things become machines and the non-living suddenly acquire ominous life.

In the late *Still-life* this point is brought forth even more mercilessly in the drawing of an angel at the bottom of the picture. As Klee's preliminary study for this figure reveals, the artist originally conceived of it as being essentially

189

ugly in nature.[21] Whether or not one sees it as retaining this quality in the final painting it must be admitted that its heavenly nature and aspirations have here been ruthlessly thwarted and that, in this sense, it too represents a perversion of the accepted order of things. Like the plants and flowers it accompanies, it remains a true contradiction in terms – a celestial being which appears anguished, earth-bound, and seemingly strangled presiding over a world in which living things wither and die and only the non-living flourish. Like any number of Klee's late birds, beasts, and fishes, it seems to represent a defunct and obsolete species momentarily summoned back from a point in oblivion to witness that moment when metal and machine will take over the world.

# 6 · Creating like Nature: The Eventual Goal

It has often been noted that the humanoid vases and pitchers of Klee's late *Still-life* closely resemble a group of cactuses at the far right of *Botanical Theatre* (fig. 177), one of the artist's supreme masterpieces and a picture which, somewhat unusually, was begun in 1924 but only completed ten years later. Although this extraordinary work does not include the puzzling mixture of thematic elements of the untitled *Still-life* or the two great fish pictures – and although its content and symbolism would therefore seem to pose a less obvious problem for the viewer – it too would appear to be primarily concerned with the natural order. Moreover, both in its technical intricacy and its richness of invention *Botanical Theatre* may arguably be seen as Klee's single greatest evocation of the overwhelming beauty and authority of nature.

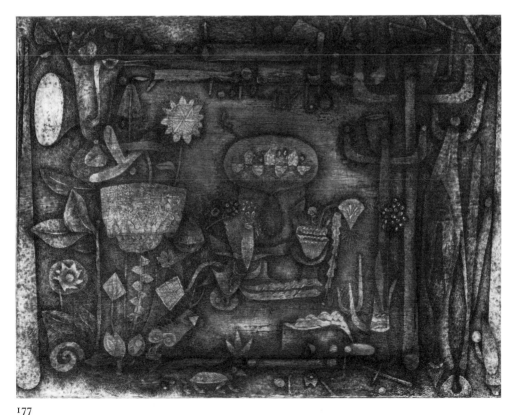

177
*Botanical Theatre* 1924–34  Städtische Galerie im Lenbachhaus, Munich

Densely gathered on to this stage is a veritable phantasmagoria of natural forms, the majority of which are clearly derived from the world of plants. In the centre foreground, however, a small animal scampers in front of the footlights of Klee's 'stage' as though eagerly seeking a way out of this strange and threatening forest. In addition, further references to the animal world peep forth in the eyes, mouths, and noses donned by certain of Klee's 'plants' and in the decidedly human forms of the aforementioned cactuses – plants which the artist was already comparing to humans in his early diary entries.[1] Indeed, so richly allusive are Klee's inventive powers in this mysterious picture that, at the upper left, one of his pitcher plants may also be read as the form of a glowering cat. No sooner has one discovered this lurking menace, however, than this selfsame cat may be seen to metamorphose itself into the pompous profile of a long-necked water bird! The result is a kaleidoscopic glimpse of the whole of the natural kingdom which affords us with the most brilliant demonstration in all of Klee's art of his avowed belief that all of nature's inventions were essentially variations on a handful of recurring types and patterns.

With the exception of Klee's regimentally posed cactuses few of the plants in this picture would appear to be even remotely identifiable, though all are almost obscenely redolent of life. Instead, the artist evokes the entire gamut of plant-like existence by resorting to some of his favourite 'a priori formulas'. Composite flowers, spiral stems (which at the bottom left also double as lethargic snails), and succulent archetypal leaves intermingle with the simpler forms of circular, triangular, and lozenge-shaped blossoms – the last group reminding us again not of the realm of the higher plants but rather of the microscopic world of the diatoms. Indeed, the hushed and secretive atmosphere which pervades this entire painting elicits in the viewer an emotion of wonder and surprise akin to that which accompanies one's first glimpse under a microscope. Suddenly one is brought face to face with a small, new world which in some uncanny way seems to parallel one's own – a world in which everything and yet nothing strikes one as familiar. As in *Botanical Theatre* it is a world which appears to obey a logic and order which mirrors that of more ordinary nature but whose inhabitants remain forever mysterious.

It is not difficult to see how Klee creates this effect. As in many other of his nature paintings the scene unfolded to us is one of a world contained and enclosed, as though seen on a stage, in one of Klee's own showcases of preserved specimens, or indeed under a microscope itself. In this guise it automatically invites the closest scrutiny; for far from being a casual glimpse of nature in disarray it is a sharply focused image of nature on display. Viewed at such close range the scene acquires the aura and intimacy of a well-kept secret suddenly divulged by the artist in a private communication with the viewer. As in any number of Klee's comparable works, too, the world of *Botanical Theatre* is devoid of references to the scale of man himself; and, indeed, it is noteworthy that, even when human figures are introduced into such pictures – as in *Fish Magic* or *Around the Fish* – they are diminished to the size of the flowers and fishes they accompany. As a result of this Klee is able to make the smallest creations of nature – whether an illuminated leaf or a meandering snail – appear immense, and even awesome. Although such an approach is fully in keeping with a century in which (as one writer has put it) artists have forsaken the world of plainly visible nature to 'descend into nature's laboratories',[2] Klee's explorations of this new realm of imagery rarely fail to startle and transfix us – doubtless because of his never-ending ability to re-invent nature and present it to us with all the clarity and authority of an age-old truth. As a result of all of these devices the mysterious beings which greet our eyes in *Botanical Theatre* provoke a response which is recurringly elicited by Klee's most penetrating nature paintings, from *The Bud* to *The Fruit*. Suddenly the humble acquires the semblance of the wondrous – and an image of the microcosm becomes a vision of the macrocosm.

This sensation becomes even more pronounced when one confronts the central motif in Klee's picture – a weird, oval-shaped platform which suspiciously resembles a fruit and which harbours within it a cluster of seed-like elements, the whole serving as a second theatre within the larger one of the picture's title. Suspended from it is the most boldly coloured form in the entire picture – a pendulous red shape which at once resembles both a heart and a tear and thereby evokes both the promise and the pathos of existence. Occupying the very heart of the canvas itself, this motif would appear to represent the life centre and animating impulse behind all of the organisms surrounding it. Once again, a more precise interpretation of this (or any other) element in Klee's picture would serve only to deprive it of its marvellous suggestiveness. But there can be little doubt that *Botanical Theatre* presents us with a microcosm of creation – both human, animal, and vegetable – and of those processes of birth, growth, and reproduction which sustain it in all of these guises. As such it may be seen as Klee's counterpart to the *Arsenal for a Creation* of his friend Franz Marc[3] – that is to say, as an armoury of archetypal forms and forces out of which all of nature might be born. And not the least remarkable feature of Klee's picture is that this impression of the awe-inspiring mystery and diversity of the natural world is vividly conveyed without recourse to a single classifiable form or species. Instead, having fully explored and absorbed the manifold secrets of nature Klee now appears able to evoke them in all their primitive power and wild luxuriance without resorting to the temptation to duplicate anything that he has actually seen. In the truest sense of the word, this is a creation parallel to nature – the product of an inventive faculty so inexhaustibly rich and so fully attuned to the forms and processes of the living world that he can summon them into being without turning his head from the canvas in front of him.

*Botanical Theatre* is a supreme demonstration of Klee's well-known belief that the artist should so completely immerse himself in nature that he will eventually be able to recreate it at will, from out of the depths of his imagination. But for Klee the lessons to be learned from a lifelong dialogue with nature did not end there. Rather, as we have seen, they moved on to illuminate and guide the creative process itself, thereby ensuring that the individual work

178
*Artistic Symbiosis* 1934
Present whereabouts unknown

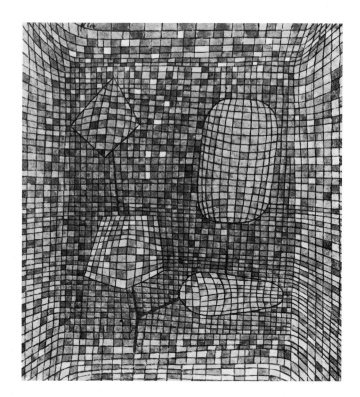

179
*Symbiosis (botanical)* 1934
Felix Klee, Bern

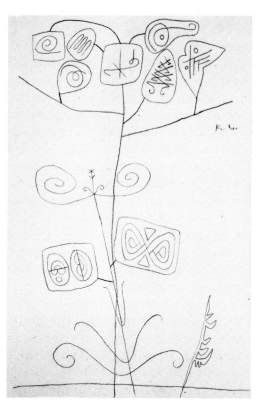

of art was born and grew under the artist's hand in a manner analogous to that of the individual organism in nature. At this point the artist became nature itself and found himself capable of instilling into his own creations a sense of logic, unity, and purpose comparable to that of the greatest of all creators. To do this, however, it was necessary to master not only nature's wide repertoire of shapes and forms but also to understand the processes which had brought them into being. After all, it was only through a knowledge of these that one could hope to explain the final form that nature's own creations took. Klee addressed himself to this problem at least as early as 1905, when he noted in his diaries: 'The real point is the law according to which "nature" functions and how it is revealed to the artist.'[4] And from there it remained only for him to uncover this law and apply it to his own artistic offspring to become a creator like nature.

A graphic example of Klee's interest in parallel phenomena in art and nature is provided by two relatively unfamiliar works of 1934 – the year of the completion of *Botanical Theatre* – entitled *Artistic Symbiosis* and *Symbiosis (botanical)* (figs. 178 & 179). The phenomenon in question here is one well known to biologists: namely, that of a mutually beneficial partnership between two different organisms such as exists, for example, between the sea anemone and the hermit crab, the former of which is accorded free transportation in return for providing camouflage for its bearer. Thus, in *Symbiosis (botanical)* Klee presents us with a similar partnership from the world of plants. Here two distinct species, one of them with delicately lyre-like leaves, cross over one another in such a way as to suggest that they enjoy an unusually compatible relationship – so much so that their fruits and flowers could almost be interchangeable.

In the even more intriguing complement to this work, *Artistic Symbiosis*, Klee offers us a parallel to this natural partnership from the realm of art. Against a mosaic-like background of small coloured planes appears a sprig of four large blossoms. As each of these superimposes itself upon this background the planes of the latter change shape, size, and rhythm, as though refracted through the transparent surface of one of Klee's blossoms. Thus, a situation of mutual interdependence is recreated on an artistic level. The flowers acquire their colour and texture from Klee's mosaic background while the latter itself suddenly acquires a measure of rhythmic individuality under their influence. Of course, the formal procedure which Klee employs here is far from unique to this one work. Rather it immediately reminds us of his favourite device of building up his pictures according to a principle of structural articulation, or '*Gliederung*'.[5] Such a device would appear to have derived much of its inspiration from Klee's discovery of the 'symbiotic' relationship which often exists in music between a freely floating melody line and its supporting accompaniment.[6] But whether the artist seeks a parallel to this principle in the language of music or in that of nature, the principle itself remains essentially the same. Through the intimate partnership of two distinct lines or beings there emerges a structure which possesses both unity and variety and in which the separate elements are woven together in a wholly organic manner. In this

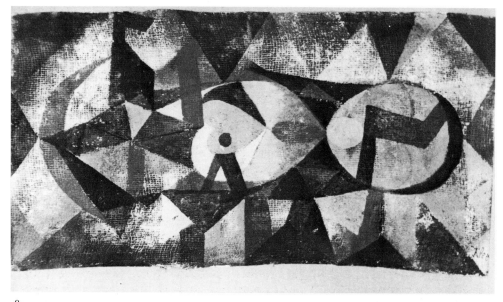

180
*ab ovo* 1917 Kunstmuseum, Bern

respect any number of Klee's most characteristic creations warrant the title (or
at least the subtitle) of 'artistic symbiosis'. But in the case of the picture which
was eventually accorded this distinction the comparison is especially apt, not
only because of the reciprocal relationship which Klee here created between
his chosen subject and its accompanying background but because that subject
itself derives from the world of nature, the inventor of that symbiotic
partnership which Klee has here realized on an artistic level.[7]

However intriguing may be Klee's application of this phenomenon in nature
to the world of art, it is negligible when compared with the frequent parallels
he drew, both in his art and his teachings, between the processes of birth and
growth in nature and art. Perhaps the most famous of these is the comparison
between the tree and the artist in *On Modern Art*.[8] But scarcely less familiar
are the many analogies between procreation in nature and creation in art to be
found throughout Klee's diaries. As early as 1903, the artist spoke of himself
as one 'pregnant with things needing form';[9] and by 1914 he was elaborating
upon this idea with such well-known statements as 'the creation lives as genesis
beneath the visible surface of the work'.[10] Several entries later Klee pursued
this analogy in a crucial account of the fundamental similarities he had
uncovered between natural and artistic creation:[11]

> Genesis as formal motion is the essential thing in a work.
> In the beginning the motif, insertion of energy, sperm.
> Works as shaping of form in the material sense: the primitive female
>     component.
> Works as form-determining sperm: the primitive male component . . .

196

The shaping of form is weak in energy in comparison with the determining of form. . . . In the beginning the male speciality, the energetic stimulus. Then the fleshly growth of the egg.

Thus, like Aristotle long before him,[12] Klee acknowledged the male and female roles in life to have their parallels in art, with the creative impulse – that is to say, the will to form – and the material substance awaiting formation comparing as do sperm and egg.

At the time Klee wrote these lines his own art was not yet ready to apply them; to put it bluntly, it was still far too closely tied to the rendering of appearances to do so. But, within three years, with the formation of his mature style, this basic principle of nature had been assimilated into Klee's creative procedure and the dialogue with the natural world advocated in *Ways of Studying Nature* had begun.[13]

One of the first examples of this new approach to creation is a remarkable little watercolour now in the Klee Foundation, Bern, entitled *ab ovo* (fig. 180). Considering its small size, the construction of this work is unusually elaborate, consisting of a cardboard base overlaid with a piece of paper and, on top of this, a piece of gauze. All three of these layers have been separately painted; and, when superimposed, they create an impression of exceptional density and richness. But Klee never indulged in such effects for their own sake; and, however unconsciously he may have pursued the earliest stages in the growth of this picture, they eventually became essential to its deeper meaning.

The latter is best approached as Klee himself almost certainly approached it – through an investigation of the purely formal drama here taking place. Centred around two large and adjoining ovals, the picture dissolves into a series of rhythmically fragmented colour planes covering the entire surface. These planes fade out towards the edges and thus firmly hold the central ovals in place without usurping attention from them. To create this impression Klee employs the coarse mesh of the gauze as a mysterious veil thrown over the periphery of the picture. For whereas the ovals are painted so as to appear to be resting on top of the gauze layer the surrounding forms are rendered as though receding below it, directly into the multi-layered support.

The resulting impression is one of growth and change – of a sequence of closely related colour planes shown at various stages of their life-cycle, with most of them still forming themselves into the fully realized state of the ripe, central ovals. It is as though Klee has here created the pictorial equivalent of a peep into a kaleidoscope, where, with each successive moment and movement, new forms, colours, and relations are brought to the fore. Nevertheless, at the moment the artist chooses to paint, the two ovals are clearly uppermost in his mind and eye. Although both of these contain within them a smaller and darker oval, they are in all other respects sharply differentiated. The large central oval, with its strong contrasts of tone and colour, is obviously the more energetic of the two; and, led by its pointed end and trailed by a heart, it moves decisively in the direction of the inert mauve oval at the right. Indeed, the latent energies

Living human ovum at moment
of *in vitro* fertilization

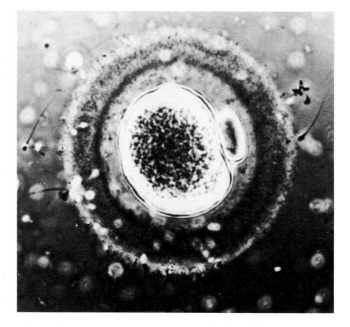

of Klee's entire design would appear to converge upon that juncture between these two forms where the deep blue spearhead pierces the small mauve oval which has migrated towards it.

It is at this stage that one is led naturally to the title which Klee gave to this picture – *ab ovo*, or 'from the egg'. Now it is well known that Klee usually titled his pictures only after completing them, at a point when it became apparent to him that the results of his pictorial researches had come to coincide with something he knew in nature.[14] It is tempting to conclude that this was the case with *ab ovo*, and that the abstract formal drama which this work had (perhaps unconsciously) come to outline was later discovered by the artist to have a parallel in nature, where a comparable infusion of energy into matter occurs when sperm and egg meet and a new life begins. The recognition of this analogy between nature and his picture thereby led Klee to achieve what he regarded as one of his highest artistic goals – namely, 'to bring architectonic and poetic painting into a fusion, or at least to establish a harmony between them'.[15] For in *ab ovo* the pictorial and the poetic focus are one; and the solution to a purely formal problem has resulted in the elucidation of a central mystery of nature.

From the stylistic point of view *ab ovo* would appear to be indebted to the discoveries of the Cubists, whose works had so deeply impressed Klee on his visit to Paris in 1912.[16] But, however abstract this picture may seem at first glance, it belongs more properly to those states of mind Klee termed 'abstract with memories';[17] and in this case the 'memories' betray a profound knowledge of the microscopic drama of procreation in nature (fig. 181). Thus, colour and form differentiate the two reproductive cells or 'gametes': the swollen shape and dull tones of the egg aptly characterizing its fleshy and sluggish nature and the lean and tapered sperm cell its complementary form and purpose. But perhaps even more importantly, the moment depicted by Klee reveals a remarkably accurate awareness of the fertilization process as it is known to biologists. A single sperm cell – its dark colour resulting from its densely packed chromosomes – has just penetrated the egg, the pronucleus of which moves to receive it. Already a characteristic bulge in the egg membrane (the so-called 'fertilization cone') has begun to engulf the sperm. Soon the two pronuclei will fuse and the long process of cell division will begin.

No sooner has one uncovered the apparent moment in this process depicted by Klee, however, than certain irregularities present themselves. For one, the sperm cell is accompanied by a heart which, with its critical placement in the exact centre of the picture, directs one back to the impulse behind every procreative act: namely, the attraction – and, to Klee's mind, the love – of one being for another. Moreover, a close look at the egg reveals within it the dimly outlined eyes and mouth of a slumbering human head. Assuming that Klee did not subscribe to the beliefs of certain early scientists that the embryo existed in a preformed state within the egg, his introduction of this motif, embedded within the fatty substance of the egg, must be seen as a poetical reminder of the eventual result of the union here taking place. Thus, with the central oval for its body and with its feet resting on a crescent moon – a traditional symbol of the promise of the future[18] – Klee's future human being slumbers in the egg, waiting to be born.

Regardless of precisely how one chooses to interpret the pictorial drama of *ab ovo* there can be little doubt that Klee's concern here is not simply with the split-second moment of fertilization but also with moments around it – with the emotion behind the urge to procreate and with the ultimate product of this union. Nor is this surprising, for Klee was acutely aware of the need of the visual artist to overcome the problem of treating more than one moment in time in a picture. 'Simple motion strikes us as banal. The time element must be eliminated,' he wrote in 1917, the very year of *ab ovo*, 'yesterday and tomorrow as simultaneous.'[19] And, accordingly, *ab ovo* prefigures such so-called 'fugal' pictures by Klee as the 1921 *Hanging Fruit* (fig. 103) in its concern to bring together on to the picture surface several distinct events which normally occur in sequence.

But perhaps the most remarkable feature of *ab ovo* is the relationship between Klee's handling of form in this picture and the processes of fertilization and cell division which are its true subject. Klee is known to have placed great emphasis upon a study of 'the embryology of forms' in his teachings;[20] and rarely can he have given more imaginative – or apposite – expression to this concept than in *ab ovo* itself. Thus, the egg is split by a prominent and divisive zigzag form which serves to provide both a nose and profile for the recumbent figure and a cleavage path for the newly-fertilized egg. From there it is not hard to relate this deep purple fissure to other broken forms in the picture and, eventually, to the phenomenon of cell division which follows the penetration of the egg. On this level the basic manipulation of form in *ab ovo* may be seen

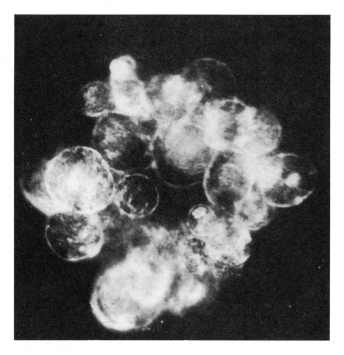

182
*Dividing human ovum after in vitro fertilization*

to re-enact the miracle of cell cleavage in nature (fig. 182). This is not to say that Klee's fragmented forms resemble animal cells, but only that they behave like them. They are the cells of the picture – germinal elements of art, growing, changing, and unleashing energy in a manner parallel to that of nature's cells. And, as though in recognition of their primordial nature and diminutive state Klee even casts his title in small letters. It is *ab ovo* and not *Ab Ovo*. Like his subject – and like his picture – Klee's title too has yet to grow.

Although *ab ovo* remains among the most memorable of all Klee's paintings of nature its sudden appearance in 1917 was not without precedent, however unpremeditated its actual conception and growth may have been. Klee spent much of that year fulfilling his military obligations as an accounting clerk at Gersthofen, near Augsburg. During that time recurring bouts of hunger led him on at least one occasion to dream about one hundred eggs;[21] and, in the course of converting such dreams and hunger pangs into art, Klee created not only *ab ovo* but the much less mysterious *With the Egg* (fig. 183), which was painted earlier that year. Already in this picture the image of the egg, at the bottom centre of the design, is seen in a cosmic context, with its yolk now doubling as a sun and its entire form being embraced by a sickle moon, as though to remind us of those cycles and rhythms which will preside over its destiny at every stage of its earthly reign, from conception to death.

Much more importantly – at least where the richly poetical language of *ab ovo* is concerned – 1917 proved to be the year in which Klee fully realized his ambition to 'make visible' rather than merely to 'render the visible' in his art.[22] Although the artist produced only about 150 works during this year, a significant number of these must be accounted among the first in his career to

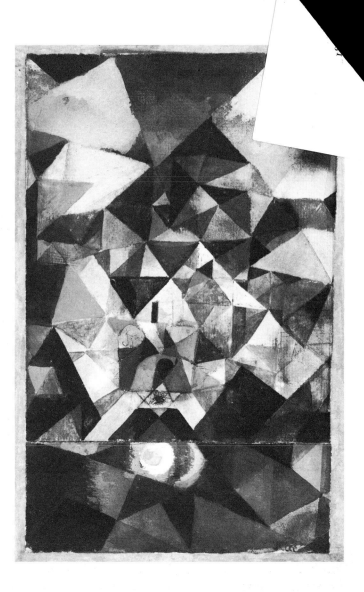

183
*With the Egg* 1917
Private Collection, Hamburg

reveal the almost mystical intensity with which he had begun to explore the inner face of nature. Moreover, such works are rendered in a formal language which is now entirely Klee's own, though this is not to say that it is not indebted to an ever-growing insight into the formal language of nature itself. *Ab ovo* may arguably be considered the masterpiece of this series, but its concern with the general theme of procreation in nature is also to be found in other works of this year. Among them is *The Idea of Firs* (fig. 184), which presents us with the visual equivalent (here perhaps still somewhat indebted to Delaunay) of the forms and forces necessary to plant the conifer forests of the world, while nestled in the middle of them is the pregnant outline of the original (or 'Ur') conifer. Similarly, in *Embryonic Elements of Abstraction*,[23] Klee affords us a glimpse of that bare armoury of formal motifs from which may be evolved the language of pictorial abstraction – in short, of the germ cells of art rather than

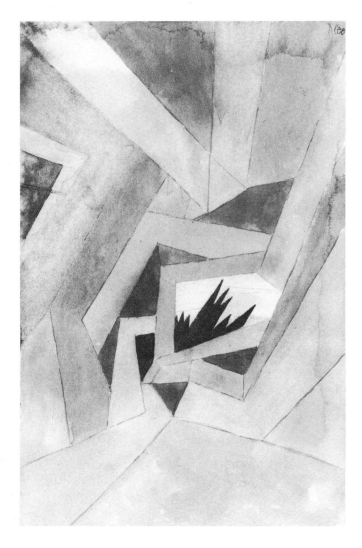

of nature. Finally, in *10 (Twin Plants)* (fig. 123), a parallel drama is enacted, this time from the world of plants. As we have already seen, this evocative little picture, which (to judge from its *œuvre* catalogue number) was conceived at the same time as *ab ovo*, offers us a combination of human and vegetable beings so potent and protean in their suggestiveness as to leave little doubt that they are endowed with a capacity to propagate the flower beds of the universe.[24] Here too, however, Klee appears so fully attuned to the essence of nature's own forms and processes that, without referring to any of them, he miraculously seems to allude to them all.

That Klee eventually succeeded in giving birth to his pictures in a manner analogous to that of nature itself is confirmed by a study of any number of his later works, where the patient pursuit of a purely pictorial problem often gives rise to an image which is then discovered to have a parallel in the world of nature. Needless to say, such parallels do not always concern themselves with

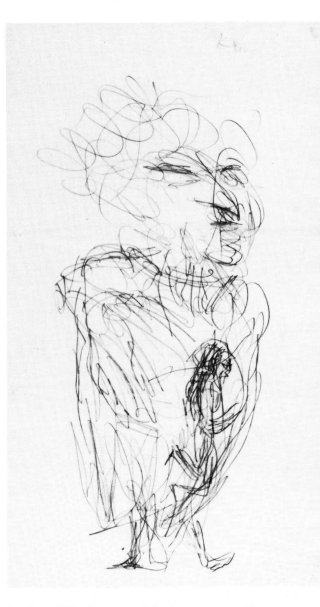

the theme of genesis; though, given Klee's avowed desire to create like nature
it is perhaps inevitable that many of his profoundest pictures – that is to say,
those which seem to well forth from the deepest levels of his being – end up
taking nature as their subject and often bring us face to face with one of its
central mysteries. On occasion, too, Klee gave unusually witty expression to
his belief that the artist should beget art as nature begets nature. In the 1933
drawing *A Pregnant Poet* (fig. 185), for instance, he presents us with an image
of a long-haired artistic type congenitally given to versifying and bearing within
him an unborn foetus, waiting to behold the light of day. Absurd though such
a combination may seem, it too illustrates this central premise of Klee's art.
For this drawing is titled with a turn of phrase which, in German, means either

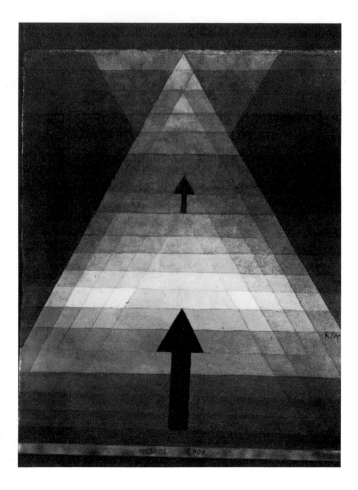

186
*Eros* 1923
Rosengart Collection, Lucerne

to be pregnant with child or to be pregnant with grand artistic ideas; and, as we have seen, the two had much in common for Klee, who repeatedly referred to his own artistic offspring as '*Kinder*', or 'children'.[25]

Moreover, on other occasions in his later art Klee returned to the theme of *ab ovo* in pictures which almost certainly began life as purely artistic problems but where the birth of the finished work once again reminded the artist of the miracle of creation in nature. Thus, in a rather constructivist watercolour of 1923 Klee divided up his sheet into a series of horizontal bands of graduated colour and superimposed upon these two overlapping triangles which approach one another from opposite ends of the design (fig. 186). The larger of these, which rises from the base of the sheet, is marked by stronger and livelier colour contrasts which suggest a more energetic character; while the smaller, which descends from above, revolves around muted tones of green and deep blue. As the two intersect, an ascending black arrow makes contact with a dimly glowing red triangle; while below this, a larger black arrow rushes upwards towards this key point in the design. Klee entitled this pictorial drama *Eros*, which is apt enough when one remembers that such arrows are Cupid's invariable attributes.

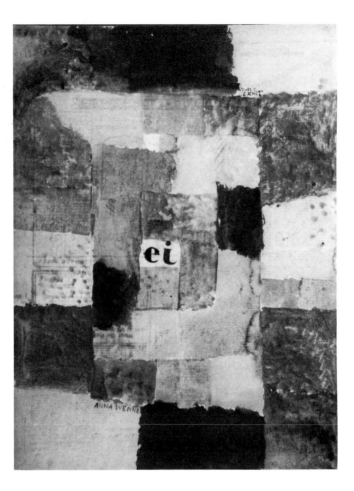

187
*Centrifugal Memory* 1923
Galerie Rosengart, Lucerne

But, from the manner in which Klee treats this meeting between arrows and triangles, it is clear that the picture's true subject is that of *ab ovo*, however decked out it here may be in mythological guise. As in *ab ovo* the formal drama again centres around the infusion of lively energy into inert matter, with the aggressive male component in the picture being greeted by a muted – but no less ardent – response from its female partner. Hence the parallel with the phenomenon of fertilization in nature is unmistakable.

   In another picture of 1923, *Centrifugal Memory* (fig. 187), Klee creates one of his familiar 'magic square' compositions and centres the design around a small white square containing the word '*ei*', or 'egg'. On a purely visual level he thus appears to acknowledge that this central kernel was the primal substance out of which all else in his picture grew. But that Klee may also have had a more personal message in mind here is suggested both by the cryptic title he bestowed upon this picture and by two names inscribed at the opposite ends of this table of colour and so aligned that a straight line connecting them would bisect the all-nourishing egg in the middle. The female name – Anna Wenne – has never been satisfactorily explained, though it appears in at least one other

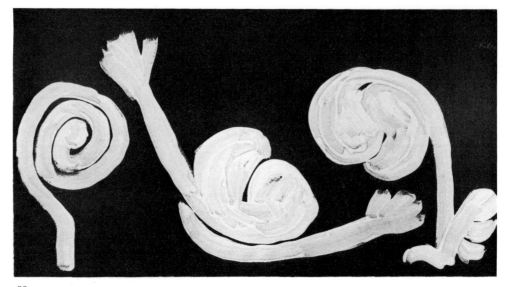

188
*Pathetic Germination* 1939 Kunstmuseum, Bern

work by Klee of these years.[26] But the male name – Paul Ernst – is none other than Paul Klee's own two Christian names. And whatever else it may mean, it suggests that the artist's concern with the phenomenon of procreation in art – as in nature – was far from impersonal.

Even more personal still are the references to this theme in Klee's late art, which is replete with depictions of the procreative instincts of nature – many of them, as we have seen, pervaded by a bitter-sweet recognition that the inevitable consequence of birth is death and that the shadow of death already looms large even at nature's happiest and most hopeful moments. Such works have always attracted less critical attention than Klee's late images of death, doubtless because the latter are more obviously confined to this phase of his career and because they are more overtly autobiographical. But, in the end, it is arguable that the depictions of birth and growth in nature are no less personal in meaning – and certainly they are no less tragic in their prevailing tone.

Among such works is the aforementioned drawing of 1937, *Germinating* (fig. 101), in which Klee portrays a single frail seedling putting forth a slender stem which struggles to release itself from the entombing earth – the whole rendered with such pathos that one is forced to wonder whether its solitary bid for life will ever really come to anything. An even more sombre mood pervades the 1939 *Pathetic Germination* (fig. 188), where three sprouting seedlings are painted – in the bold and pasty manner of the late Klee – against a stark black background. One, at the right, already plays at being a flower with its accompanying leaves; while another, at the left, cautiously prepares to unfurl its spiralling stem. Between them a third sprouts arms and hands instead of stems and leaves and pathetically gropes its way towards the light. A year later, in 1940, Klee draws *As if two Blossoms . . .* (fig. 189), where two beings – which

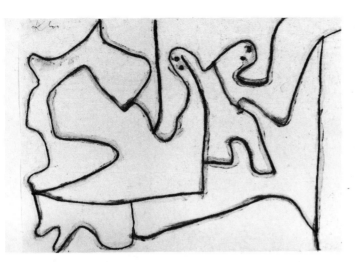

189
*As if two Blossoms . . .* 1940
Felix Klee, Bern

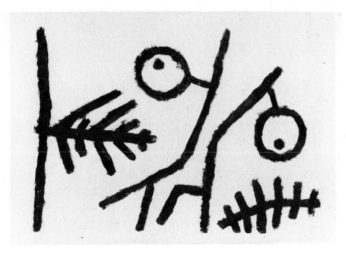

190
*Dancing Fruit* 1940
Kunstmuseum, Bern

could be anything from blossoms to flatworms to humans – meekly raise their heads above their almost overpowering surroundings in a pained and seemingly desperate attempt at self-assertion. Finally, in *Dancing Fruit* (fig. 190), drawn later that same year, Klee gives us another of nature's fertility symbols and another of his favourite late pairs of beings.[27] Now two fruits don arms and legs to perform a ritualistic dance of life – or death – watched over by a conifer and a louse, the differences between these two hardly seeming to matter any more. 'It must be a kind of shipwreck when someone is old and still grows excited about something,' observed Klee from the comfort and security of his youth, in 1905.[28] And in these final meditations on burgeoning nature there is something of both the excitement and the shipwreck.

In the last analysis this may also be said of the picture which stands at the head of this group of works – *ab ovo*. We have already seen that this picture makes visible not only a secret of nature but a capsule history of man who, conceived in love, develops from the fertilized egg to the fully-fledged human

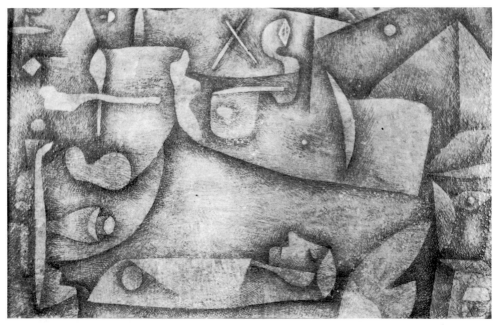

191
*De-Soulment* 1934 Kunstmuseum, Bern

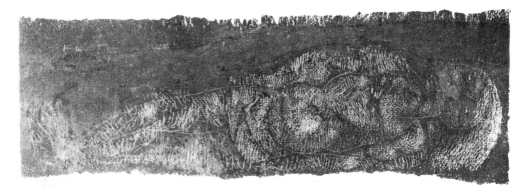

192
*Female Patient* 1933 Kunstsammlung Nordrhein-Westfalen, Düsseldorf

being. But dare one go further than this? Is the face worn by Klee's figure here really that of a young child or of a fully-grown adult? And is the sleep of this figure simply that of the unborn – or that of the dead? One cannot be sure, of course; but the mature cast of this figure's features together with the sombre pathos of its expression are surely more befitting to an adult. With this, the solemnity of the figure's sleep and the stiffness and torpor of its pose are less obviously reminiscent of one awakening to life than of one who has departed from it. In fact the closest analogies in Klee's art for the mood of this figure are all to be found in representations of the dead or the dying – for example,

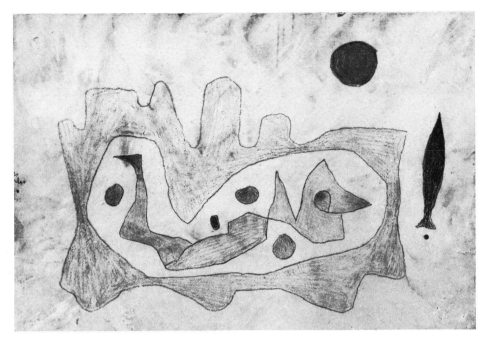

193
*Rock Grave* 1932 Felix Klee, Bern

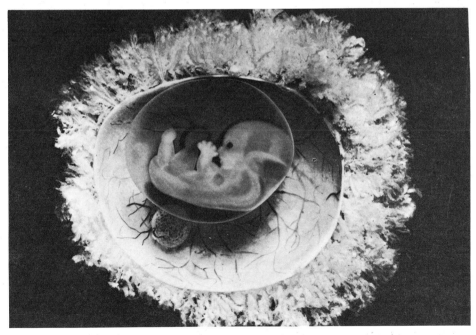

194
Human embryo, 48 days old  Photo courtesy of the Carnegie Institution of Washington, Department of Embryology, Davis Division

in the petrified form of the youth embedded in thick paint in the 1939 *Graveyard* (fig. 157), in the mummified figure which surrenders its soul in the 1934 *De-Soulment* (fig. 191), and (perhaps most strikingly of all) in the rejected and incurably diseased *Female Patient* of 1933 (fig. 192).

Moreover, one need only reconsider Klee's title to realize that *ab ovo* may be made to refer not only to the prenatal period of man's life but to its entire span. The origins of that title are in the *Satires* of Horace (I, 111, 6) – 'ab ovo usque ad mala' – and are widely translated either as 'from the egg to the fruit' (i.e. to the developed human being) or 'from the beginning to the end'. By the latter reading the figure in Klee's picture would be seen at two points in oblivion and the temporal span of the work would become even wider than originally suspected. And, far from being a symbol of hope, the crescent moon which supports Klee's figure would now require to be read as a traditional harbinger of the apocalypse[29] – that is to say, of those cyclical forces in nature which return living matter to infernal chaos.

Nor is the analogy Klee may be drawing here between the opposite ends of man's life unique to this one work. In a little known watercolour of 1932 entitled *Rock Grave* (fig. 193) he gave an even more unequivocal expression to this idea. Despite the fact that the figure in this picture is apparently depicted as dead and buried, the tomb in which it sleeps its eternal sleep assumes the unmistakable form of a uterus, with the surrounding landscape doubling as a kind of placenta (fig. 194). Imprisoned within these, Klee's figure opens its mouth and releases a cry which is at once both anxious and anguished. It is as though the first scream of the newborn is here blending imperceptibly into the last scream of the dying.[30] Only an artist who could 'live just as well with the dead as with the unborn' could have created an image such as this. And only the lines which follow these words on Klee's own gravestone could describe the vantage point from which he did so –

Somewhat closer to the heart of creation than usual
But far from close enough.[31]

# Postscript: **Towards a Wider Context**

Klee was not alone in his view of the world. Others, both of his own time and of long before, shared his desire to penetrate as closely as possible to the 'heart of creation' and to bring themselves face to face with the central mysteries of existence. Like Klee, many of them believed that Nature was both orderly and indissoluble and that a true insight into any one of her workings would often provide the key to the whole. From the study of a single leaf could be gleaned an image of the entire tree; and from an immersion in the microcosm could come a vision of the macrocosm. In this sense Klee's view of nature had a long and distinguished ancestry. But whether the discoveries of his predecessors and contemporaries in this field had much direct influence upon Klee himself is another matter; and here one must frankly proceed with greater caution. After all, when the infant Klee recorded his first artistic impressions of a snail in 1883 he is unlikely to have been inspired by anything but his own innate curiosity about nature. And even as he embarked upon a more systematic exploration of the natural world during his adolescence and maturity Klee would appear to have remained largely untouched by developments outside of himself. Indeed, where his periodic dialogues with the humble snail are concerned it is hard to think of any such developments – at least in the artistic sphere – which could have touched him, for Klee was alone among the painters of his time in turning his attentions to this simple creature.

In the broader evolution of both his art and his thought, too, Klee would appear to have been guided by a purely private muse, with the result that his art possesses an internal logic and consistency which seems largely self-willed. This is doubtless why he has come to be seen as one of the great 'originals' among twentieth-century painters – as an 'independent master'[1] whose achievement ultimately defies classification and demands instead to be explored and explained on its own terms. To be sure, Klee eventually became aware that his own ideas on nature were shared by certain of the greatest thinkers of his own time and of much earlier; and this discovery can only have confirmed him in the belief that his own efforts to come to terms with the totality of creation were essentially correct. But to speak of 'influences' where Klee and nature are concerned is probably unwise. Rather, it would be better to speak of 'confluences'. Klee's approach to nature belonged to a tradition – an established way of seeing the world – which had its origins deep in the past and of which Klee himself was to become an important twentieth-century disciple. But, rather than being schooled in that tradition Klee would appear to have been schooled by nature itself and to have emerged with a set of beliefs and intuitions about the organization of the universe which inevitably paralleled those of others who had followed this same path.

Somewhat surprisingly, Klee's fellow painters are among the least helpful in providing us with a framework from which to understand his own paintings and drawings of natural themes. Admittedly, the world of nature had afforded a rich source of imagery for the generation of painters which reigned at Klee's birth – namely, the Impressionists and Post-Impressionists – and it was also to prove a major inspiration to those two movements in twentieth-century art with which Klee's own name would most often be linked, Expressionism and Surrealism. But any attempt to uncover deeper affinities between Klee's paintings of nature and those of the artists traditionally grouped under any of these headings will soon lead to only one conclusion. Klee's understanding of the living world was unequalled by that of any other painter of his time and was ultimately turned towards quite different creative ends.

Despite the fact that the mainstream of modern art is usually seen as having turned its back upon the world of nature so lovingly depicted by the Impressionists to concern itself instead with the world of the city, the psyche, or just with the world of pure form, in the German-speaking countries at least an interest in nature persisted among a diverse group of early twentieth-century masters, many of whom were known and admired by the young Klee. Different though their modes of expression were, all of these artists turned to nature in reaction against the more dehumanizing aspects of modern urban life, with its increasing materialism and mechanization.[2] Like the great Romantic painters and thinkers with whom they had so much in common these artists discovered in nature a purity, harmony, and instinctual freedom which were man's rightful domain – a domain from which he had grown progressively alienated through the soulless advances of modern industrialization. An art based on nature, then, became a means of rediscovering man's own soul and of re-establishing a long-lost link between himself and the original creative force. In this belief that nature was but the visible manifestation of something both invisible and all-powerful such artists may well have provided an inspiration to Klee, who likewise sought constantly to probe beneath the physical surface of things to uncover a transcendent reality. But there the relationship ends; for in one way or another all of the great painters of nature contemporary with Klee may be said to have used it in an attempt to revive and reform the bankrupt spiritual condition of modern man. Klee alone had no such motives and remained content to see nature on its own terms.

Klee's unique position among the artists of his generation has been aptly summarized by Peter Selz, who observed of him: 'Unlike most of the expressionist painters, Klee was not occupied merely with the state of his own mind, nor did he express an explosive image of an unresolved conflict with society.'[3] These more typically expressionist attitudes are exemplified in the art of his close friends, Emil Nolde and Franz Marc; and, as it happens, they are also the two painters of Klee's time whose choice of natural subjects most closely accords with his own. Like Klee, Nolde had a deep attachment to birds

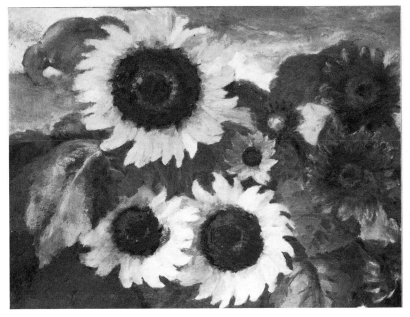

195
*Large Sunflowers II* by Emil Nolde 1940 Present whereabouts unknown

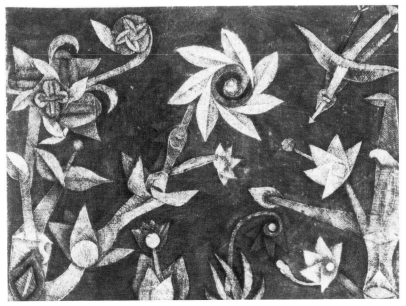

196
*Cross and Spiral Blossoms* 1925 Present whereabouts unknown

and flowers, which became the subjects of a brilliant series of paintings and watercolours spanning much of his career. A comparison of any of these with Klee's characteristic birds or flowers will immediately reveal the essential differences between the two (figs. 195 & 196). Nolde's flowers, which openly declare his admiration for Van Gogh, ultimately afford the artist with an

213

opportunity to explore deeply passionate – and essentially human – emotions, whether of ecstasy, torment, or despair. As such they betray an emotional involvement in nature which is alien to Klee's more impersonal vision. Klee himself saw Nolde as a creature of the earth and of the 'lower regions' but presumably not of the empyrean, where Klee alone resided.[4] And this purely terrestrial relationship with the world of nature is apparent in Nolde's own remarks on flowers. 'The blossoming colors of the flowers and the purity of those colors – I love them,' he confessed, 'I loved the flowers and their fate: shooting up, blooming, radiating, glowing, gladdening, bending, wilting, thrown away and dying.'[5] It is hard to imagine so impassioned a love – or so human a gloom – emanating from the crystalline Klee. Accordingly, if Nolde prefers to paint the *pathos* of his wild blooms Klee prefers to paint their *ethos*. His flowers remain mere cyphers – or ideographs – which point us in the direction of universal truths. Like the stars which they so often resemble in Klee's paintings, they illuminate the earth from a point in the heavens.

We have already seen how Klee likewise regarded Marc's vantage point upon nature as being an essentially 'earthly' one and have observed how Klee's own animal paintings avoid that pantheistic identification with nature which is one of the most compelling attractions of Marc's art.[6] In the latter's desire to 'penetrate to the soul' of his animal subjects and to uncover the 'inner spiritual side of nature' there lies hidden, too, a desire to recover something of both of these for modern man.[7] Marc himself admitted that his initial attraction to animals was prompted by the realization that mankind was 'ugly' and that the animal world appeared 'more beautiful, more pure';[8] and it was in an effort to reclaim such qualities for the repressed and inhibited society of his day that Marc held his mirror up to nature in his pictures. At least until the very last years of his life Marc discovered there an image of Paradise – the vision of an unsullied world in which creature and creation lived as one. In the paintings of Klee, on the other hand, one senses no such feeling of the artist existing outside of nature and seeking reunion with it. Eternal truths – and not what Klee himself called 'current contingencies'[9] – are the prevailing concern of his art; and, accordingly, Klee paints not the lost pleasures of Paradise but the continuing mysteries of Genesis. Nature for him is not a realm from which mankind has been banished but one to which it is ineluctably bound, whether it knows it or not.

Both in their choice of natural subjects and in their treatment of these Nolde and Marc inevitably betray a sensuous involvement in the living world which is likewise avoided by Klee. Although the creations of nature may often appear to us greatly transformed in their art, these always retain an earthiness and a tangibility which remind us that they are the visions and products of essentially human goals and needs. It is as though in painting such subjects both artists seek to possess and inhabit them and thereby to escape to a better world. This yearning and nostalgia for nature, which again links both Nolde and Marc more firmly with their Romantic predecessors, may also explain why both artists draw their subjects from those realms of nature where such identification appears not

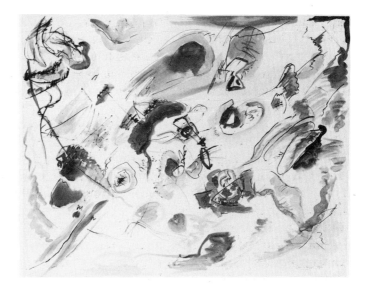

only possible but preferable – from the most beautiful and benevolent of its creations or from those closest to man himself. Along with the nature paintings of any number of their fellow Expressionists, then, those of both Nolde and Marc afford us with a vision of something to which we should aspire – with what Marc himself called 'symbols that belong on the altars of a future spiritual religion'.[10] Klee, on the other hand, does not reach out to embrace nature in his pictures but only to encompass it. His art reveals no desire to touch, be, or feel with his subjects. Instead, Klee's gaze upon nature is emptied of desire; and far from seeking to lose himself in the subjects of his pictures, Klee self-effacingly disappears behind them. By his own admission he remains a mere medium – the trunk of a tree – and the works which stem from his brush present themselves to us as so many conjuring tricks from an undisclosed source.

In keeping with this less anthropomorphic approach to creation Klee also presides over a natural domain which is infinitely greater than that of any of his contemporaries. Thus, his vision encompasses not only the soulful deer and stormy sunflowers so beloved by a Marc or a Nolde but the puny snail, the seed, and the crystal. Seen on their own terms – as Klee chooses to see them – Nature invests as much energy and artistry in the creation of such apparently insignificant creatures as these as she does in her more spectacular creations. Like Klee himself she does not discriminate but works with equal determination in all directions. For in the end all of her creations are reducible to one level – that of the single cell, or the crystal. And the crystal, as we know, is the level to which Klee himself descended in order to be on an equal footing with the rest of creation.

In certain respects Klee's vision of nature has more in common with that of Kandinsky than with any other of his Expressionist contemporaries. In his abstract paintings of the period 1911–14 Kandinsky often evokes the world of microscopic creation and (as Klee himself would seek to do) calls to mind nature's formative processes rather than its finished forms. Although the natural world often provided the initial inspiration for even the most 'non-objective' of these works Kandinsky shared with Klee an ability to penetrate beneath the 'outer shell' of objects in nature to uncover their hidden essence; and these 'inner sounds' (as Kandinsky preferred to call them) became the true subject of his mature paintings.[11] Inevitably these sounds often take on decidedly organic shapes and seem to lay bare the protoplasmic basis of all life and to depict it in a state of perpetual ferment – of becoming rather than being (fig. 197). As one critic has astutely observed, we expect such forms 'to flow or extend like parts of a tissue culture'.[12] Although there is no evidence that Kandinsky himself sought inspiration in the world of microscopic nature, it is perhaps inevitable that his desire to express his own inner feelings or emotions in the most direct manner possible should have led him to approach such elemental statements in his art and to evolve a pictorial language which recalls the basic constituent of all organic life – the single cell – together with those capacities for growth and change which mark nature's workings at every stage. In such apparent incursions into the world of microscopic nature Kandinsky occasionally anticipates Klee's interests and imagery in such pictures as *ab ovo* or *Plant-like Strange*. But, given Kandinsky's increasing reluctance to introduce natural objects into his paintings, this is where the relationship ends. For whereas Kandinsky's cellular shapes vividly evoke the formative forces and processes of the living world Klee's alone introduce us to the myriad beings which nature has created out of these.[13]

Kandinsky's protoplasmic forms – which so often seem to call to mind all of life and yet no particular form of life – prefigure the use of similarly biomorphic forms by that other major group of artists with whom Klee has often been linked, namely the Surrealists. Although Klee was never an official member of this group the importance which he placed upon unconscious creation and the rich store of imagery which he discovered in the hidden crevices of nature find obvious parallels in the art of certain of the Surrealists, and especially of Ernst, Miró, and Masson. Moreover, Klee's art is known to have had a decisive impact upon the work of all three of these masters. In the case of Ernst – whose art forms perhaps the most interesting parallel and comparison with his own – this influence may be documented to a meeting between the two painters which took place in Munich in 1919.[14] Within three years of this Masson too had become familiar with Klee's work, which he subsequently introduced to Miró.[15] Both are likewise known to have felt the effect of Klee's work. But, once again, the differences are more revealing than the similarities; for measured by the standards set by Klee himself even the most biologically inclined of the Surrealists seem essentially disinterested in nature.

As has often been observed, one of the chief stylistic innovations of Surrealism was a return to the use of biomorphic imagery – that is to say, of imagery derived from the forms and processes of organic life. Such imagery may be seen as a reaction against the prevailingly geometric mode of expression of Cubism; and, as William Rubin has noted, this biomorphism 'would be the nearest thing to a common form-language for the painter-poets of the Surrealist generations'.[16] The same critic has also observed that this new mode of expression 'had its roots in Art Nouveau, although there it was primarily linear in style and botanical in its associations'; and in this respect it has clear links with Klee. For Klee's own early nature imagery had derived from the German equivalent of Art Nouveau – *Jugendstil* – and thereby shared its formal sources with the art of the Surrealists themselves. In both cases the search for an organic mode of expression – one which recalled the creations of nature rather than the constructions of man – resulted from a desire to redirect art back to a renewed concern with the processes of life itself.

But to what different ends! For the true Surrealists the hidden world of microscopic nature afforded a storehouse of suggestive images which, when wrenched from their context and magnified into art, would have a disorientating effect upon the eye and mind and would bring man into closer touch with his own primal processes, whether physical or emotional. In an effort to reawaken man's contact with these processes such painters often discovered in nature's repertoire of primordial shapes an 'obscure correspondence to his inner state'.[17] The fantastic, the irrational, the amorphous, and the ambiguous in nature's imagery thus came to be seen as a visible reflection of the human unconscious – of the unexplored depths of man's own thoughts and feelings. Once again, the contrast with Klee could hardly be greater. For while the Surrealists may be said to have plundered nature for shapes and images which mirrored their own irrational emotions and experiences, Klee went to it instead not to illuminate his own inner unreason but rather its own supreme reason.

Inevitably the very different uses to which Klee and his Surrealist contemporaries put their natural images are apparent in their very choice of imagery. Unlike Klee, with his encyclopaedic interest in the living world, his contemporaries in this sphere typically show an obsession with certain favourite forms or beings which came to acquire a purely private significance for them. Thus, the ubiquitous bird which forms one of the leitmotifs of Max Ernst's art has acknowledged origins in his own life and became a kind of alter ego, that is to say an image of himself in another guise.[18] Much the same is also true of both Miró and Masson's obsessive concern with birds, fishes, and insects. Rather than seeking to say something about these creatures and their place in the world, both artists employ them as surrogates for man himself, or at least for his own inner states. Through the very ambiguity with which they enter the art of either of these masters such creatures take on associations with mankind's biological functions and origins – with his violence, his sexuality, or his preconscious mental life. Seen in this way even such a drawing as Masson's *Birth of the Birds* (fig. 44) becomes less an image of avian evolution than a seismographic record of the inner ferment and embryonic chaos of the artist's own mind. In either case, then, nature serves these artists as a means of unlocking the floodgates of man's mind and of releasing it beyond the bounds

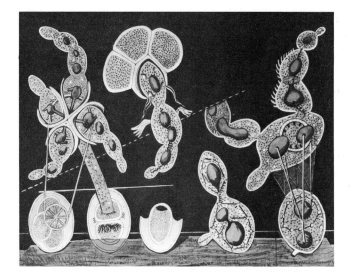

198
*The gramineous bicycle garnished
with bells . . .* by Max Ernst 1920–1
Collection, The Museum of Modern
Art, New York, Purchase

of rational thought. Although Klee too may initially have been drawn to nature
as a means of freeing himself from some of the more inhibiting aspects of life
around him, once drawn there he appears to have resolved to confront and
explore this new world not for the light it might shed upon man's own condition
but only for that which it reflected back on to itself.[19]

There can be no better demonstration of the crucial differences which
distinguish Klee from his contemporaries in this regard than a comparison of
the uses to which he and Max Ernst put the imagery of microscopic nature.
Perhaps under the inspiration of Klee himself Ernst was led during the early
1920s to investigate the nooks and crannies of unseen nature and to create from
these a series of collages in which isolated fragments from biological charts and
diagrams are rearranged in a manner which is unnervingly evocative of the
world of microscopic life. As such, these works may be seen as Ernst's
counterpart to Klee's embryonic images of the late 1910s – to such works as
*ab ovo* and *10 (Twin Plants)* (figs. 123, 180), though the verisimilitude of
Ernst's collages more readily calls to mind Klee's later *Plant-like Strange*
(fig. 68).

One such example is Ernst's *The gramineous bicycle garnished with bells . . .*
of 1920–1 (fig. 198), which is based on an illustration of echinoderm cells here
transplanted from their dryly factual surroundings in a biological diagram and
metamorphosed into a mechanism which calls to mind the form of a many-
wheeled bicycle. In another collage of this period Ernst converts the tiny
skeletons of an insect and a fish into the massive and mobilized forms of a
battleship and an airship floating in an indeterminate realm somewhere between
sea and sky.[20] And in yet a third work of these years he transforms a series
of illustrations of modish children's hats into the spectre of a sandworm slowly
making its way across a beach.[21] In all of these instances the dividing line
between the organic and inorganic worlds is subtly effaced through an ingenious
process of free association upon a given form in which the artist then comes

to discover analogies with other, very different forms. Klee himself likewise engaged in this process and often uncovered hidden links between the most diverse facets of creation. But the differences between him and Ernst far outweigh the apparent similarities. For when Klee draws such comparisons they inevitably serve to instruct and enlighten us in nature's own ways – in its formal vocabulary or its creative strategy. This is because they are invariably founded upon an understanding of what is truly comparable in nature itself rather than upon what the artist has decided may be metaphorically so. In the case of Ernst, however, the appeal of such images lies precisely in their illogicality and their absurdity – in their ability to disturb and disorientate the mind and to evoke the realm of dreams and dream images. Ernst himself admitted that the attraction of such images lay in the extent to which they revealed the hallucinations and 'secret desires' that were visible within him;[22] and in this he differed fundamentally from Klee. For along with all of the other painters of nature contemporary with Klee, Ernst ultimately went to nature in search of man. Klee alone sought nature itself.

If one contemplates Klee's writings on nature without looking at his pictures one is reminded not of the painters of his own day but of the great natural scientists and philosophers of the German Romantic age, and especially of Goethe. That Klee was familiar with the writings of Goethe – whom he deemed 'the only bearable German'[23] – is clear; and, as we have already seen, certain of these find obvious parallels in Klee's own depictions of archetypal plants and flowers of the 1920s.[24] But the relations go much deeper than this and reveal a consistent world view in both men which at times tempts one to regard Klee's paintings and drawings of natural subjects as the ideal accompaniment to Goethe's writings. That such a pictorial counterpart to Goethe's theories should only have come into being a century after his death is understandable when one remembers that the artistic conventions of Goethe's own day were still bound to the outward appearance of things whereas he was already viewing nature with both a 'bodily eye' and an 'intellectual eye'.[25] Goethe himself was aware of the fact that even the most painstaking description of the 'outward resemblance' of things was 'not Nature herself'.[26] Indeed, the former precluded the latter, as Goethe admitted[27] – and as Klee's own art, with its well-developed 'inner eye', was one day to demonstrate.

Although a full account of the many striking parallels between Klee's view of nature and that of his most important predecessors and contemporaries in this field is beyond the scope of this book, some of the most obvious of these demand consideration here; for no attempt to understand the intellectual background of Klee's ideas on nature can ignore the fact that, in many respects, he was a child of the eighteenth century and that his approach to nature shares more in common with that strain of scientific mysticism which originated with Goethe – and which has attracted disciples right up to our own day – than it does with any more recent developments in the history of ideas. In common with Klee's own approach to the living world, the Goethean view of nature finds in all aspects of existence an intimation of the whole and patiently pursues a study of the visible world of Nature until it comes face to face with her invisible secrets and, ultimately, with the original creative spirit itself. For the sake of convenience only those aspects of this tradition which bear most directly upon Klee's own ideas or imagery may concern us here as they appear in the writings of a representative group of major figures from Goethe to Klee's own time. Even from so selective an approach as this, however, it will become apparent that Klee's view of nature was a widely shared and sanctioned one, and that many of its basic premises were so inherently logical as to seem self-evident. But this is not to say that Klee's ability to give artistic expression to these fundamental truths was not in itself of the highest originality.

In his epoch-making *Essay on the Metamorphosis of Plants* of 1790 Goethe set out to trace 'the manifold specific phenomena in the magnificent garden of the universe back to one simple general principle'.[28] To do this he approached the world of plants in a way which was unusual for its day but which exactly anticipates that of Klee. To begin with he divorced himself from any concern with the beauty or utility of plants and sought instead simply to uncover the truth about them. 'Like the sun that lures forth and illuminates each and every plant', Goethe set out to 'survey them all with the same calm glance.'[29] For him this was the only way to discover the everlasting truths about nature and, in this, Klee would surely have agreed. For Klee too sent his rays equally in all directions – and far from concerning himself with the beauty or utility of plants, he remained content to portray the most ordinary and unassuming varieties.

In addition, Goethe largely ignored the multitude of different plants to be found in nature; and in this respect his approach was exactly opposite to that of the great taxonomist of his time, Linnaeus. Rather than losing himself in the endless varieties of such beings to be seen around him, Goethe sought to discover the underlying features which united them all. His way, as one critic noted, was not to recount 'the history of plants' but, rather, 'the history of *the plant*'.[30] Thus, instead of seeking to describe the differences between individual species Goethe went in search of a common and characteristic symbol of plant life: the archetypal plant, which would exist only in the mind's eye – until, that is, Klee's art would seek to approach it. As Goethe saw it the way towards this goal was, firstly, through the intensive study and observation of as many different plant types as possible and, secondly, through the application of thought and reflection to the evidence of the senses until one acquired an intuitive understanding of the common features which pervaded all of plant life. Here again Klee was to follow him and to apply both sight and insight in his own dialogues with nature.

Goethe's principal concern, then, was with form rather than with function. Yet for him form was never something static but always something becoming, something changing. Recognizing that all of nature was in a state of 'ceaseless flux' Goethe concluded that a true understanding of any of its creations could only come through a familiarity with the processes which had brought them into being – in short, with the phenomenon of formation. To discover, 'the law whereby the formations are produced' thus became his declared aim;[31] and in this he obviously anticipated Klee's search for 'the law according to which "nature" functions'.[32] Inevitably a concern with the processes of formation also led both men to introduce a temporal dimension into their thinking about nature. In an idea about an organism, Goethe observed, 'the simultaneous and successive are intimately bound up together, whereas in an experience they are always separated'.[33] The parallels with Klee are once more self-evident; for time and again in his mature art – and not least when he compresses the entire plant life-cycle into a single painting (fig. 95) – Klee succeeds in making 'yesterday and tomorrow . . . simultaneous'[34] to afford us with a vision of all moments in the life of his chosen subject. Thus, in their search for the essence of forms in nature both men acknowledged that this was only to be discovered through a consideration of the workings of time upon any one of its creations. The living processes of nature – the phenomena of genesis, growth, and transformation – thereby became the focus of both of their investigations.

Among the most important discoveries which Goethe himself was to make by turning his attentions to the temporal development of the typical plant were two which, as we have seen, are particularly relevant to Klee's treatment of this theme in such paintings as *The Bud* (fig. 93).[35] The first of these was his recognition that the development of the plant is governed by alternate processes of expansion and contraction;[36] and the second, that the two basic tendencies which shape the growth of the living plant are the vertical and the spiral.[37]

In his desire to come as close as possible to an understanding of nature's creative strategy Goethe soon discovered that this was best approached through a careful study of the individual parts of a plant. Although he acknowledged that 'each living creature is a complex, not a unit' Goethe realized that it was only by penetrating to the smaller units which made up that complex that one could confront the secrets of its inner being.[38] When applied to the form of a flower this led him to the discovery that all the organs of the flower were essentially modified leaves and that these in turn had been transformed by nature into the more specialized and diversified flower parts. Through all of this, however, these parts revealed their origins in the basic leaf – a phenomenon which Goethe noted to be particularly apparent in the composite flowers,[39] and one which Klee's own buds and composite flowers repeatedly reveal to us.[40] Carrying these observations even further Goethe discovered that, if one concerned oneself with the essence of an entire plant rather than merely with its appearance one would soon discover that all of its parts were essentially modifications of the leaf. The latter, he noted, contains within it the structural blueprint for the entire organism, from the branch to the tree, and from the flower to the fruit[41] – a secret which nature likewise vouchsafed to the creator of *Illuminated Leaf* (fig. 97). 'In organic life,' Goethe observed, 'nothing is unconnected with the whole, and even if the phenomena *appear* isolated to us . . . it does not prove that they actually *are* isolated. The question is merely how to find the interrelation of these phenomena'.[42] Thus Goethe set out to lift the veil from the various disguises worn by nature's creations in order to discover their essential oneness. As Klee would one day seek to do he sought to penetrate to the very 'womb of Nature', where her invisible archetypes lay hidden.[43]

Inevitably Goethe's method of discovering such hidden affinities in nature relied upon an approach which Klee himself was later to explore to the full: namely, that of uncovering analogies between apparently dissimilar things. In this sense both men were comparative thinkers, more interested in those features which united all of creation than in those which diversified it. But Goethe himself admitted that one could carry such analogies too far and reach a point of fantasy or absurdity which transgressed the boundaries of science and moved instead into the realm of poetry. Thus, whereas Goethe found it permissible in general to compare the seed capsule of a plant with an ovary, or the seed itself with an egg, a more detailed comparison between the parts of these two elements seemed to him to stray too far from the truth since it ignored the fundamental differences between the plant and animal kingdoms.[44] In his most searching paintings of nature Klee may likewise be seen to respect these boundaries and rarely to present us with analogies which can be considered absurd. Thus he too will compare a fruit to a womb (figs. 104 & 105) but not a developing seed to a developing foetus. In the former case both the form and function of such beings may be seen as analogous, but in the latter only the purpose is so.

Goethe's strictures, which may here seem reasonable enough to us, were clearly directed by him against that prevailing tendency of many eighteenth-century naturalists to make indiscriminate comparisons between all aspects of the animal and vegetable kingdoms. This was a favourite pastime in an age which sought repeatedly for a comprehensive explanation of all of life,[45] and one which is even apparent in the writings of such major scientists of the day as Linnaeus, whose efforts to explain the life processes of the plants often led him to compare these to the more familiar – and more visible – biological functions of the higher animals.[46] Goethe provides one such instance of this when he cites Linnaeus's description of the petals of a flower as 'curtains of the nuptial bed'.[47] 'A parable that would do honour to a poet,' he admits. 'But after all! The discovery of the true physiological nature of such parts is completely blocked in this way'.[48] Similarly, Goethe disapproved of any attempt to describe the sexual lives of plants in a graphic and essentially human manner[49] – an approach which calls to mind Klee's more poetical and fantastic treatments of this theme in such works as *A Table set with strange Flowers* or *Erotic Super-plant* (figs. 131 & 132). In such inventions as these Klee must be admitted to have more in common with certain of Goethe's contemporaries than with Goethe himself. For such fanciful analogies were another preoccupation of the eighteenth century and find their fullest expression in Erasmus Darwin's *The Loves of the Plants* of 1789, which sought to restore to the plants some of their 'original animality' and, with this, much of their blatant sexuality.[50]

One intriguing species whose curious sexual habits attracted the attention of both Goethe and Erasmus Darwin also sheds interesting light on certain of Klee's more purely poetical renderings of the love lives of the plants. This is the shallow-water variety *Vallisneria*, which is unusual in bearing its male flowers underwater and its female ones above it, on spiralling stems. As Goethe observed, the two sexes meet on the surface of the water itself, where the female flowers come to rest and to receive the pollen which the male flowers have distributed over the surface.[51] This explanation, noted Goethe, did away with the 'current fairy tale' about the male *Vallisneria* detaching itself from the plant 'to go hunting lasciviously for the female' and confirmed him in his belief that the spiralling tendency in the plant was a female one and the vertical tendency a characteristic of the male. Erasmus Darwin, on the other hand, perpetuated that 'fairy tale' in his oft-quoted lines on the lovelorn *Vallisneria*, which curiously anticipate certain of Klee's many depictions of unrequited love among the plants:[52]

> Vallisner sits, up-turns her tearful eyes,
> Calls her lost lover, and upbraids the skies;
> For him she breathes the silent sigh, forlorn,
> Each setting day; for him each rising morn. –

Accompanying this passage Darwin includes a drawing of this strange species, which shows the spiralling female blossoms hovering above the water in search of a mate (fig. 199). For all its elegance and finesse, Darwin's drawing remains an accurate botanical illustration which captures nothing of the fantasy – or the 'fairy tale' – of his poem. For that one had to await such drawings by Klee as *The Flower as Object of Love* (fig. 114), which affords us with an image of just such a love match as Darwin had described. Thus Klee's curvacious female flower floats freely in the breeze, flaunting her attractions and clearly on the lookout for a mate; while from below a thrusting male already advances towards her. Along with any number of Klee's other depictions of amorous plants and flowers of the period 1914–23,[53] this drawing belongs more to the realm of fantasy than of fact and finds its nearest analogies in the writings of such eighteenth-century naturalists as Erasmus Darwin, who willingly attributed human forms and feelings to the plants – and who ultimately concerned himself more with the lore of nature than with its law. Yet it is noteworthy that Goethe's more scientific explanation of this phenomenon in *Vallisneria* was also intuitively appreciated by Klee, whose female flowers often display that spiralling waywardness which Goethe had discovered in their real-life counterparts and whose male blossoms likewise prefer to adopt a more no-nonsense verticality in their stance and movement. As befits the more aggressive sex they prefer to travel the distance between two points in the most direct manner possible.

Goethe's admonitions against so purely fanciful an interpretation of nature were, of course, made while he was wearing his botanist's cap. But he was also the greatest German poet. And in his occasional poetical incursions into the

199
*Vallisneria spiralis* from
Erasmus Darwin's *The Loves
of the Plants* 1789

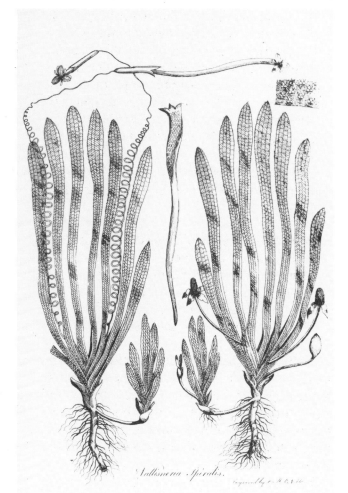

botanical world Goethe explored the inner poetry of natural life itself in a
manner which has nothing to do with the pure fantasy of Erasmus Darwin or
of Klee's own erotic plants but which does anticipate certain of Klee's most
profound depictions of nature's hidden truths. One such instance may be found
in the elegy which Goethe composed for 'well-disposed ladies' who had
complained that his scientific discourses on flowers and plants had reduced
these creatures of form, colour, and fragrance to mere 'wraithlike figures'.[54]
Taking up this challenge Goethe composed a poem which fully restored them
to life and which repeatedly brings Klee to mind. Indeed, the student of Klee's
nature imagery might find it hard to read the following lines from Goethe's
poem without illustrating them in his mind's eye with Klee's own *Germinating*
or *A new Face* (figs. 101, 130):[55]

Asleep within the seed the power lies,
Foreshadowed pattern, folded in the shell,
Root, leaf, and germ, pale and half-formed.
The nub of tranquil life, kept safe and dry,
Swells upward, trusting to the gentle dew.
Soaring apace from out the enfolding night.
Artless the shape that first bursts into light –
The plant-child, like unto the human kind –

Still less might he find it possible to contemplate the following passage
without remembering Klee's many renderings of umbilical fruits (figs. 104 &
105):

Deep in the bosom of the swelling fruit
A germ begins to burgeon here and there,
As nature welds her ring of ageless power,
Joining another cycle to the last,
Flinging the chain unto the end of time –
The whole reflected in each separate part.

As in all of Klee's most penetrating nature paintings Goethe's images strike
us as the products of a truly informed imagination – one which speaks at once
to the heart and the mind. 'All the things an artist must be,' wrote Klee in
1911; 'poet, explorer of nature, philosopher!'[56] Following Goethe's great
example Klee eventually succeeded in becoming all three of these. As a result
his greatest paintings of nature invariably afford us with a rare mixture of both
poetry and truth.

Finally, mention should also be made here of one last parallel between
Goethe and Klee's attitudes towards Nature – and this, perhaps, an inevitable
one given the obvious reverence in which they held her. Like Klee, Goethe saw
in Nature 'a model of everything artistic'[57] and, therefore, the supreme model
for the creative artist himself. 'Through contemplation of ever-creative Nature,'
observed Goethe, 'we might make ourselves worthy of participating
intellectually in her productions' and 'in evolving a method in harmony with
Nature.'[58] Inevitably, such a statement recalls Klee's own belief that, through
repeated contemplation of the living world, the artist himself would 'become
just as resourceful, flexible, and determined as great Nature'.[59] Although this
notion was not new with Goethe, and was soon to become a commonplace of
Romantic critical theory,[60] it is more likely to have reached Klee from Goethe
than from any other source. Yet if Goethe conceded that Nature's creative
methods were the artist's best sourcebook, he also admitted that those methods
were destined to remain forever unfathomable. One could 'eavesdrop' upon
Nature in the hope of coming a step or two closer to her creative secrets;[61]
but in the end Goethe confessed that she worked according to no knowable
system but merely 'from an unknown center toward an unknowable goal'.[62] In

this respect her methods mirror those of Klee's creative artist, who, for all his knowledge and experience of the natural world, faces his blank canvas and finds himself forced to play 'an unwitting game with ultimate things'. Whether in nature or in art, the creative process remained eternally mysterious for both men. All one could hope to do was to break it down until some, at least, of its parts became known.

'We are encompassed and embraced by her – powerless to withdraw, yet powerless to enter more deeply into her being,' declared Goethe of Nature; 'we live within her, yet are foreign to her.'[63] Such a view of creation could equally have come from Klee himself, the 'observer above the world or [the] child in the world's totality'.[64]

So much that is central to Klee's vision of nature is to be found in Goethe that it may seem unnecessary to look elsewhere for precedents for his own ideas on organic creation. Nevertheless, it is fair to note that many of Goethe's views on nature survived into our own century and that in certain instances they may have reached Klee through the writings of more recent thinkers. This is particularly the case with Goethe's search for the common denominators underlying all forms of life, which, as we shall see, has remained a preoccupation of many of his more recent followers. But even the parallels Goethe drew between natural and artistic creation have likewise preoccupied a diverse range of later writers, especially during the Romantic period, when a reverence for all aspects of nature led poets and critics as different as Schlegel and Shelley to posit just such a link between these two forms of creation. Klee is almost certain not to have read Shelley; yet the latter's account of the creative act in man affords us with a striking presentiment not only of Klee's 'unwitting game' but, on a more graphic level, of his *Pregnant Poet* (fig. 185):[65]

A great statue or picture grows under the power of the artist as a child in the mother's womb; and the very mind which directs the hands in formation is incapable of accounting to itself for the origin, the gradations, or the media of the process.

Despite the fact that Goethe had regarded Nature as 'the All-in-One',[66] his own efforts to come to terms with her totality were chiefly directed towards the visible world – and above all towards the higher plants and animals. A number of his disciples, however, extended their vision of this totality towards the two great invisible realms – those of microscopic nature and of the cosmic domain. Descending on the one hand towards the level of the single cell or the crystal and ascending, on the other, towards the realm of the stars they sought an all-embracing vision of creation such as one finds reflected in certain of Klee's 'cosmic compositions'. Klee himself was familiar with the ideas of many of these men; and although it would once again be unwise to assume that he was directly influenced by them, it is not hard to imagine him nodding his head in agreement as he read their thoughts on the invisible bonds which link heaven and earth and all living things.

One scientist who did much to introduce Klee's generation to the world of microscopic creation was Ernst Heinrich Haeckel (1834–1919), a self-confessed disciple of Goethe whose pioneering studies of the diatoms and radiolarians have already been mentioned in connection with Klee's depictions of these crystalline creatures.[67] Where Klee's nature imagery in general is concerned Haeckel's importance lies chiefly in the fact that he extended the Goethean view of nature to encompass the world of microscopic life; that he showed a lifelong interest in uncovering analogies between the organic and inorganic worlds; and, perhaps most importantly of all, that he published many of his findings in illustrated form. For although Haeckel was a notable biologist, he was also a great lover of art; and in the magnificent portfolio of lithographs in which he combined these pursuits, *Art Forms in Nature* (1899–1904) may be found some of the most remarkable nature illustrations of this period. Haeckel's work formed part of Klee's library; and in view of the fact that Klee himself did not use a microscope until relatively late in his career,[68] this volume may have afforded one of his chief sources of inspiration where the hidden wonderland of microscopic forms of life was concerned. Certainly Haeckel's exquisitely drawn and designed plates must have opened up new creative vistas for any number of impressionable young artists of Klee's generation; and, as the title of his work suggests, this is exactly what Haeckel set out to do by introducing them to hitherto uncharted regions of nature's artistry and by making them aware of the aesthetic possibilities of organic forms.[69] In addition to this, however, Haeckel's explorations of microscopic life provided him with tangible evidence that, at the most elementary level, nature created its forms in accordance with principles of symmetry, regularity and structural simplicity which yet contained within them the possibilities of infinite variation. Moreover, in the lucidly geometrical forms which Haeckel discovered amongst creatures as diverse as the diatoms and radiolarians he approached that point in creation where plant, animal, and crystal meet and the bare vocabulary of nature may be glimpsed in its purest state.[70] Klee, of course, was to follow him in this pursuit in any number of works of the middle years of his career, among them *Botanical Theatre* and *Around the Fish* (figs. 169, 177).

In the writings of another of Goethe's avowed disciples, Rudolf Steiner (1861–1925), an even more all-encompassing vision of nature prevails. This may best be summarized in Steiner's own words: 'For in great Nature – again and again I must say it – everything, everything is connected'.[71] Seeing more often with his inner eye than with his 'bodily' one, Steiner put forward a view of the universe in which all elements are in mutual interaction and in which everything is ultimately linked – plants and animals, earth and cosmos. Even the humble larvae and earthworms burrowing deep beneath the surface of the earth, observes Steiner, may be seen to have their effect upon the forests which clothe it.[72] And, indeed, it is above all in one's contact with these creatures and with the even humbler plants that Steiner finds himself in closest touch with the cosmic domain – a domain from which man had outwardly (but *only* outwardly) emancipated himself through the benefits of civilization.[73]

Klee was generally dismissive of Steiner's writings, which he read in the very year – 1917 – that he was himself setting an earthworm in a cosmic context in his *Mystical Landscape with a Worm in the Ground* (fig. 159). Nevertheless Steiner was the foremost exponent among Klee's generation of the Goethean approach to nature; and, in certain respects, his view of the universe does undoubtedly accord with Klee's own. Both see all of creation as subject to cosmic and earthly influences, and both imagine the balance of life to be maintained by an oscillation between opposing rhythms or forces, from chaos to order and then back again. Such a view even makes it possible for both men to compare the development of a seed to that of the entire universe, which alike had its origins in inchoate matter and became an ordered whole. Thus for Steiner the growth of a single plant recapitulates the birth of the cosmos itself; while for Klee the same essential processes mark 'every sort of beginning', with the seed – the 'charged point' in nature – standing as 'a kind of sum total of the infinite'.[74] Such correspondences in their thinking may well explain Klee's principal objection to Steiner's writings: namely, that they were full of 'commonplaces'.[75] 'Commonplaces' they may have seemed to one with Klee's metaphysical turn of mind, who was already well-grounded in Goethe – and who had been busy uncovering such hidden affinities in the world about him from his earliest years. But to others of Klee's generation Steiner's view of nature afforded an alternative to the more orthodox scientific thinking of its day. For, as Steiner himself admitted, the aim of his approach was to free mankind from the increasingly specialized and fragmented vision of much of modern science and to encourage it to adopt a more comprehensive attitude towards nature:[76]

> What does science do nowadays? It takes a little plate and lays a preparation on it, carefully separates it off and peers into it, shutting off on every side whatever might be working into it. We call it a 'microscope'. It is the very opposite of what we should do to gain a relationship to the wide spaces. No longer content to shut ourselves off in a room, we shut ourselves off in this microscope-tube from all the glory of the world. Nothing must now remain but what we focus in our field of vision.

> By and by it has come to this: scientists always have recourse, more or less, to their microscope. We, however, must find our way out again into the macrocosm. Then we shall once more begin to understand Nature – and other things too.

Although Klee also wished 'to be anchored in the cosmos',[77] the above-quoted passage from Steiner makes it clear that both men sought this destination by different routes and goes far towards explaining Klee's objections to Steiner's writings. For if Steiner saw the microscope as impeding one's progress towards this goal, Klee found in it instead an image of the wider whole.

Although Steiner's cosmic view of creation accords with certain aspects of

Klee's own thinking there is one important feature of the latter's approach to nature which is not encompassed by such a theory. This is the emphasis which Klee places upon Nature's logic and reason or, to put it another way, upon the order and method with which she designs and builds her creations. In Klee's own art this belief most often expresses itself on a purely formal level and leads him to uncover certain basic patterns and principles which, as we have seen, may be found to pervade the entire hierarchy of life. If this pursuit is yet another example of Klee's interest in comparative science, it is also one area of his thinking which can be readily demonstrated in nature itself, providing one has the patience and diligence to survey the entire domain of organic life and to attempt to reduce it to order.

Contemporary with Klee's own investigations of this facet of nature, a number of writers and scientists were likewise devoting themselves to this problem and seeking to uncover the formal and mathematical principles which underlay much of creation. Whether or not Klee was aware of their findings is immaterial, though in at least one case there can be no doubt that he was. But what is more important is that many of these findings tend to corroborate Klee's own discoveries regarding Nature's reason, consistency, and economy, and to confirm his belief that she created according to clearly established rules and that those rules were ultimately knowable.

Probably the most significant of all studies of this broad theme is that put forward by D'Arcy Thompson in his now-classic *On Growth and Form*, first published in 1917. Where Klee at least is concerned the most important discovery of this great work was the realization 'that forms mathematically akin may belong to organisms biologically remote'[78] – in other words, that nature often repeats its basic forms throughout the entire range of its creations, from the apple to the snail-shell. The latter, of course, is Klee's example of this phenomenon in action and not D'Arcy Thompson's. But in D'Arcy Thompson's discovery that there are physical reasons why only certain forms are possible in nature, and which explain the spiralling tendencies of a plant as well as of a snail, Klee would doubtless have found much support for his own efforts to uncover the constant and irreducible patterns of organic creation.

D'Arcy Thompson was not alone in discovering such broad analogies amongst the most diverse forms of life and in seeking to provide a scientific explanation of them. Three years before his classic study appeared, in 1914, T. A. Cook published a book devoted to the spiralling principle alone as it pervades nature and recognized in this form 'one of the great cosmic laws'.[79] In a wealth of accompanying illustrations Cook demonstrated this law in action, finding it alike in the seeds, seed cases, cells, stems, flowers, and fruits of the living plant and in the sperm cells, heart muscle, umbilical cord, and inner ear of the animal body.[80] In all cases he noted that the spiralling pattern arose in response to certain specific physical laws which forced unlike things to develop along similar paths. Extending beyond these familiar examples, Cook discovered the identical formal principle in the structure of the tiniest protozoans and in 'the gigantic nebula in the immeasurable heavens'.[81] On this basic formal level at least, he – and others of his generation – had forged a tangible link between the microcosm and the macrocosm. 'Nature has no watertight compartments,' insisted Cook in the introduction to his study, 'every phenomenon affects and is affected by every other phenomenon . . . A Nautilus growing in the Pacific is affected by every one of the million stars we see – or do not see – in the universe.'[82]

In the decade following the publications of both Cook and D'Arcy Thompson a Swiss musician and musicologist named Hans Kayser (1891–1964) published the first of a series of books dedicated to subsuming all branches of science and art into a universal harmony.[83] Kayser was a friend of Klee's and performed string quartets with the artist during the 1930s;[84] and although many of his most important works were not published until after the artist's death, the broad lines of his thinking were apparent from the start and must surely have been known to Klee. Central to Kayser's vision of the universe was his belief that all forms were similar to all other forms and that, in the last analysis, nature creates according to simple numerical patterns or multiples thereof. In his search for these patterns Kayser was inevitably led to explore the most rudimentary forms of life – the flowers, radiolarians, and crystals, which revealed most clearly to him the secret geometry of nature. At that point where animal and plant meet, at the bottom of the hierarchy of life, Kayser uncovered formal patterns which could also be found in crystals themselves and concluded that, on this level, the formative processes acting upon organic and inorganic creation were essentially the same. Whether or not Klee was familiar with these discoveries his own art of these years certainly supports them; for in the cave blossoms and *Dynamoradiolaren* which suddenly make an appearance in Klee's works in 1926 (figs. 77, 80) there are unmistakable formal similarities to a series of snow crystals which Kayser had published in this same year (fig. 200). Once again it is not necessary to assume a direct influence, but perhaps only a coincidence. Klee was by this time sufficiently familiar with nature's basic shapes and patterns to realize that these were not exclusive to any one or other of its creations.

Kayser's search for the laws pervading all facets of life – from music to painting and from nature to religion – ultimately transgresses the bounds of science (if not of credibility) and moves into domains where Klee is unlikely to have followed him. But the basic tenets of his thinking, which inevitably draws much inspiration from Goethe, appear sympathetic to Klee's own aims. For underlying the investigations of both men is a desire to rid oneself of that blinkered vision which automatically confronts everything in the world as distinct and individual and proceeds to catalogue and classify it accordingly. Instead, Kayser seeks to restore to his readers a sense of life's oneness – of its hidden congruences, its unalterable truths, and its 'pure being'.[85] To lead them towards this goal Kayser observes in the preface to his first book that there are two ways of looking at any organism in nature: either by probing deeper and deeper into its form, function, and development or by seeing it in relation to things beyond itself – to the general ebbing and flowing of the life force as it

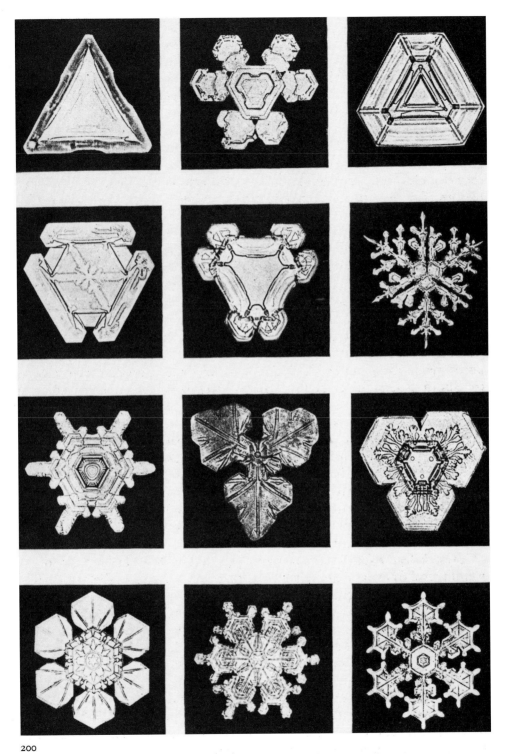

200
Snow crystals published by Hans Kayser  1926

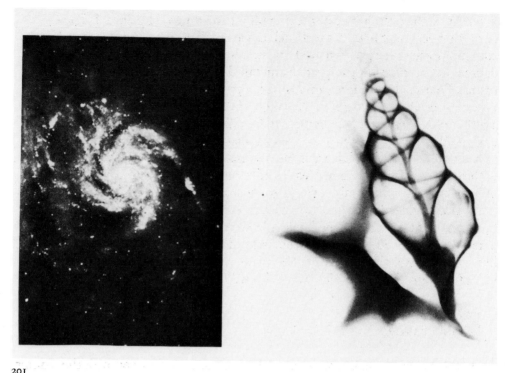

201
Spiral nebula and X-ray of a Snail shell, published by Hans Kayser 1946

permeates all of existence, or to the motions of the planets floating high above it.[86] In short, one may direct one's gaze in towards the plant or bird, or out from it. The latter course alone, however, will disclose the deepest secrets of existence and lead one to a truly comprehensive understanding of all things.

Klee's gaze, of course, moved in both directions. Like the highly sensitized antennae of his beloved snails, his own antennae scanned both the damp earth and the dark heavens. But it was the latter of these alone – the cosmic vantage point upon creation – which made it possible for him to float a snail in the heavens and make us see it as a nebula (fig. 15). Nor was Klee alone in perceiving this connection. For six years after his death Kayser published a long account of the spiralling principle in nature and accompanied it with a plate showing a photograph of a snail-shell alongside one of the constellation of the Great Bear (fig. 201). 'Even the most distant and yet recognizable world-systems are of a spiral nature to our telescopic vision,' noted Kayser, who then proceeded to draw the attention of his readers to the essential similarities between this vast astral body and the spiralling snail.[87] If Klee's view of nature had ever needed vindicating, Kayser's discovery had done just this. For here at last the earthly and the cosmic stood side by side, their inner bond visible for all to see.

To be able merely to place them side by side on the page is the predicament of the scientist or the philosopher. To set one's snail afloat in the heavens,

232

however, is the prerogative of the painter – providing that painter is Klee – or of the poet. As it happens just such a poet could also be found among Klee's contemporaries – one who shared his interests and imagery to so unerring a degree that at times they appear as one mind expressing itself in two different forms. That poet was Hermann Hesse (1877–1962), whom we have already encountered in our discussion of *Around the Fish*[88] and who was to recall another of Klee's great fish pictures in his *The Glass Bead Game*, when he described the moon as 'the great, near, moist orb, the fat magic fish in the sea of heaven'.[89] Although Klee and Hesse apparently never met, each was familiar with the other's work;[90] and Hesse's admiration for Klee is recorded in several of his writings, most notably *The Journey to the East* (1931), where Hesse makes the acquaintance of Klee and later discovers his 'signature' in the archives of the East. 'I found there a small gold-plated dish on which a clover was either painted or engraved,' he writes, 'the first of its three leaves represented a small blue sailing-boat, the second a fish with coloured scales and the third looked like a telegram-form on which was written:[91]

As blue as snow,
Is Paul like Klee.'

If Hesse never actually met Klee he had so much in common with the painter that many of the most salient features of their biography seem almost interchangeable. Thus Hesse too passed part of his life in Bern, from 1912–19 – a period when Klee, alas, was resident in Munich. During these years he was introduced to a number of the artist's friends, among them Louis Moilliet, with whom Klee had journeyed to Tunisia in 1914.[92] Such coincidences are, to be sure, far from correspondences. But the latter are, if anything, even more numerous. Like Klee, Hesse had a passion for cats, gardening, and fishing[93] – though, like Klee too, he abandoned the last of these in later life, when the tormenting and killing of fishes began to trouble his conscience.[94] In his cultural allegiances Hesse was, by his own admission, a disciple of the eighteenth century – a worshipper of Goethe and Mozart, who were also two of Klee's greatest loves.[95] In the careers of both men, too, a journey to an exotic land (in Hesse's case, India) fundamentally altered the course of their creative lives. Finally, those lives were themselves not so dissimilar; for if Klee tried his hand at writing poetry, Hesse also practised as a painter – a painter, moreover, of pictures which are at times suspiciously Klee-like and in which 'the trees have faces and the houses laugh or dance or weep'.[96] Although this realm of fantasy may occasionally be encountered in Hesse's art,[97] his more characteristic landscape watercolours remain closer in style to those which Moilliet was painting in Tunis with Klee.[98] In their views on art, however, both men were in broad agreement, with Hesse likewise viewing the creative process as one subject to both male and female influences, which he deemed spiritual and instinctual,[99] and describing art itself as 'a striving for totality, an attempt to enclose chaos in a nutshell'.[100] It is hard to imagine a description which accords more fully with Klee's own aims – or, indeed, with his pictures. Moreover, on the most fundamental level of all the creative vantage points of both men made them kindred spirits; for, in company with Klee, Hesse described himself as one who had escaped from the world about him and had taken 'refuge in the cosmic'.[101]

From an early age Hesse identified closely with the changing moods and patterns of Nature and confessed to being taught by her more than by any human being.[102] No less than Klee himself Nature confided in Hesse and afforded a background for the most diverse of his soul's emotions. In later life Hesse admitted that this close identification with Nature may occasionally have led him to project his own inner life on to her, rather than the reverse;[103] but even in his maturity he never lost his 'child's sense of wonder'[104] at her unfolding spectacle or her smallest creation. Like Klee he appears to have had the capacity to be born anew with each day, his senses ever wiser but never dulled. Accepting that his was an 'insignificant life caught up in one great rhythm'[105] Hesse willingly submitted the one to the other and allowed 'the estimable I to disappear once more into the universe' where he took his place 'in the eternal and timeless order'.[106] Like Klee, then, he anchored himself in the cosmos and became 'a creature on a star among stars'.[107]

As an inhabitant of both earth and sky Hesse did not place himself at the top of the hierarchy of life – that is to say, where man presumably belongs – but somewhere near the middle, in the company of birds and fishes.[108] From this position he could glimpse the entire domain of Nature and could imagine himself taking on the life of any one of her creations – a phenomenon of metamorphosis which occurs throughout Hesse's writings and leads him to assume the form of a bird, a fish, or a flower.[109] In company with Klee, then, Hesse's regard upon creation is neither anthropomorphic nor sentimental, though his sensuous delight in it is greater than Klee's and links Hesse even more firmly with his German Romantic predecessors. This is above all apparent in Hesse's admission that he could not live in cold climates but only in sun-drenched zones.[110] Klee, as we have seen, preferred the opposite.[111] Detached and crystalline, he sought not even the beauty in nature which constantly appealed to Hesse, but simply truth. Yet, whatever the object of their search, both men accepted that Nature's deepest secrets would only be vouchsafed to one who confronted her without desire, from a point of view which Hesse called 'pure contemplation'[112] and Klee 'distant and religious'.[113] Goethe, on the other hand, had called it simply a 'calm glance'.[114] But whatever the turn of phrase the result in all three cases was to bring about a state of inner illumination before nature which transformed the seeker after truth into a true seer.

From this vantage point Hesse discovered that the greatest joy and wisdom to be revealed to man was 'from the thousands of relationships, correspondences, analogies, and echoes that speak to us eternally from things great and small'.[115] Foremost among these for Hesse was the indissoluble partnership between life and death, the latter of which he saw as 'one of the great and eternal forms of life and transformation'.[116] Such rebirth and transformation into another form is a constant theme in Hesse's work and forms an obvious parallel to Klee's many physiognomic landscapes of the 1920s and '30s. Thus for Hesse too the dead and dying take on other forms as flowers or trees, while the soul may awaken from death to find itself assuming the form of a bird or a fish, of the world itself, or even of God. Dead and entombed in the earth it yet finds itself freely floating and arranging a constellation in the heavens.[117] Death, then, is not a single irrevocable event in man's life for Hesse. Rather it is a constant occurrence because it is constantly being followed by rebirth – rebirth in the garden or grave, both of which Hesse repeatedly refers to as 'mother'.[118] The parallels with Klee need no underlining here, especially when one confronts such lines as these by Hesse: 'Death agony, no less than childbirth, is a life process, and often one can mistake the one for the other'.[119] Here as elsewhere throughout his writings Hesse appears to us as an unelected spokesman for Klee's pictures, for Klee himself had reached just such a realization as this in his own *Rock Grave* (fig. 193).

In addition to this most fundamental of all correspondences to be revealed by nature Hesse also discovered there that inner kinship between the part and the whole which likewise preoccupied Klee. To be sure, Hesse's attempts to derive the macrocosm from the microcosm are seldom as scientific as Klee's. Rather, like the original Romantics themselves, he was more often given to seeing 'A Heaven in a wild flower' than an image of an entire tree in one of its leaves. 'How wonderful,' exclaims Hesse's Goldmund, 'that each of these thousand tiny leaves should have a whole starry heaven hidden in it.'[120] But on other occasions in his writings Hesse makes it clear that he too sought to plumb the wellsprings of Nature's creativity and to explore the destiny of any one of her creations in a way which calls to mind both Goethe and Klee. Witness the following passage from Hesse's *Wandering* of 1920, with its uncanny reminiscences of Klee's *Illuminated Leaf* and *Germinating* (figs. 97, 101):[121]

> A tree says: A kernel is hidden in me, a spark, a thought. I am life from eternal life. The attempt and the risk that the eternal mother took with me is unique, unique the form and veins of my skin, unique the smallest play of leaves in my branches and the smallest scar on my bark. I was made to form and reveal the eternal in my smallest special detail . . . I live out the secret of my seed to the very end.

Moreover, Hesse also shared with Klee a firm belief that one could glimpse the eternal through a regular communion with the ephemeral and likewise echoed the painter's view that, through a constant communication with Nature the creative spirit would eventually find her residing within himself. Indeed, Hesse's account of this process could hardly be bettered as an explanation of Klee's own creative position:[122]

We see the boundaries between ourselves and nature waver and melt away and can no longer tell whether the images on our retina spring from outward or from inner impressions. An experience of this kind is the simplest means of discovering how creative we are, how deeply our soul participates in the perpetual creation of the world. The same indivisible divinity is indeed at work in us and in nature, and if the outside world were to perish, one of us would be capable of rebuilding it, for mountain and stream, leaf and tree, root and flower, everything that has ever been formed in nature lies preformed within us, springs from the soul whose essence is eternity.

Inevitably one is reminded here not only of Klee's desire to recreate nature from out of the depths of his imagination but of his claim upon reaching early maturity: 'I am God. So much of the divine is heaped in me that I cannot die'.[123]

And it was this contact with the divine – with the original creative spirit itself – that both men saw as the ultimate goal of their perpetual dialogues with nature. To glimpse the unknowable from the knowable appeared to be the only way forward in either case. Thus Klee abandoned his attempts to find God and concentrated instead upon one of his flower beds – a step, it would seem, along the way.[124] And Hesse's Goldmund chose a similar path. 'I believe,' he observed, 'that the cup of a flower, or a little, slithering worm on a garden path, says more, and has more things to hide, than all the thousand books in a library. . . . God writes the world with them.'[125] So too did Klee write his world with them.

For both Hesse and Klee, then, all aspects of nature bore the mark of the divine and symbolized his eternal presence. In this respect every one of nature's creations could be seen as representing something else – something greater and forever invisible. All one could do was to glean this 'something greater' in the wayward motions of the fishes and flowers; or, as Klee himself was to do, rearrange those selfsame fishes and flowers until they brought one face to face with the divine mystery itself – until, that is, the ordinary beings of this world unlocked the gate to another. 'Each phenomenon on earth is an allegory,' wrote Hesse in 1918:[126]

and each allegory is an open gate through which the soul, if it is ready, can pass into the interior of the world where you and I and day and night are all one. In the course of his life, every human being comes upon that open gate, here or there along the way; everyone is sometime assailed by the thought that everything visible is an allegory and that behind the allegory live spirit and eternal life. Few, to be sure, pass through the gate and give up the beautiful illusion for the surmised reality of what lies within.

236

The creator of *Fish Magic* needs no special pleading for consideration among these few, even if he preferred to think of his allegories as 'ultimate things'. What is more, Klee not only passed through that open gate but he ushered others into the world which lay beyond it by rendering its invisible secrets visible in his art. As Hesse himself acknowledged, this was the greatest service that those who gained entrance to this realm could perform for those who stood outside:[127]

As long as there is life on earth, men will not cease to tell each other what they have experienced and communicate that part of their experience which has remained an inner possession. And among these men there will always be some whose experience becomes for them an expression and symbol of age-old cosmic laws, who in the perishable perceive the eternal and in the changing and contingent the imprint of the divine. It will not matter very much whether such writers call their works novels, memoirs, confessions, or something else.

Paul Klee was likewise of this company, and he called his 'works' pictures.

# Biographical Outline

| | |
|---|---|
| 1879 | Born 18 December at Münchenbuchsee near Bern, to Hans Klee (1849–1940), a music teacher, and Ida Maria Frick Klee (1855–1921), a singer. |
| 1886–98 | Schooling in Bern; graduates from the Literarschule, 1898. |
| 1898–1900 | Munich; studies with Knirr and, at the Academy, with Franz von Stuck. |
| 1901–2 | Travels to Italy, visiting Genoa, Pisa, Rome, Naples, and Florence. |
| 1902–6 | In Bern, living with his parents; completes a set of fifteen satirical etchings (1903–5) – his 'Opus One'. |
| 1906 | Marriage to the pianist Lily Stumpf; moves to Munich. A son, Felix, born 30 November 1907. |
| 1911 | First one-man exhibition at the Thannhauser Gallery. Makes contact with the *Blaue Reiter* group and begins to compile a catalogue of his own works. |
| 1912 | Trip to Paris; visits Delaunay and sees pictures by Picasso, Braque, and Rousseau. |
| 1914 | Trip to Tunisia with Auguste Macke and Louis Moilliet. |
| 1916–18 | Service in the German Army. |
| 1920 | Publication of the *Creative Credo* and the *Candide* illustrations. Appointed to the faculty of the Weimar Bauhaus by Walter Gropius, 25 November |
| 1921 | Moves to Weimar. |
| 1923 | Publication of *Ways of Studying Nature*. |
| 1924 | Lecture *On Modern Art* delivered at the Jena Kunstverein. |
| 1925 | The Bauhaus moves to Dessau. Participates in the first group exhibition of the Surrealists in Paris. |
| 1926 | Moves to Dessau. Summer holiday in Italy. |
| 1927 | Summer in Corsica and the Isle of Porquerroles. |

| 1928 | Trip to Egypt, December 1928 – January 1929. |
|------|---------------------------------------------|
| 1929 | Fiftieth birthday marked by a large one-man exhibition at the Flechtheim Gallery, Berlin. |
| 1930 | Klee exhibition at the Museum of Modern Art, New York. |
| 1931 | Appointed Professor at the Düsseldorf Akademie, 1 April. Exhibits at the Düsseldorf Kunstverein. |
| 1933 | Dismissed by the Nazis; returns to Bern in December. |
| 1934 | First Klee exhibition in England (Mayor Gallery, London). |
| 1935 | Large Klee exhibition at the Kunsthalle, Bern, and in Basel. Onset of fatal illness (scleroderma). |
| 1936 | Summer in Switzerland, at Tarasp and Montana. |
| 1937 | Visited by Picasso, Braque, and Kirchner. Seventeen of his pictures included in the Nazi exhibition of 'Degenerate Art'; 102 of his works confiscated from German public collections. |
| 1940 | Major exhibition of the late works at the Kunsthaus, Zurich, to mark the artist's sixtieth birthday. |
|      | Dies, 29 June, at the clinic of St Agnese in Muralto-Locarno. Klee's ashes interred in the Schosshalden Cemetery, Bern, after the death of his wife in 1946. |

# Footnotes

## Abbreviations

Works cited in brief in the footnotes

| | |
|---|---|
| *Briefe I & II* | Paul Klee, *Briefe an die Familie*, ed. Felix Klee, Cologne, 1979. Vol. I (1893–1906); Vol. II (1907–1940). |
| Cologne 1979 | *Paul Klee, Das Werk der Jahre 1919–1933, Gemälde, Handzeichnungen, Druckgraphik*, Kunsthalle, Cologne, 1979. |
| *Colored Works* | Jürgen Glaesemer, *Paul Klee, The Colored Works in the Kunstmuseum, Bern*, trans. Renate Franciscono, Bern, 1979. |
| *Diaries* | *The Diaries of Paul Klee, 1898–1918*, ed. Felix Klee, Berkeley and Los Angeles, 1964. |
| Grohmann 1954 | Will Grohmann, *Paul Klee*, New York, 1954. |
| *Handzeichnungen I* | Jürgen Glaesemer, *Paul Klee, Handzeichnungen I, Kindheit bis 1920*, Sammlungskataloge des Berner Kunstmuseums (Bd. 2), Bern, 1973. |
| *Handzeichnungen III* | Jürgen Glaesemer, *Paul Klee, Handzeichnungen III, 1937–1940*, Sammlungskataloge des Berner Kunstmuseums (Bd. 4), Bern, 1979. |
| London 1974 | Arts Council of Great Britain, *Paul Klee, The Last Years, An exhibition from the collection of his son*, London, 1974. |
| Munich 1979 | *Paul Klee, Das Frühwerk 1883–1922*, Städtische Galerie im Lenbachhaus, Munich, 1979. |
| New York 1967 | *Paul Klee 1879–1940, A retrospective exhibition*, The Solomon R. Guggenheim Museum, New York, 1967. |
| *Notebooks I* | *Paul Klee: The Thinking Eye*, The Notebooks of Paul Klee, Vol. I, ed. Jürg Spiller, London and New York, 1964 (2nd ed.). |
| *Notebooks II* | *Paul Klee, Notebooks, Volume 2, The Nature of Nature*, ed. Jürg Spiller, London and New York, 1973. |
| Osterwold I | *Paul Klee, Die Ordnung der Dinge*, ed. Tilman Osterwold, Stuttgart, 1975. |
| Osterwold II | Tilman Osterwold, *Paul Klee, Ein Kind träumt sich*, Stuttgart, 1979. |
| Pasadena 1967 | *Paul Klee 1879–1940, A retrospective exhibition*, organized by the Solomon R. Guggenheim Museum in collaboration with the Pasadena Art Museum, 1967. |
| P.N. | Klee's pedagogical papers (Pädagogischer Nachlass), a collection of manuscripts comprising his theoretical writings at the Bauhaus and the Akademie in Düsseldorf; now preserved in the Klee Foundation, Kunstmuseum, Bern. |

## Chapter 1 The Artist as Naturalist

1 *Diaries*, p. 4, no. 8.

2 *Ibid.*, p. 7, no. 25.

3 In the thematic index of Klee's titles compiled by the Klee Foundation the word '*Schnecke(n)*' – or 'snail(s)' – appears fourteen times. In addition to the works on this theme illustrated here, the following are readily available in reproduction: *Exit of the Snails* (*Ausgang der Schnecken*), 1915, 109 (*Handzeichnungen I*, p. 238, no. 568) and *Forkings and Snail* (*Gabelungen und Schnecke*), 1937, N2(82), (Felix Klee, Bern; repro. London 1974, p. 19, no. 56).

4 *Infra*, pp. 123 ff.

5 Closely related to this watercolour in both style and theme is Klee's *Leaf of Memory about a Conception* (*Erinnerungs-Blatt an eine Empfängnis*), also of 1918 (75; Pasadena Art Museum, repro. Pasadena 1967, p. 27, no. 19).

6 This sketchbook of 1889–90 is now in the collection of Felix Klee, Bern. For a convenient selection of illustrations from it, together with a number of Klee's other childhood drawings, see Osterwold II, pp. 32 ff.

7 *Diaries*, p. 77, no. 323.

8 All three of these works remain in the possession of Felix Klee: *Butterfly* (1892N, Inv. 1302), *Skeleton of an Eagle* (1894N, Inv. 1330; repro. Munich 1979, p. 302, no. 11), and *Toucan* (1895N, Inv. 1156).

9 *Diaries*, p. 256, no. 895.

10 Cf. *Colored Works*, , p. 59, no. 7, and *Handzeichnungen I*, p. 130, no. 303 a-d (for a series of cat studies of 1905). Two watercolours of asters date from 1908 (53, 63); see also the stylistically related *Flowers in a Vase* of this year (repro. Munich 1979, p. 343, no. 108). An undated oil of *Cactuses* (*c.* 1912) is reproduced in the same catalogue, p. 379, no. 185.

11 *Diaries*, p. 229, no. 834.

12 *Ibid.*, p. 125, no. 429.

13 See *Handzeichnungen I*, p. 138, n. 4, for the distribution of works in these categories between 1905–11.

14 For Klee and Cubism, see especially Jim M. Jordan, *Paul Klee and Cubism, 1912–1926*, Ph.D. dissertation, New York University, 1974 (Ann Arbor, Michigan, 1974), 2 vols.

15 Ludwig Grote (ed.), *Erinnerungen an Paul Klee*, Munich, 1959, pp. 19, 104.

16 *Diaries*, p. 41, no. 112.

17 *Ibid.*, p. 38, no. 103. (See also *Briefe I*, p. 10.)

18 *Briefe I*, p. 41.

19 *Ibid.*, p. 264.

20 *Ibid.*, p. 313.

21 *Briefe II*, p. 1114.

22 *Ibid.*, p. 700.

23 *Ibid.*, p. 891.

24 *Diaries*, p. 190, no. 713/14.

25 *Briefe I*, p. 329 and *passim* (see the index, p. 1311, under 'Bimbo I'). For a documentary record of Klee's cats see the catalogue of the photographic exhibition *Paul Klee e il privato* (*Paul Klee, the private life*) by Paola Watts, Rome: Palazzo Braschi, 1979.

26 *Infra*, p. 39.

27 *Briefe I*, p. 173 and *passim*.

28 *An Owl* (*Eine Eule*), 1937, V13 (sold Klipstein and Kornfeld, 25–26 May 1962, lot 535); *Two Kinds of Tortoise* (*Zweierlei Schildkrot*), 1938, 357, V17 (Felix Klee, Bern; repro. *Il Bestiario di Paul Klee, ventiquattro disegni della collezione di Felix Klee*, Lugano: Sergio Grandini, 1978, no. 15). *Ibid.*, no. 24, for a 1940 drawing of Bimbo. For other late studies of cats by Klee, see *Handzeichnungen III*, p. 66, no. 38; p. 126, no. 248; p. 139, nos. 296–7; and p. 247, nos. 627–8.

29 *Infra*, p. 29.

30 *Infra*, p. 82.

31 *Briefe I*, pp. 161, 164, 212; *II*, p. 1075. *Diaries*, pp. 89 f., no. 372.

32 *Briefe I*, p. 149.

33 *Ibid.*, p. 301.

34 *Ibid.*, p. 484.

35 *Briefe II*, p. 1114.

36 *Diaries*, p. 91, no. 375.

37 *Ibid.*, p. 196, no. 753.

38 See *Briefe I*, p. 458; *Diaries*, p. 387, no. 1104; and *infra*, pp. 113 ff.

39 E.g. *Briefe I*, pp. 603, 623; *II*, p. 1075.

40 *Diaries*, p. 83, no. 357; *Briefe II*, pp. 1048, 1052, 1118 f., 1127; and *infra.* pp. 93 ff., 191 ff.

41 Information from Felix Klee (conversation with the author, 25 July 1981).

42 *Infra*, p. 81

43 Grote, *op. cit.*, pp. 73, 78.

44 *Notebooks I*, intro. p. 24; *II*, p. 289 (for Klee's portfolio of natural wonders and his collection of mollusc shells).

45 *Infra*, pp. 107 ff.

46 *Diaries*, p. 39, no. 109.

47 *Briefe I*, p. 53.

48 *Briefe II*, pp. 1072 f.

49 *Briefe I*, p. 152.

50 *Briefe II*, p. 919.

51 *Diaries*, p. 39, no. 109.

52 *Ibid.*, p. 14, no. 51.

53 *Infra*, pp. 149 ff., 161 ff.

54 *Briefe I*, p. 535.

55 *Diaries*, p. 18, no. 58.

56 *Ibid.*, p. 39, no. 108.

57 *Briefe I*, p. 482.

58 *Ibid.*, pp. 638 f.

59 *Ibid.*, p. 603; *II*, p. 683; and *infra*, pp. 99 f.

60 *Briefe I*, p. 83.

61 *Diaries*, p. 123, no. 421.

62 *Briefe I*, p. 154.

63 *Diaries*, p. 185, no. 675.

64 *Ibid.*, p. 194, no. 748.

65 *Ibid.*, p. 308, no. 931.

66 *Ibid.*, p. 313, nos. 950–1.

67 In addition to the examples illustrated here, see Klee's *With the Rainbow* (*Mit dem Regenbogen*), 1917, 56 (Felix Klee, Bern; repro. Munich 1979, p. 447, no. 321), *Zoological Garden* (*Tiergarten*), 1918, 42, and *With the Eagle* (*Mit dem Adler*), 1918, 85 (both in the Kunstmuseum, Bern; repro. *Colored Works*, pp. 113, no. 65, and 117, no. 68.)

68 Paul Klee, *Gedichte*, ed. Felix Klee, 2nd ed., Zurich, 1980, p. 9.

69 Cf. *Notebooks I*, pp. 63 ff. First published in *Staatliches Bauhaus Weimar 1919–1923*, Bauhaus Verlag Weimar-Munich, 1923, pp. 24 f. Original text reprinted in *Paul Klee, Schriften, Rezensionen und Aufsätze*, ed. Christian Geelhaar, Cologne, 1976, pp. 124 ff.

70 *Notebooks II*, pp. 149, 289. Grote, *op. cit.*, p. 64. *Briefe II*, p. 1020 (21 June 1926).

71 *Infra*, pp. 115 ff., 143, 229 ff.

72 See also *Snail Signs* (*Schnecken Zeichen*), 1921, 161, and *Measured Heights* (*Gemessene Höhen*), 1934, 87, N7 (repro. *Notebooks II*, p. 74).

73 Grote, *op. cit.*, p. 73.

74 *Diaries*, p. 52, no. 155.

75 *Infra*, pp. 60 ff., 171 ff.

76 *Infra*, pp. 116 ff., 161.

77 Information from Felix Klee (conversation with the author, 25 July 1981).

78 In the alphabetical index of Klee's, titles referred to in note 3 above, the following natural subjects occur most frequently:
　Flower, Flora, Blossom, Blooming, etc. – 194 times
　Garden – 185
　Animal – 166
　Bird – 117
　Tree – 103
　Planting, etc. – 93
　Park – 80
　Fish – 77
　Fruit, Fruitful, etc. – 70
　Forest – 69
　Cat – 32
　Snake – 26
　Lion – 17
　Rose – 15
　Aurochs – 14
　　(*infra*, p. 46)
　Snail – 14

79 Paul Klee, *On Modern Art*, introduction by Herbert Read, London, 1969 (first published 1948), p. 9. See also Grohmann 1954, p. 63.

80 Grote, *op. cit.*, p. 91.

81 See especially the various accounts of Klee's teachings in Grote, *op. cit.*, and Petra Petitpierre, *Aus der Malklasse von Paul Klee*, Bern, 1957.

82 Grote, *op. cit.*, p. 97.

83 *Ibid.*, p. 64.

84 *Notebooks I*, p. 169.

85 *Diaries*, p. 177, no. 640. Further to this analogy with music in Klee's art and theory, see R. Verdi, 'Musical Influences on the Art of Paul Klee', *Museum Studies 3*, The Art Institute of Chicago, 1968, pp. 81 ff.

86 *Infra*, pp. 70, 105 ff., 111 f., 197 ff.

87 *Notebooks I*, pp. 217 ff., and Grote, *op. cit.*, p. 98.

88 Klee, *On Modern Art*, p. 51.

89 Grote, *op. cit.*, p. 91.

90 *Infra*, pp. 111, 196 ff.

91 Klee, *On Modern Art*, pp. 13 ff. This lecture was delivered at the Jena Kunstverein on 26 January 1924 and first published in 1945. For an alternative translation of it to the one used here, see *Notebooks I*, pp. 81 ff.

92 Klee, *On Modern Art*, p. 19.

93 *Supra*, p. 16

94 One drawing in particular summarizes Klee's situation in 1933: *Emigrating* (*Auswandern*), 1933, U1 (Kunstmuseum, Bern; repro. Grohmann 1954, p. 287). Among the many other works in this vein from the same year are *Struck from the List* (*Von der Liste gestrichen*), 1933, G4, *Head of a Martyr* (*Kopf eines Märtyrers*), 1933, V20, and '*HE*', also, *Dictator!* (*Auch 'ER' Diktator!*), 1933, B19 (all in the collection of Felix Klee, Bern; repro. London 1974, p. 10, nos. 12–13, and p. 29, no. 116).

95 *Briefe II*, p. 1242.

96 Werner Haftmann, *The Mind and Work of Paul Klee*, London, 1967, p. 205.

97 *Briefe II*, p. 1247.

98 *Ibid.*, pp. 1252, 1254.

99 *Ibid.*, pp. 1271 f.

100 *Diaries*, p. 15, no. 54.

101 *Briefe II*, p. 1280.

102 *Ibid.*, p. 1298.

103 Grote, *op. cit.*, p. 54.

## Chapter 2　The Animal Kingdom

1 Klaus Lankheit (ed.), *Franz Marc im Urteil seiner Zeit*, Cologne, 1960, p. 47.

2 Grote, *op. cit.*, pp. 74, 107; and *Briefe I* and *II*, *passim*.

3 *Diaries*, pp. 343 ff., no. 1008.

4 *Paul Klee par lui-même et par son fils Félix Klee*, Saverne, 1963, p. 71.

5 Klaus Lankheit, *Franz Marc*, Berlin, 1950, p. 18. Further to Franz Marc's ideas on art and nature, see Frederick S. Levine, *The Apocalyptic Vision, The Art of Franz Marc as German Expressionism*, New York, 1979. On Marc and Klee, cf. *infra*, pp. 212 ff.

6 Examples of all these may be found in most well-illustrated books on Klee (e.g. Grohmann 1954 or Gualtieri di San Lazzaro, *Klee*, New York, 1957); but for a publication devoted exclusively to Klee's animal subjects, see *Il Bestiario di Paul Klee, ventiquattro disegni della collezioni di Felix Klee*, Lugano: Sergio Grandini, 1978.

7 Grohmann 1954, pp. 192 ff.

8 The German word for monkey appears ten times among the titles of Klee's works according to the thematic index of these compiled by the Klee Foundation. For four late drawings of monkeys, see *Handzeichnungen III*, p. 150, no. 322; p. 158, no. 347; p. 166, no. 379; and p. 288, no. 752.

9 *Study after a very old Dromedary, sketched in Hammamet* (*Studie nach einem greisen Dromedar, in Hammamet scizziert*), 1914, 208 (Felix Klee, Bern; repro. Munich 1979, p. 416, no. 265). Cf. *Diaries*, p. 292, no. 926m.

10 Cf. Klee's own *Rosinante's Grandchild* (*Rosinantes Enkel*) of this same year (1939, RR20; Felix Klee, Bern; repro. Grohmann 1954, p. 320.)

11 Grote, *op. cit.*, p. 50. Cf. Klee's *Mount of the Sacred Cat* (*Der Berg der heiligen Katze*), 1923, 190 (Private Collection, repro. Douglas Cooper, *Paul Klee*, London, 1949, Plate 9) or *Idol for Housecats* (*Götzenbild für Hauskatzen*), 1924, 14 (Pasadena Art Museum, repro. New York 1967, p. 62, no. 69).

12 *Briefe I*, pp. 173, 177.

13 *Briefe II*, p. 693.

14 For which, see Eberhard W. Kornfeld, *Verzeichnis des graphischen Werkes von Paul Klee*, Bern, 1963, no. 18. Cf. also Klee's *Cat and Bird* (*Katze und Vogel*), 1928, 73, Qu3 (Museum of Modern Art, New York; repro. Carola Giedion Welcker, *Paul Klee*, London, 1952, p. 72).

15 See, for example, the two drawings of 1889–90 reproduced in Osterwold II, p. 44.

16 Wassily Kandinsky and Franz Marc (ed.), *The Blaue Reiter Almanac*, edited and with an introduction by Klaus Lankheit, London, 1974, p. 18.

17 On the *Candide* illustrations and related works on this theme, see especially *Handzeichnungen I*, pp. 178 ff.

18 Cf. Haftmann, *op. cit.*, pp. 194 ff. and Max Huggler, *Paul Klee, Die Malerei als Blick in den Kosmos*, Frauenfeld/Stuttgart, 1969, pp. 223 f.

19 *Bestie, ihr Junges säugend*, 1906, 13 (Felix Klee, Bern; repro. Grohmann 1954, p. 110.)

20 On the sources and significance of these early satirical etchings and drawings, see especially *Handzeichnungen I*, pp. 104 ff.; Alessandra Comini, 'All Roads lead (reluctantly) to Bern: Style and Source in Paul Klee's early "sour" Prints', *Arts Magazine*, Vol. 52, No. 1, September 1977, pp. 105 ff.; and Marcel Franciscono, 'Paul Klee und die Jahrhundertwende', in Munich 1979, pp. 51 ff.

21 Jürgen Glaesemer, 'Paul Klee: Die Kritik des Normalweibes', *Berner Kunstmitteilungen*, 131/132, Jan.-Feb. 1972, pp. 2 ff.

22 *Diaries*, p. 143, no. 513. (Cf. *Briefe I*, p. 335.)

23 *Was für ein Pferd!*, 1929, AE4(264), (repro. New York 1967, p. 79, no. 105).

24 *Esel aus der Hand fressend*, 1937, 7(7), (Kunstmuseum, Bern; repro. *Handzeichnungen III*, p. 53, , no. 4). For an earlier treatment of this theme, see *Eats out of the Hand* (*Frisst aus der Hand*), 1920, 5, (repro. Leopold Zahn, *Paul Klee, Leben, Werk, Geist*, Potsdam, 1920, p. 79).

25 Typical of such works are *A Dog insults poor People* (*Ein Hund beschimpft arme Leute*), 1912, 171; *The Poisonous Animal* (*Das giftige Tier*), 1913, 34; and *The Malicious Bird* (*Der boshafte Vogel*), 1915, 5 (all in the Kunstmuseum, Bern; repro. *Handzeichnungen I*, pp. 210–11, nos. 483 and 489, p. 232, no. 544). See also *The Dangerous Bird* (*Der gefährliche Vogel*), 1913, 59 (repro. Wilhelm Hausenstein, *Kairuan oder eine Geschichte vom Maler Klee und von der Kunst dieses Zeitalters*, Munich, 1921, p. 53). For the greatest of all such treatments of the theme of natural cataclysm by one of Klee's contemporaries – Franz Marc's *Fate of the Animals* (*Tierschicksale*) of 1913 (Kunstmuseum, Basel) – see especially Levine, *op. cit.*, pp. 76 ff. and *passim*.

26 Cf. Roland Penrose, *Picasso, His Life and Work*, Harmondsworth, 1971, pp. 282 ff., and the same author's 'Beauty and the Monster', *Picasso in Retrospect*, ed. Sir Roland Penrose and Dr. John Golding, London and New York, 1973, pp. 157 ff.

27 Cologne 1979, p. 16.

28 Cf. *Handzeichnungen III*, pp. 166, no. 379, and 356, no. 921

29 *Unternehmendes Tier*, 1940, W19 (Felix Klee, Bern; repro. London 1974, p. 32, no. 137). Cf. *Scepticism about the Steer* (*Skepsis dem Stier gegenüber*), 1938, F19(79), (Felix Klee, Bern; repro. Osterwold I, p. 35, no. 38). For a series of further works in this vein, see *Handzeichnungen III*, pp. 338, no. 871, and 351 ff., nos. 909–13.

30 *Bellum Gallicum*, VI, 28. The species in question was *Bos primigenius*, one of the ancestors of the modern cattle. Somewhat misleadingly, most modern writers on Klee describe the aurochs (German: *Urochs*) as a mythical beast.

31 Cf. *Handzeichnungen III*, pp. 44 ff., 291 ff., nos. 753–7; p. 295 f., nos. 762, 765–6; pp. 300 f, nos. 774–6; p. 338, no. 867; and *Il Bestiario di Paul Klee* no. 20, for other members of this series.

32 *Supra*, p. 33.

33 *Diaries*, p. 416.

34 *Supra*, p. 2, and *Diaries*, p. 13, for a characteristic example.

35 *Ibid.*, p. 144, no. 514. Further to this important early etching, see the article by J. Glaesemer cited in note 21 above.

36 *Diaries*, p. 109, no. 403. Cf. Max Friedländer and Jakob Rosenberg, *The Paintings of Lucas Cranach*, London, 1978, nos. 402–4. Closer in design – though not in theme – to Klee's *Virgin in a Tree* is Pisanello's *Allegory of Luxury* (Albertina, Vienna), which is commonly cited as a source for this etching (cf. James Thrall Soby, *The Prints of Paul Klee*, New York, 1945, iv).

37 On partridge symbolism, see especially *Lexikon der Christlichen Ikonographie, Dritter Band, Allgemeine Ikonographie*, ed. Engelbert Kirschbaum SJ, Freiburg im Breisgau, 1971, pp. 503 f.

38 Kornfeld, *op. cit.* no. 16, and *Diaries*, p. 162, no. 585.

39 *Mehr Vogel* (*als Engel*), 1939, YY19 (Kunstmuseum, Bern; repro. *Handzeichnungen III*, p. 266, no. 689).

40 The latter of these is based on Klee's *Hot Place* (*Heisser Ort*) of 1933 (440), (Private Collection, repro. *Notebooks II*, p. 158).

41 Klee, *Gedichte*, p. 9.

42 *Ibid.*, p. 50. (This translation from Kathalin de Walterskirchen, *Paul Klee*, New York, 1975, p. 28.)

43 For which, see *Diaries*, p. 375, no. 1081a. The works concerned are *Trilling Nightingale* (*Schlagende Nachtigall*), 1917, 81 (Private Collection, repro. Grohmann 1954, p. 389, no. 36); *Love-Death Song of the Persian Nightingale*, (*Liebestod der persischen Nachtigall*), 1917, 83 (Kunstmuseum, Bern; repro. *Handzeichnungen I*, p. 249, no. 606); *Three black Nightingales* (*Drei schwarze Nachtigallen*), 1917, 84 (repro. Munich 1979, p. 197); and *Persian Nightingale* (*Persische Nachtigall*), 1917, 92 (present whereabouts unknown).

44 *Vogel-Flugzeuge*, 1918, 210 (Felix Klee, Bern; repro. Munich 1979, p. 217). For an excellent account of the importance of this theme in Klee's art of the war years, see the article by O. K. Werckmeister ('Klee im Ersten Weltkrieg', in Munich 1979, pp. 166 ff.), in which this drawing is reproduced (especially pp. 196 ff.).

45 Among them *Travelling Bird* (*Reisender Vogel*), 1918, 176 (Kunstmuseum, Bern; repro. *Handzeichnungen I*, p. 263, no. 621); *Travelling Birds* (*Reisende Vögel*), 1917, 21 (reused for a monotype of 1923, Collection Anneliese Itten, Zurich), and *Flying Bird* (*Fliegender Vogel*), 1923, 224 (Felix Klee, Bern; repro. Nürnberg, Albrecht-Dürer-Gesellschaft, *Paul Klee, Zeichnungen, Aquarelle*, 1966, no. 29).

46 Cf. *Travelling Birds* (*Reisende Vögel*), 1921, 2 (Private Collection), or *Bird Drama* (*Vogel Drama*), 1923, 219 (repro. Will Grohmann, *Paul Klee, Handzeichnungen*, Wiesbaden, 1951, Pl. 16).

47 For a related painting of 1923 (89) entitled *From Gliding to Climbing* (*Von Gleiten zu Steigen*), see Grohmann 1954, p. 393, no. 73.

48 For which, see especially William Rubin and Carolyn Lanchner, *André Masson*, New York, The Museum of Modern Art, 1976, p. 109. Further to Masson and Klee, *infra*, pp. 216 ff.

49 *Wasservögel*, 1919, 195 (Private Collection, repro. Grohmann 1954, p. 137); *Exotische Flusslandschaft*, 1922, 158 (sold Klipstein and Kornfeld, Bern, 20 June 1973); *Vogelgarten*, 1924, 223 (repro. Cologne 1979, p. 220).

50 *Briefe I*, p. 10.

51 A preparatory drawing for this well-known picture, entitled *Concert on a Twig* (*Konzert auf dem Zweig*), 1921, 188, is in the Kunstmuseum, Bern.

52 Maurice L. Shapiro, 'Klee's *Twittering Machine*', *The Art Bulletin*, L, March 1968, pp. 67 ff.

53 E.g. *Scene with Birds* (*Szene mit Vögeln*), 1937, 6 (Kunstmuseum, Bern; repro. *Handzeichnungen III*, p. 52, no. 3) or *Bird Couple* (*Vogelpaar*), 1939, FG17 (Felix Klee, Bern; repro. London 1974, p. 32, no. 135).

54 *Der Geier hat ihn*, 1939, H3(43), (Felix Klee, Bern; repro. *Paul Klee (1879–1940)*, Museum der Modernen Kunst, Kamakura, 1969, no. 168). Cf. also *Bird of Prey* (*Raub-vogel*), 1938, 5 (Stedelijk Museum, Amsterdam).

55 Klee's *Wasserturm Vogel*, 1937, 259(W19), (Felix Klee, Bern) is reproduced in London 1974, p. 31, no. 126.

56 No systematic study of the significance of this theme in Klee's late art has yet been undertaken, but a sensitive account of selected examples of these works may be found in Huggler, *op. cit.*, pp. 223 f., and (above all) Haftmann, *op. cit.*, pp. 194 ff.

57 Many of the most important of these are conveniently brought together in Werner Schmalenbach, *Paul Klee, Fische*, Stuttgart (Reclam), 1958.

58 *Notebooks I*, pp. 67, 313 ff. Klee's fullest treatment of this theme occurs in P.N. 26, 45/19 – 45/25 (February–March 1924).

59 *Notebooks I*, pp. 313 ff.

60 On these works, see especially Franciscono, *op. cit.*, pp. 38 f.

61 *Infra*, pp. 180 ff.

62 *Diaries*, p. 98, no. 390; *Briefe I*, pp. 219 f.

63 According to Felix Klee (Grote, *op. cit.*, p. 29).

64 *Infra*, pp. 171 ff.

65 Robert Musil, *The Man without Qualities*, trans. E. Wilkins and E. Kaiser, London (Pan Books Ltd.), 1979, Vol. II, pp. 385 f. (Originally published as *Der Mann ohne Eigenschaften*, Berlin, 1930–33.) Klee himself expresses a remarkably similar sentiment in his P.N. 26, 45/23 (p. 146), when he observes: 'We stand here spellbound at the boundary between two elemental realms and in between two forces of equal power'. For his own thoughts on the 'utopian' realms of the water and air, see *Colored Works*, pp. 149 f.

66 Typical examples of these are conveniently illustrated in *Handzeichnungen III*, pp. 212 f., nos. 521–4.

67 See the examples cited in the preceding note and, especially, *Aquarium* (1938, M1, Private Collection, repro. Schmalenbach, *op. cit.*, Pl. 14).

68 The former of these – *Raupenfisch*, 1938, N5 (Private Collection) – is reproduced in *Notebooks II*, p. 195. Cf. also Klee's *Leaf-Fish* (*Blattfisch*), 1937, 263(X3), (sold Klipstein and Kornfeld, Bern, 7–8 June 1978, lot 470). Although the German title of *Mud-Louse Fish* is usually interpreted as a pun on the words 'Schlamm-Assel' ('Mud-Louse' or 'boxed-up'), it is worth noting that, though there is no such creature as a mud-louse fish, there is a mud fish (genus *Protopterus*), which is known in German as a *Schlammfisch*. As this creature is among the most primitive and degenerate of all living fishes, Klee's title may be seen to contain more than a grain of truth. Yet another of the artist's fishes of these years – *Blue-eyed Fishes* (*Blauäugige Fische*), 1938, N6 (Private Collection, repro. Schmalenbach, *op. cit.*, Pl. 15) – call to mind such lower forms of life as the familiar flatworms of the genus *Planaria* (for which, *infra*, pp. 72 ff.).

69 *Supra*, pp. 25 f.

70 Cf. *The Beetle* (*Der Käfer*), 1925, 237 (Kunstmuseum, Bern; repro. Haftmann, *op. cit.*, p. 31) and *Green Plant-Blood-Louse* (*Grüne Pflanzenblutlaus*), 1924, 124 (sold Klipstein and Kornfeld, Bern, 25–26 May 1962, lot 530).

71 The most important of these not illustrated here is *Wood Louse in an Enclosure* (*Assjel im Gehege*), 1940, 353(F13), (Kunstmuseum, Bern; repro. *Colored Works*, p. 438, no. 253).

72 P.N. 26, 45/24(149).

73 *Toter Katarakt*, 1930, 184 (Private Collection, repro. Huggler, *op. cit.*, Pl. 18).

74 On this great picture, see especially Christian Geelhaar, 'Et in Arcadia Ego – zu Paul Klees "Insula dulcamara",' *Berner Kunstmitteilungen*, No. 118, May–

June 1970, pp. 1 ff., and *Colored Works*, pp. 320 ff.

75 Cf. *The Snake Goddess and her Foe* (*Die Schlangengöttin und ihr Feind*), 1940, 317(H7), (Private Collection); *The Biblical Snake shortly after the Curse* (*Die biblische Schlange kurz nach dem Fluch*), 1940, 319(H9) (Private Collection); and (*Metamorphoses*) *The Collapse of the Biblical Snake* (*Metamorphosen, der Zusammenbruch der biblischen Schlange*), 1940, 324(G4) (Kunstmuseum, Bern) – all reproduced in *Colored Works*, pp. 332 and 432.

76 Similar in style to *Spirits of the Air* are Klee's *Group under Trees* (*Gruppe unter Bäumen*), 1929, 298 (Omega 8), (Felix Klee, Bern; repro. *Colored Works*, p. 153, d.) and his etching *Without End* (*Nicht endend*) of 1930 (20), for which see Kornfeld, *op. cit.*, no. 106. Another invertebrate species which appears in Klee's art for the first (and only) time in this year is the starfish (cf. *Dynamized Starfish* (*Dynamisierter Seestern*), 1930, 157(Z7), (Felix Klee, Bern; repro. London 1974, p. 29, no. 109)

77 Among the latter one thinks especially of the vase and bell-shaped colonial species of the order *Peritrichida*, many of which are stalked and all of which bear cilia. Among the most familiar such creatures are those of the genus *Vorticella*.

78 *Briefe II*, p. 1058.

79 For a parallel phenomenon among fungi see the discussion and diagram of sexual reproduction in *Pythium aphanidermatum* in C. J. Alexopoulos, *Introductory Micology*, New York and London, 1962 (2nd ed.), p. 25 and fig. 15.

80 Klee, *On Modern Art*, pp. 47 ff.

81 Further to *Plant-like Strange* in the context of Klee's art of the late 1920s, see *Colored Works*, pp. 154, 168. In purely formal terms this picture is closest to the watercolour which immediately follows it in Klee's catalogue of works – *In the Land of Precious Stones* (*Im Lande Edelstein*), 1929, 3, H18, now in the Kunstmuseum, Basel (repro. *Katalog der Sammlung Richard Doetsch-Benziger*, Kunstmuseum, Basel, 1956, no. 180). As the title of

this work suggests, Klee is here concerned with a meeting between heaven and earth rather than between two single cells. A comparison of these two works alone serves to remind us of the extent to which the artist discovered the same forms and forces at work in both the macrocosm and the microcosm (*infra*, pp. 219 ff.)

## Chapter 3  The World of Plants

1 *Diaries*, pp. 7, no. 25; 14, no. 50; 20, no. 62; 47, no. 134.

2 *Ibid.*, pp. 59, no. 178; 87, no. 366. *Infra*, pp. 123 ff.

3 For the garden theme in Klee's art see especially Huggler, *op. cit.*, pp. 92 ff., and Christian Geelhaar, *Paul Klee and the Bauhaus*, Bath, 1973, pp. 89 ff. A small group of characteristic works on this subject may be found in Osterwold I, pp. 134 ff.

4 *Garten-Rhythmus*, 1932, T5(185), (Felix Klee, Bern; repro. San Lazzaro, *op. cit.*, p. 165); *Garten-Plan*, 1922, 150 (Kunstmuseum, Bern; repro. *Colored Works*, p. 187); *Plan einer Gartenarchitektur*, 1920, 214 (Kunstmuseum, Bern; repro. *Colored Works*, p. 127); *Nach Regeln zu pflanzen*, 1935, 91(N11), (Kunstmuseum, Bern; repro. *Colored Works*, p. 353).

5 For which, see Grohmann 1954, pp. 213 ff., Geelhaar, *Klee and the Bauhaus*, pp. 44 ff., and (above all) Eva-Maria Triska, 'Die Quadratbilder Paul Klees – ein Beispiel für das Verhältnis seiner Theorie zu seinem Werk', in Cologne 1979, pp. 45 ff.

6 *Ibid.*, p. 67, for Klee's *Harmony of the Northern Flora* (*Ein Klang der nördlichen Flora*) of 1924 (74).

7 *Infra*, pp. 212 ff. for a comparison of the two artists' approaches to this subject.

8 *Goethe's Botanical Writings*, trans. Bertha Mueller, Honolulu, University of Hawaii Press, 1952, pp. 42 ff. (Hereafter: *Goethe, Botany*.) Cf. Johann Wolfgang Goethe, *Gedenkausgabe der Werke, Briefe und Gespräche*, ed. Ernst Beutler, Zürich and Stuttgart (Artemis-Verlag), Vol. XVII

(*Naturwissenschaftliche Schriften, Zweiter Teil*), 1952, pp. 29 ff. (Hereafter: *Gedenkausgabe*).

9 See, for example, Klee's *Flower in the Valley* (*Blume im Tal*) of 1938 (381, X1), repro. *Paul Klee*, Fondation Maeght, Saint-Paul, 1977, p. 147; or, for analogies with the human face, *infra*, pp. 138 ff.

10 *Infra*, pp. 171 ff.

11 *Tor im Garten*, 1926, 81(R1), (Kunstmuseum, Bern; repro. *Colored Works*, p. 233).

12 *Goethe, Botany*, pp. 127 ff. (*Gedenkausgabe*, XVII, pp. 153 ff.)

13 Huggler, *op. cit.*, p. 84.

14 J. W. Goethe, *Italian Journey (1786–1788)*, trans. W. H. Auden and Elizabeth Mayer, Harmondsworth (Penguin Books), 1970, pp. 310 f. (*Gedenkausgabe*, XI, p. 353).

15 Johann Peter Eckermann, *Conversations with Goethe*, trans. John Oxenford, London (Everyman's Library), 1971, p. 171. (*Gedenkausgabe*, XXIV, p. 237.)

16 Agnes Arber, *The Natural Philosophy of Plant Form*, Cambridge, 1950, p. 62.

17 For a well-illustrated introduction to this broad theme see Peter S. Stevens, *Patterns in Nature*, Boston and Toronto, 1974. *Infra*, pp. 229 ff.

18 These drawings bear consecutive numbers in Klee's *œuvre* catalogue (1926, 126 C6–133, D3).

19 Cf. *Windmill Blossoms* (*Windmühlenblüten*), 1926, 120 c null (Felix Klee, Bern; repro. Cologne 1979, p. 259, no. 189).

20 Oral communication from Felix Klee. For a modern edition of Haeckel's classic work, see Ernst Haeckel, *Art Forms in Nature*, New York (Dover Publications), 1974. Further to Haeckel and Klee, see p. 227 below.

21 E. Haeckel, *Die Radiolarien*, Berlin, 1862.

22 For an intelligent summary of Haeckel's ideas and of their significance for twentieth century art, see Philip C. Ritterbush, *The Art of Organic Forms*, Washington, DC, 1968, pp. 63 ff.

23 *Diaries*, p. 236, no. 857.

24 Anthony Huxley, *Plant and Planet*, Harmondsworth (Pelican Books), 1978, pp. 109 ff.

25 Cf. *Fantastic Cactus* (*Phantastischer Kaktus*), 1925, 101, A1 (Private Collection), and *infra*, pp. 191 ff.

26 The last of these is a preparatory drawing for a work of the same name of 1922 (77), which is now lost. For Klee's *Pflanzen auf dem Acker I* (1921, 68), see Kunstsammlung Nordrhein-Westfalen, *Paul Klee, Bilder, Aquarelle, Zeichnungen*, Düsseldorf, 1977, p. 25.

27 *Diaries*, p. 47, no. 134.

28 The title of this work is not listed in Klee's catalogue of works and its *œuvre* catalogue number is illegible. Together with the imitative style of the drawing this suggests that it is a forgery.

29 *Supra*, p. 11.

30 *Infra*, pp. 187 ff.

31 Klee had previously employed the clover-leaf (or 'Kleeblatt') as a monogram in certain of his early satirical etchings (cf. Kornfeld, *op. cit.*, nos. 6–11, 13.)

32 *Infra*, pp. 126 ff.

33 *Diaries*, pp. 20, no. 62; 34, no. 86; 126, no. 431.

34 *Garten nachts*, 1918, 55 (repro. Norbert Lynton, *Paul Klee*, London, 1964, Pl. 11).

35 *Dämmer-Blüten*, 1940, X2(42), (Felix Klee, Bern; repro. New York 1967, p. 134, no. 177). For one of Klee's finest works on this theme – *Garden by the Full Moon* (*Vollmond im Garten*), of 1934 (214, U14) – see Huggler, *op. cit.*, pp. 149 ff., and *Colored Works*, pp. 305 f., 350, no. 186.

36 Cf. *Night Blossoms* (*Blüten in der Nacht*), 1930, 207(E7), (San Francisco Museum of Art; repro. Grohmann 1954, p. 397, no. 105).

37 Closely related to this watercolour in both style and theme are: *Ribbon Flower* (*Band Blume*), 1915, 146; *Plant-like Abstract* (*Pflanzlich-Abstrakt*), 1915, 174 (repro. Munich 1979, p. 269); *Plant* (*Pflanze*), 1915, 183; and *Three Blossoms* (*Drei Blüten*), 1915, 235 (Kunstmuseum, Bern; repro. *Handzeichnungen I*, p. 243, no. 584).

38 *Goethe, Botany*, p. 77, no. 115. (Cf. *Gedenkausgabe*, XVII, p. 56).

39 *Ibid.*, pp. 42. ff. (*Gedenkausgabe*, XVII, pp. 30 ff).

40 *Infra*, pp. 219 ff. (for Goethe and Klee).

41 *Notebooks II*, p. 64.

42 *Supra*, p. 28.

43 *Diaries*, p. 147, no. 536.

44 *Supra*, pp. 24 f.

45 *Notebooks II*, pp. 5 ff.

46 For which, see especially Geelhaar, *Klee and the Bauhaus*, pp. 129 ff., and *Colored Works*, pp. 153 f., 166 ff.

47 *Notebooks II*, p. 5.

48 Arber, *op. cit.*, pp. 70 ff., and *passim*.

49 *Notebooks II*, p. 23.

50 Klee's sudden interest in 1929 in depicting individual elements of the living plant which fill the picture space as though seen under a microscope may owe something to an exhibition of photographs of similarly magnified plant specimens by Professor Karl Blossfeldt of Berlin, which was shown at the Bauhaus between 11–16 June 1929 and entitled 'Archetypal Forms of Art'. Blossfeldt's photographs were subsequently published in two volumes as *Art Forms in Nature*, London, 1929 & 1932. In this form they remain among the most striking photographic parallels to Klee's numerous paintings of single fruits, flowers, and leaves of the 1930s.

51 Cf. *Trees* (*Bäume*), 1938 M4(184) (Felix Klee, Bern; repro. *Notebooks II*, intro. (p. 69), in which the central 'tree' is reminiscent of such lower forms of life as the brown marine algae of the family *Laminariaceae*.

52 *Diaries*, p. 221, no. 809.

53 *Notebooks II*, p. 25 ff.

54 Cf. *Air-borne Seeds* (*Flugsamen*), 1925, 230, x null (Kunstmuseum, Bern) or *The Wind distributes Seeds* (*Der Wind streut Samen*), 1934, T12(192), repro. Osterwold I, p. 181, no. 363.

55 *Notebooks II*, p. 25.

56 *Ibid.*, pp. 253 ff.

57 *Infra*, pp. 191 ff.

58 For a representative selection of these see *Notebooks II*, intro. pp. 68 ff.

59 The first three of these are reproduced in *Notebooks II*, intro. p. 77 and text, pp. 24 & 132.

60 *Infra*, pp. 161 ff.

61 Cf. Grohmann 1954, pp. 221 f.

62 *Notebooks II*, pp. 39 ff.

63 See, for example, *Flower and Fruit* (*Blume und Früchte*), 1927, 275 (Oe5) and *Temperaments* (*Blossoms and Fruit*) (*Temperamente, Blüten und Früchte*), 1927, 281 (Ue1), both repro. *Notebooks II*, pp. 120, 122.

64 Cf. P.N. 20/11, for a related pedagogical drawing of the preceding decade.

65 Photographed on Klee's easel after his death (cf. *Notebooks II*, intro., p. 42). *Fruitfulness* (*Fruchtbarkeit*), 1937, 115(p15) (Guggenheim Museum, New York; repro. *Paul Klee, 1879–1940, in the collection of the Solomon R. Guggenheim Museum, New York*, 1977, p. 74, no. 59); *Coelin Fruit* (*Coelin-Frucht*), 1938, 28(D8) (Kunstmuseum, Bern; repro. *Colored Works*, p. 375); *Voluptuous Fruit* (*Üppige Frucht*), 1939, X19 (Felix Klee, Bern; repro. London 1974, p. 23, no. 77). For a selection of late drawings on this theme, see *Handzeichnungen III*, pp. 122, no. 235; 219, no. 544; 229, no. 575; and 333, no. 856.

## Chapter 4    The Two Realms Meet

1 Cf. Magritte's *La chambre d'écouté* of 1952 (Private Collection, Houston, Texas). Other works by Klee in this manner include *Pineapple Pear* (*Ananasbirne*), 1933, 244, X4 (Private Collection); *Negro Fruit* (*Neger-Frucht*), 1934, R8; *Prizewinning Apple* (*Prämierter Apfel*), 1934, UIS (both Coll. Felix Klee, Bern; repro. London 1974, p. 13, no. 16, and p. 18, no. 48); and *Artistic Fruit* (*Künstliche Frucht*), 1935, 34, K14.

2 *Supra*, pp. 40 ff., 49.

3 *Supra*, pp. 18 ff.

4 Grote, *op. cit.*, p. 64.

5 *Supra*, p. 69.

6 *Infra*, p. 207.

7 P.N. 26, 45/24(149), and *supra*, p. 70.

8 Reprinted in *Notebooks I*, pp. 76 ff. For an even more striking application of this principle than the 1934 *Snake Paths* see Klee's *The Snake* (*Die Schlange*) of 1929, 341 3 H 41 (Private Collection; repro. *Colored Works*, p. 321), which is a true walking line (cf. *Notebooks I*, pp. 105 ff.).

9 *Notebooks I*, pp. 17 ff., and *passim*; *II*, pp. 3 ff., 149 ff., and *passim*. See also above, pp. 17 ff.

10 For all of these, see above, pp. 10, 78.

11 Carl Linnaeus, *The Elements of Botany*, London, 1775, p. 194 f. Cf. Rubin and Lanchner, *op. cit.*, p. 146, for André Masson's punning drawing *La Pensée* (1938), which gives overt expression to this idea by converting the form of a pansy into that of a vulva.

12 The companion drawing, *Pflanzenweisheit*, 1915, 77, is in the Hannover Museum (Sammlung Sprengel).

13 *Supra*, pp. 20 f.

14 For a well illustrated introduction to such foliate heads in medieval art, see Kathleen Basford, *The Green Man*, Ipswich, 1978. For Grandville's works in this vein, see *The Court of Flora (Les Fleurs Animées)*, *The Engraved Illustrations of J. J. Grandville*, intro. Peter A. Wick, New York (George Braziller), 1981.

15 *Die Knospe des Lächelns*, 1921, 159 (repro. Geelhaar, *Klee and the Bauhaus*, p. 60, pl. 27).

16 *Physiognomie einer Blüte*, 1922, 88 (present whereabouts unknown).

17 *Die Alte*, 1926, 161, G1 (Private Collection, USA; repro. Grohmann 1954, p. 252).

18 Closely related to this work in style, theme, and date, is *Helical Flowers I (Spiralschrauben-blüten I)*, 1932, v 17 (repro. *Notebooks I*, p. 376).

19 *Klee and the Bauhaus*, p. 65.

20 Kornfeld, *op. cit.*, nos. 54–56, 61. Further to these works see especially Charles Werner Haxthausen, 'Klees künstlerisches Verhältnis zu Kandinsky während der Münchner Jahre', in Munich

1979, pp. 119 f. and Jim M. Jordan, 'Garten der Mysterien, Die Ikonographie von Paul Klees expressionistischer Periode', *Ibid.*, pp. 227 ff.

21 *Supra*, pp. 12 ff.

22 *Diaries*, p. 221, no. 809.

23 Further to Klee's *Menu without Appetite*, see *Colored Works*, pp. 305 f. Perhaps the closest analogies to the forms Klee creates here are to be found in such drawings by Picasso as his 1933 *Two Figures on the Beach* (Museum of Modern Art, New York), for which see William Rubin, *Picasso in the Collection of the Museum of Modern Art, New York*, New York, 1972, pp. 141 ff.

24 Cf. *Handzeichnungen III*, pp. 140 ff., nos. 300–15. The drawings are reproduced in the order discussed here.

25 *Ibid.*, p. 34.

26 For Klee's *Figur im Garten*, 1937, QU9(129) (Felix Klee, Bern), see Grohmann 1954, p. 315.

27 *Diaries*, p. 14, no. 51.

28 This is immediately apparent if one turns the painting ninety degrees to the right (cf. *Colored Works*, p. 327, fig. c).

29 *Legende vom Tod im Garten*, 1919, 244 (repro. Grohmann 1954, p. 390, no. 49).

30 Although it hardly seems necessary to seek specific sources for Klee's many paintings and drawings devoted to the theme of death and rebirth in nature, it may be worth noting that this theme also figures prominently in a work which made a deep impression upon the young Klee, Mascagni's opera *Iris* (1898), which Klee saw twice in Rome in 1902 (*Diaries*, pp. 96, no. 388, and 104, no. 397; cf. also *Briefe I*, pp. 218, 225–7). In the last act of this now-forgotten opera – which Klee described as 'the finest stage-work since Wagner' (*Ibid.*, p. 225) – the heroine dies in a field suffused with warmth and light only to be 'reborn' in the many flowers which proceed to bloom around her. Klee was particularly impressed by this concluding scene in the opera, when 'the entire stage was covered with one thousand blossoms' (*Ibid.*, p. 218) – a curious (and perhaps significant?) anticipation of the

themes and imagery of many of his later physiognomic landscapes and of the equally numerous botanical stage landscapes familiar from all phases of his career.

## Chapter 5 Cosmic Compositions

1 P.N. 26, 45/19 (p. 143) and 45/21.

2 Many of the points raised here are treated more fully in the text and notes of the author's 'Paul Klee's *Fish Magic*; an interpretation', *The Burlington Magazine*, CXVI, 852, March 1974, pp. 147 ff.

3 As a technical analysis of the support of this picture has never been made, it is impossible to say whether the added patch of material conceals an underlying layer of paint. The complicated history of the picture set out below (pp. 176 ff.), however, would suggest that it does.

4 *Supra*, pp. 64 ff.

5 Cf. Grohmann 1954, pp. 200 f., or Schmalenbach, *op. cit.*, pp. 13 f.

6 Grohmann 1954, p. 200.

7 Among the most important of these not discussed here are: *Fishes (Fische)*, 1921 (no number), (Private Collection; repro. Schmalenbach, *op. cit.*, Pl. 3); *Goldfish Wife (Goldfisch Weib)*, 1921, 93 (Philadelphia Museum of Art; repro. New York 1967, p. 42, no. 41); *Aquarium with Silvery Blue Fishes (Aquarium mit Blausilberfischen)*, 1924, 211 (Private Collection; repro. San Lazzaro, *op. cit.*, p. 51); *Fish-Physiognomic (Fisch-physiognomisch)*, 1926, 30 (Private Collection; repro. Haus der Kunst, Munich, *Paul Klee, 1879–1940*, 1970–71, No. 79); *Aquarium*, 1927, 8 (sold Sotheby's 23 April 1968, lot 17); and *Fish People (Fisch-Leute)*, 1927, 11 (K1) (Kunstmuseum, Bern; repro. *Colored Works*, p. 235, no. 119). For the role and importance of fishes in Klee's teachings of these years, see *Notebooks I*, pp. 230, 264 f., and *II*, pp. 189, 213.

8 *Supra*, pp. 60 ff., 82.

9 Cf. *Notebooks I*, p. 118, for the theme of interwoven figures in Klee's art. For a selection of double-faced figures of the early 1930s, see Verdi, '*Fish Magic*', p. 153, n. 32.

10 *Diaries*, p. 310, no. 937. (Original: 'Eine Auge, welches sieht, das andere, welches fühlt'.)

11 *Ibid.*, p. 310, no. 938. (Original: 'Menschentier, Uhr aus Blut'.)

12 *Colored Works*, pp. 133 f.

13 *Diaries*, p. 176, no. 636.

14 Most notably by C. S. Kessler, 'Science and Mysticism in Paul Klee's *Around the Fish*', *Journal of Aesthetics and Art Criticism*, XVI, 1957, pp. 76 ff., and Siegfried Gohr, 'Symbolische Grundlagen der Kunst Paul Klees', in Cologne 1979, pp. 90 ff.

15 *Supra*, p. 62. For a treatment of a similar theme by an old master see Pieter Bruegel's drawing *Big Fish eat little Fish* (1556) in the Albertina, Vienna (cf. Ludwig Münz, *Bruegel, The Drawings (Complete Edition)*, London, 1968, Pl 125, Cat. 128, and H. Arthur Klein, *Graphic Worlds of Pieter Bruegel the Elder*, New York (Dover Publications), 1963, pp. 76 f., no. 29).

16 Hermann Hesse, *Siddhartha*, trans. Hilda Rosner, Pan Books, 1977, p. 118.

17 Cf. Osterwold II, pp. 79, 144 f., 225 and (above all) the 1935 (K 11) *Child Consecrated to Suffering* (*W-geweihtes Kind*), Albright Knox Art Gallery, Buffalo (repro. Grohmann 1954, p. 403, no. 155).

18 For two comparable treatments of flowers from the end of Klee's life see his *Stone Flowers* (*Blumen im Stein*), 1939, gg 18(638) (Private Collection; repro. New York 1967, p. 128, no. 170); and *Flora on the Rocks* (*Flora am Felsen*), 1940, 343(F3) (Kunstmuseum, Bern; repro. *Colored Works*, p. 437).

19 Cf. *Handzeichnungen I*, pp. 13 ff., nos. 7, 9, 12–15.

20 *Revolution des Viaduktes*, 1937, R13(153) (Kunsthalle, Hamburg; repro. Grohmann 1954, p. 295). Further to this important picture, see Huggler, *op. cit.*, pp. 166 ff., and the bibliography cited there.

21 *Angel, still ugly* (*Engel, noch hässlich*), 1940, 26(Y6) (Kunstmuseum, Bern; repro. *Handzeichnungen III*, p. 335, no. 858).

**Chapter 6  Creating like Nature: The Eventual Goal**

1 *Diaries*, p. 83, no. 357.

2 Leo Steinberg, 'The Eye is a Part of the Mind', *Partisan Review*, 1953, p. 210.

3 Cf. Franz Marc, *Skizzenbuch aus dem Felde*, intro. Klaus Lankheit, Berlin, 1956, no. 12.

4 *Diaries*, p. 185, no. 677.

5 *Notebooks I*, pp. 217 ff. For a lucid account of the importance of this principle in Klee's artistic theory and practice, see Huggler, *op. cit.*, pp. 29 ff.

6 Cf. R. Verdi, 'Musical Influences . . .', and the references cited there.

7 As might be expected Klee's two late drawings of this subject are concerned less with a shared existence between different species than with a shared fate and are inevitably much more personal in tone. These are *Symbiose*, 1939, 817 (RR17) (Kunstmuseum, Bern; repro. *Handzeichnungen III*, p. 250, no. 636) and *Symbiose?*, 1940, 23(Y3) (Felix Klee, Bern).

8 *Supra*, p. 28

9 *Diaries*, p. 141, no. 505.

10 *Ibid.*, p. 308, no. 932.

11 *Ibid.*, pp. 310 ff., nos. 943–4.

12 *De generatione animalium*, I, 20–1.

13 *Supra*, pp. 16 ff.

14 Petitpierre, *op. cit.*, p. 53.

15 *Diaries*, p. 125, no. 429.

16 *Ibid.*, pp. 267 ff., nos. 907–14.

17 *Ibid.*, p. 315, no. 952.

18 Guy de Tervarent, *Attributs et symboles dans l'art profane, 1450–1600*, Geneva, 1958, p. 254.

19 *Diaries*, p. 374, no. 1081.

20 Grote, *op. cit.*, p. 98.

21 *Diaries*, p. 370, no. 1074. Cf. *Briefe II*, pp. 822, 857, 866, 871.

22 Cf. *Notebooks I*, p. 76.

23 *Embryonale Abstractionselemente*, 1917, 119 (Felix Klee, Bern; repro. Cologne 1979, p. 145, no. 8).

24 See also Klee's *Spirit of Fruitfulness* (*Geist der Fruchtbarkeit*) from this same year (1917, 78) in the Kunstmuseum, Bern (repro. *Handzeichnungen I*, p. 248, no. 604).

25 E.g. *Briefe II*, p. 1295, or Petitpierre, *op. cit.*, p. 62.

26 *Show-window for Ladies' Lingerie* (*Schaufenster für Damen Unterkleidung*), 1922, 125 (present whereabouts unknown, but repro. *Paul Klee*, Curt Valentin Gallery, New York, 1953, no. 8).

27 Cf. figs. 152 & 153 and the numerous late pairs and groups in *Handzeichnungen III*. Klee's preoccupation with such themes during his last years has often been remarked upon but never fully explored. A convenient selection of his many late groups may be found in Osterwold II, pp. 172 ff.

28 *Diaries*, p. 191, no. 726.

29 Cf. Levine, *op. cit.*, pp. 116 ff.

30 A similar theme and mood would appear to pervade Klee's equally poignant *Wandering Soul* (*Irrende Seele*) of 1929, 3 h 11 (Private Collection; repro. Grohmann 1954, p. 400, no. 128).

31 The full inscription reads as follows (*Diaries*, p. 419):
   I cannot be grasped in the here and now
   For I live just as well with the dead
   As with the unborn
   Somewhat closer to the heart of creation than usual
   But far from close enough.

**Postscript: Towards a Wider Context**

1 See, for example, Herbert Read, *The Meaning of Art*, Harmondsworth, 1963 (orig. 1931), p. 168, or George Heard Hamilton, *Painting and Sculpture in Europe 1880–1940*, Harmondsworth, 1967, pp. 333 ff.

2 Peter Selz, *German Expressionist Painting*, Berkeley and Los Angeles, 1957, pp. 39 ff. and *passim*.

3 *Ibid.*, pp. 296 f.

4 'Beitrag für die "Festschrift für Emil Nolde,"' *Paul Klee, Schriften . . .*, p. 129.

5 Quoted in Peter Selz, *Emil Nolde*, New York, The Museum of Modern Art, 1963, p. 49.

6 *Supra*, pp. 33 ff.

7 Franz Marc, *Briefe, Aufzeichnungen und Aphorismen*, Berlin, 1920, Vol. I, p. 123. Idem., 'Die Neue Malerei', *Pan II*, 1912, p. 556.

8 Franz Marc, *Briefe aus dem Felde*, Munich, 1966, p. 60.

9 *Diaries*, p. 345, no. 1008.

10 Kandinsky and Marc, *op. cit.*, p. 64.

11 *Ibid.*, pp. 147 ff., and Wassily Kandinsky, *Concerning the Spiritual in Art*, New York (Documents of Modern Art, Vol. 5), 1970, pp. 49 f.

12 Ritterbush, *op. cit.*, p. 79.

13 For an admirable account of the relations between Kandinsky and Klee during their formative years, see C. W. Haxthausen, *op. cit.*, pp. 98 ff. For a comparison of the two artists' use of nature imagery during the 1920s, see Sixten Ringbom, 'Paul Klee and the Inner Truth to Nature', *Arts Magazine*, Vol. 52, No. 1, September 1977, pp. 112 ff. On Kandinsky and Klee in general, see also: Beeke Sell Tower, *Klee and Kandinsky in Munich and at the Bauhaus*, Ann Arbor, UMI Press, 1981. Another artist of Klee's acquaintance who shared his belief in the parallels between natural and artistic creation was Hans Arp. 'Art is a fruit that grows in man', wrote Arp, 'like a fruit in a plant, or a child in its mother's womb'. (Hans Arp, *On My Way: Poetry and Essays, 1912–1947*, trans. R. Manheim, New York, 1948, p. 50.)

14 William Lieberman, *Max Ernst*, New York, The Museum of Modern Art, 1961, p. 25. For Ernst as a collector of Klee's works, see *Colored Works*, p. 112.

15 Rubin and Lanchner, *op. cit.*, p. 19.

16 William S. Rubin, *Dada, Surrealism, and their Heritage*, New York, The Museum of Modern Art, 1968, p. 40.

17 Leo Steinberg, *op. cit.*, p. 210. (Quoted in Ritterbush, *op. cit.*, p. 85). Chapter V of Ritterbush's book provides a valuable summary of the role and importance of nature imagery in the art of many of the major twentieth-century masters. Further to this theme see: G. Schmidt and R. Schenk(eds), *Kunst und Naturform – Form in Art and Nature*, Munich, 1960.

18 John Russell, *Max Ernst, Life and Work*, London, 1967, pp. 16, 107. Cf. Max Ernst, *Beyond Painting and other Writings*, New York (Documents of Modern Art), 1948, pp. 9 f.

19 One comparison may suffice to outline the fundamental differences between Klee and his contemporaries in this regard: namely, that between his own *Illuminated Leaf* of 1929 (fig. 97) and André Masson's *Meditation on an Oak Leaf* of 1942 (repro. Rubin and Lanchner, *op. cit.*, p. 60). Notwithstanding the title of Masson's painting, it is Klee's work alone that remains a meditation on the ways of nature. Masson's *Leaf*, on the other hand, affords him with a pretext to gaze within himself. 'As the artist contemplates the leaf', observe Rubin and Lanchner (p. 59), 'he thinks of the cycle of nature and the rapport of that mystery with the traumas and fantasies in the deepest recesses of the labyrinth of his own mind'.

20 *Here everything is still floating* (1920, The Museum of Modern Art, New York; repro. Russell, *op. cit.*, Pl. 15).

21 *The Sandworm which reties its sandal . . .* (1920, Private Collection; repro. Russell, *op. cit.*, Pl. 14). Further to Ernst and Klee, see Jordan, 'Garten der Mysterien', in Munich 1979, pp. 241 ff.

22 Ernst, *op. cit.*, p. 14.

23 *Diaries*, p. 91, no. 375.

24 *Supra*, pp. 82 ff. On Goethe as a natural scientist, see especially Rudolf Magnus, *Goethe as a Scientist*, New York, 1949 (orig. 1906), a book which Klee is known to have read (cf. Sara Lynn Henry, *Paul Klee, Nature, and Modern Science, the 1920s*, Ph.D. thesis, University of California, Berkeley, 1976, p. 89, n. 15). For an excellent introduction to the intellectual background to Goethe's theories, see Philip C. Ritterbush, *Overtures to Biology, The Speculations of Eighteenth-Century Naturalists*, New Haven and London, 1964, pp. 57 ff., and Arber, *op. cit.* Further to Goethe and Klee, see W. Hofmann, 'Ein Beitrag zur morphologischen Kunsttheorie der Gegenwart', *Alte und Neue Kunst*, II, 1953, pp. 63 ff., and A. Mösser,

*Das Problem der Bewegung bei Paul Klee*, Heidelberg, 1976.

25 *Goethe, Botany*, p. 180. (*Gedenkausgabe*, XVII, p. 85.)

26 *Ibid.*, p. 97. (*Gedenkausgabe*, XVII, p. 104.)

27 *Ibid.*

28 *Ibid.*, p. 168. (*Gedenkausgabe*, XVII, p. 85.)

29 *Ibid.*, p. 220. (*Gedenkausgabe*, XVI, p. 845.)

30 *Ibid.*, p. 208.

31 *Ibid.*, p. 85. (*Gedenkausgabe*, XVII, p. 111.)

32 *Diaries*, p. 185, no. 677.

33 *Goethe, Botany*, p. 219. (*Gedenkausgabe*, XVI, p. 872.)

34 *Diaries*, p. 374, no. 1081.

35 *Supra*, pp. 101 ff.

36 *Goethe, Botany*, p. 77, no. 115. (*Gedenkausgabe*, XVII, p. 56.)

37 *Ibid.*, pp. 127 ff. (*Gedenkausgabe*, XVII, p. 153 ff.)

38 *Ibid.*, pp. 24 ff. (*Gedenkausgabe*, XVII, p. 14 ff.)

39 *Ibid.*, pp. 43 f., no. 35. (*Gedenkausgabe*, XVII, p. 31.)

40 *Supra*, p. 82.

41 *Goethe, Botany*, pp. 33 ff., and 77, no. 119. (*Gedenkausgabe*, XVII, pp. 24 ff., 57.) Goethe's most famous statement of this principle is his oft-quoted aphorism 'Alles ist Blatt' – 'All is leaf'. (*Gedenkausgabe*, XVII, p. 189.)

42 *Ibid.*, p. 225. (*Gedenkausgabe*, XVI, p. 851.)

43 *Ibid.*, p. 94. (*Gedenkausgabe*, XVII, p. 124.)

44 *Ibid.*, pp. 78 f. (*Gedenkausgabe*, XVII, p. 59.)

45 Cf. Ritterbush, *Overtures*, pp. 57 ff. on this phenomenon in eighteenth-century thinking.

46 Linnaeus, *op. cit.*, pp. 148 ff. and *passim*.

47 *Goethe, Botany*, p. 79. (*Gedenkausgabe*, XVII, p. 60.)

48 Cf. Linnaeus, *op. cit.*, pp. 219 ff.

49 *Goethe, Botany*, p. 109.

50 Erasmus Darwin, *The Botanic Garden Part II, containing The Loves of the Plants*, II, Lichfield, 1789, vi.

51 *Goethe, Botany*, pp. 143 ff. (*Gedenkausgabe*, XVII, pp. 171 ff.)

52 E. Darwin, *op. cit.*, p. 33, lines 341–4.

53 For which, see above pp. 126 ff.

54 *Goethe, Botany*, pp. 172 ff. (*Gedenkausgabe*, XVII, pp. 90 ff.)

55 Goethe's unceasing pursuit of nature's own inner poetry is nowhere better demonstrated than in a comparison of this passage from his poem with his more purely scientific account of this same principle: 'Thus, in the early infancy of the plant, we already see a foreshadowing, as it were, of the natural force by which the inflorescence and infructescence will be effected at a more advanced age'. (*Goethe, Botany*, p. 43, no. 33. *Gedenkausgabe*, XVII, p. 30.)

56 *Diaries*, p. 256, no. 895.

57 *Goethe, Botany*, p. 168. (*Gedenkausgabe*, XVII, p. 85.)

58 *Ibid.*, p. 233. (*Gedenkausgabe*, XVI, pp. 878 f.)

59 *Supra*, p. 26.

60 The standard treatment of this subject is M. H. Abrams, *The Mirror and the Lamp: Romantic Theory and the Critical Tradition*, New York, 1958, pp. 184 ff.

61 *Goethe, Botany*, pp. 117 f. (*Gedenkausgabe*, XVII, p. 179.)

62 *Ibid.*, p. 116. (*Gedenkausgabe*, XVII, p. 177.)

63 *Ibid.*, p. 242. (*Gedenkausgabe*, XVI, pp. 921 f.)

64 *Diaries*, p. 190, no. 713/14.

65 'A Defence of Poetry', *The Complete Works of Percy Bysshe Shelley*, ed. R. Ingpen and W. E. Peck, London and New York, 1965, Vol. VII, p. 136.

66 *Goethe, Botany*, p. 244. (*Gedenkausgabe*, XVI, p. 924.)

67 *Supra*, p. 90

68 Conversation with Felix Klee (25 July 1981).

69 Further to the importance of Haeckel's book for artists and architects at the turn of the century, see *Art Nouveau, Art and Design at the Turn of the Century*, ed. P. Selz and Mildred Constantine, New York, The Museum of Modern Art, 1959, pp. 14 ff. For a comparable anthology of wonders from the plant world of these same years, which likewise aimed to put these forms at the disposal of the artist, architect, and designer, see Moritz Meurer, *Pflanzenbilder*, Dresden, 1897–1903. 2 vols.

70 Ernst Haeckel, *The Wonders of Life*, London, 1904, pp. 176 ff.

71 Rudolf Steiner, *Agriculture, a course of eight lectures*, trans. George Adams, London, 1977, p. 130.

72 *Ibid.*, p. 135.

73 *Ibid.*, pp. 22 f.

74 *Ibid.*, pp. 35 ff. Cf. *Notebooks I*, p. 4; *II*, p. 149.

75 *Diaries*, p. 378, nos. 1087–8. (Cf. *Briefe II*, pp. 880 ff.)

76 Steiner, *op. cit.*, p. 119. For an important disciple of Steiner – and, thereby, of Goethe – whose botanical writings provide us with the closest twentieth-century parallel to Klee's botanical paintings, see Gerbert Grohmann, *The Plant, A Guide to Understanding its Nature*, trans. K. Castelliz, London, 1974. Klee may well have been familiar with this classic treatment of the Goethean view of nature, which first appeared in 1929 and was revised and republished as *Die Pflanze* in 1933.

77 *Diaries*, p. 123, no. 421.

78 D'Arcy Wentworth Thompson, *On Growth and Form*, Cambridge, 1977 (abridged edition), p. 151. For D'Arcy Thompson's discoveries in the context of twentieth-century art, see Ritterbush, *The Art of Organic Forms*, pp. 87 ff.

79 Theodore Andrea Cook, *The Curves of Life*, London, 1914, p. 11. See also the same author's *Spirals in Nature and Art*, London, 1903.

80 Cook, *Curves*, p. 8.

81 *Ibid.*, p. 407.

82 *Ibid.*, viii.

83 Hans Kayser, *Orpheus, vom Klang der Welt, Morphologische Fragmente einer allgemeinen Harmonik*, Potsdam, 1926. A leaflet announcing the publication of this book appears at the end of Klee's P. N. 9; and, according to Jürg Spiller (*Notebooks I*, p. 519), Kayser's *Orpheus* was eventually owned by Klee. Among Kayser's many later works on this theme are his *Harmonia Plantarum*, Basel, 1943, and *Grundriss eines Systems der harmonikalen Wertformen*, Zurich, 1946.

84 *Briefe II*, pp. 1253 ff. Kayser had earlier written a brief but favourable account of Klee's pictures: 'Paul Klee', *Hohe Ufer*, Hannover, 2, 1920, p. 14.

85 Kayser, *Orpheus*, xxiv.

86 *Ibid.*, p. 1.

87 Kayser, *Grundriss*, p. 246. One artist to follow Klee in this regard was Max Ernst, whose *frottage* of 1964, *Un autre monde* (repro. Russell, *op. cit.*, p. 95), depicts a chambered nautilus suspended in space in a manner which recalls Klee's *In the Sign of the Snail*. Ernst's work was made as a frontispiece for the 1963 reprint of Grandville's *Un autre monde* (Paris; orig. 1844).

88 *Supra*, pp. 183 f.

89 H. Hesse, *The Glass Bead Game*, trans. Richard and Clara Winston, Harmondsworth, Penguin Books, 1972 (orig. 1943), p. 443.

90 Information kindly provided by Felix Klee. For a short review by Hesse of W. Hausenstein's *Kairuan oder eine Geschichte vom Maler Klee*, see *Vivos Voco*, 3, Nov.–Dec. 1922, p. 224.

91 H. Hesse, *The Journey to the East*, trans. Hilda Rosner, London, Panther Books, 1977, p. 91. (There mis-translated: for 'book like' read 'looked like', i.e. 'sah aus'.)

92 Two other friends that both men shared were the painters Albert Welti (1862–1912) and Ernst Morgenthaler (1887–1962).

93 Cf. H. Hesse, *Hours in my Garden and other Poems*, trans. Rika Lesser, London, Jonathan Cape, 1980, pp. 7 ff., 33 ff., 69 ff.

94 *Ibid.*, p. 71.

95 Significantly these are also the two greatest loves of the autobiographical hero of Hesse's *Steppenwolf*, Harry Haller, (H. Hesse, *Steppenwolf*, trans. Basil Creighton, Harmondsworth, Penguin Books, 1979, p. 152).

96 H. Hesse, *Autobiographical Writings*, trans. Denver Lindley, London, Pan Books, 1977, p. 64.

97 See especially Hesse's illustrations to his *Piktors Verwandlungen* (1925).

98 For Hesse as a painter, see *Hermann Hesse als Maler*, Münster, Landesmuseum, 1973, and Joseph Mileck, *Hermann Hesse, Life and Art*, Berkeley and Los Angeles, 1980, pp. 67 f. (with further bibliography).

99 H. Hesse, *Narziss and Goldmund*, trans. Geoffrey Dunlop, Harmondsworth, Penguin Books, 1976, p. 164.

100 H. Hesse, *Reflections*, Selected from his books and letters by Volker Michaels, London, Triad/Panther Books, 1979, p. 132, no. 484.

101 H. Hesse, *If the War Goes On . . . Reflections on War and Politics*, trans. Ralph Manheim, London, Picador Books, 1972, p. 26.

102 Hesse, *Autobiographical Writings*, p. 23.

103 H. Hesse, *Wandering*, trans. James Wright, London, Picador Books, 1979, p. 84.

104 H. Hesse, *Peter Camenzind*, trans. W. J. Strachan, Harmondsworth, Penguin Books, 1977, p. 80.

105 H. Hesse, *The Prodigy*, trans. W. J. Strachan, Harmondsworth, Penguin Books, 1978, p. 143.

106 Hesse, *Autobiographical Writings*, p. 65.

107 *Supra*, p. 17.

108 Hesse, *Autobiographical Writings*, p. 106. Cf. Hesse, *Reflections*, pp. 62 f., no. 225.

109 See especially Hesse's short stories *Vogel* (H. Hesse, *Die Märchen*, Frankfurt, Suhrkamp, 1980, pp. 252 ff.) and *Iris* (in H. Hesse, *Strange News from another Star*, trans. Denver Lindley, Harmondsworth, Penguin Books, 1980, pp. 104 ff.).

110 Hesse, *Autobiographical Writings*, p. 54.

111 *Supra*, pp. 14 f.

112 H. Hesse, *My Belief, Essays on Life and Art*, ed. T. Ziolkowski, St. Albans, Herts., Triad/Panther Books, 1979, p. 37. The whole of this passage is worth comparing with Goethe's approach to the natural world as discussed above, pp. 219 ff.

113 *Supra*, p. 33.

114 *Supra*, p. 220.

115 Hesse, *Reflections*, pp. 63 f., no. 230.

116 *Ibid.*, p. 175, no. 637.

117 H. Hesse, *Poems*, selected and translated by James Wright, London, Jonathan Cape, 1978, pp. 78 f., and *Idem, Strange News*, pp. 75 f.

118 E.g. Hesse, *Wandering*, pp. 14, 35, 53 and *Iris* (in *Strange News*, pp. 104 ff.), *passim*.

119 Hesse, *Reflections*, p. 175, no. 635.

120 Hesse, *Narziss and Goldmund*, p. 71.

121 Hesse, *Wandering*, p. 52.

122 Hesse, *Reflections*, p. 128, no. 464. (Cf. H. Hesse, *Demian*, trans. W. J. Strachan, London, Panther Books, 1976, p. 99.)

123 *Diaries*, p. 52, no. 155.

124 *Ibid.*, p. 221, no. 809.

125 Hesse, *Narziss and Goldmund*, p. 61.

126 Hesse, *Strange News*, p. 107.

127 Hesse, *Reflections*, p. 141, no. 520.

# Select Bibliography

This list includes only those sources which have proved particularly helpful in exploring the theme of Klee and nature. For a more comprehensive bibliography on the artist, with a full list of exhibitions, see 'Words and Images for Klee, A Bibliography', by Bernard Karpel, in *Paul Klee, Notebooks, Volume 2, The Nature of Nature*, ed. Jürg Spiller, London and New York, 1973, pp. 431–54. Equally extensive – and more up-to-date – is the bibliography to be found in *Paul Klee, Das Werk der Jahre 1919–1933, Gemälde, Handzeichnungen, Druckgraphik*, Kunsthalle, Cologne, 1979, pp. 405–22.

## Klee's own Writings

Paul Klee, *Briefe an die Familie*, ed. Felix Klee, Cologne, 1979. Vol. I (1893–1906); Vol. II (1907–1940).
*The Diaries of Paul Klee, 1898–1918*, ed. Felix Klee, Berkeley and Los Angeles, 1964.
Paul Klee, *Gedichte*, ed. Felix Klee, Zurich, 1980 (2nd ed). (For a selection of Klee's poems translated into English see *Some Poems by Paul Klee*, trans. Anselm Hollo, Lowestoft, Suffolk, 1962.)
*Paul Klee: The Thinking Eye*, The Notebooks of Paul Klee, Vol. I, ed. Jürg Spiller, London and New York, 1964 (2nd ed).
*Paul Klee, Notebooks, Volume 2, The Nature of Nature*, ed. Jürg Spiller, London and New York, 1973.
Paul Klee, *On Modern Art*, With an introduction by Herbert Read, London, 1969.
Paul Klee, *Pedagogical Sketchbook*, Introduction and translation by Sibyl Moholy-Nagy, New York, 1953.
Paul Klee, *Schriften, Rezensionen und Aufsätze*, ed. Christian Geelhaar, Cologne, 1976.

## Books, Articles, and Major Catalogues on the Artist

Cologne, Kunsthalle, *Paul Klee, Das Werk der Jahre 1919–1933, Gemälde, Handzeichnungen, Druckgraphik*, Kunsthalle, Cologne, 1979.
Düsseldorf, Kunstsammlung Nordrhein-Westfalen, *Paul Klee, Bilder, Aquarelle, Zeichnungen*, Catalogue of the Klee collection in the Kunstsammlung Nordrhein-Westfalen, Düsseldorf, 1977 (4th ed).
Geelhaar, Christian, *Paul Klee and the Bauhaus*, Bath, 1973.
Giedion-Welcker, Carola, *Paul Klee*, trans. Alexander Gode, London, 1952.
Giedion-Welcker, Carola, *Paul Klee in Selbstzeugnissen und Bilddokumenten*, Hamburg (Rowohlt), 1962 (2nd ed).
Glaesemer, Jürgen, *Paul Klee, The Colored Works in the Kunstmuseum, Bern*, trans. Renate Franciscono, Bern, 1979. (Original edition: *Paul Klee. Die farbigen Werke im Kunstmuseum Bern*, Bern, 1976. Sammlungskataloge des Berner Kunstmuseums, Paul Klee Bd. 1)
Glaesemer, Jürgen, *Paul Klee, Handzeichnungen I, Kindheit bis 1920*, Sammlungskataloge des Berner Kunstmuseums, Paul Klee Bd. 2, Bern, 1973.
Glaesemer, Jürgen, *Paul Klee, Handzeichnungen III, 1937–1940*, Sammlungskataloge des Berner Kunstmuseums, Paul Klee Bd. 4, Bern, 1979.
Grohmann, Will, *Paul Klee*, New York, 1954.
Grohmann, Will, *Paul Klee, Handzeichnungen*, Cologne 1959.
Grohmann, Will, *Paul Klee*, New York (The Library of Great Painters), 1967.
Grote, Ludwig (ed.), *Erinnerungen an Paul Klee*, Munich, 1959.
Haftmann, Werner, *The Mind and Work of Paul Klee*, London, 1954.
Henry, Sara Lynn, *Paul Klee, Nature, and Modern Science, the 1920s*, Ph.D. thesis, University of California, Berkeley, 1976.
Huggler, Max, *Paul Klee. Die Malerei als Blick in den Kosmos*, Frauenfeld/Stuttgart, 1969.
Huggler, Max, 'Die Kunsttheorie von Paul Klee', *Festschrift Hans R. Hahnloser*, Basel/Stuttgart, 1961, pp. 425–41.
Kessler, Charles S., 'Science and Mysticism in Paul Klee's *Around the Fish*', *Journal of Aesthetics and Art Criticism*, XVI, 1957, pp. 76–83.
Klee, Felix, *Paul Klee: His Life and Work in Documents*, New York, 1962.

Klee-Gesellschaft (Bern), *Paul Klee, 1 Teil: Dokumente und Bilder aus den Jahren 1896–1930*, Bern, 1949.

Kornfeld, Eberhard W., *Verzeichnis des graphischen Werkes von Paul Klee*, Bern 1963.

London, Arts Council of Great Britain, *Paul Klee, The Last Years, An exhibition from the collection of his son*, London, 1974.

Munich, Städtische Galerie im Lenbachhaus, *Paul Klee, Das Frühwerk 1883–1922*, Städtische Galerie im Lenbachhaus, Munich, 1979.

New York, The Solomon R. Guggenheim Museum, *Paul Klee 1879–1940, A retrospective exhibition*, The Solomon R. Guggenheim Museum, New York, 1967.

New York, The Solomon R. Guggenheim Museum, *Paul Klee 1879–1940, A retrospective exhibition*, Organized by The Solomon R. Guggenheim Museum in collaboration with The Pasadena Art Museum, New York, 1967.

New York, The Solomon R. Guggenheim Museum, *Paul Klee 1879–1940 in the collection of The Solomon R. Guggenheim Museum, New York*, New York, 1977.

Osterwold, Tilman (ed.), *Paul Klee, Die Ordnung der Dinge*, Stuttgart, 1975.

Osterwold, Tilman, *Paul Klee, Ein Kind träumt sich*, Stuttgart, 1979.

Petitpierre, Petra, *Aus der Malklasse von Paul Klee*, Bern, 1957.

Plant, Margaret, *Paul Klee, Figures and Faces*, London, 1978.

Ringbom, Sixten, 'Paul Klee and the Inner Truth to Nature', *Arts Magazine*, Vol. 52, No. 1, September 1977, pp. 112–17.

San Lazzaro, Gualtieri di, *Klee, A Study of his Life and Work*, trans. Stuart Hood, London and New York, 1957.

Schmalenbach, Werner, *Paul Klee, Fische*, Stuttgart (Reclam), 1958 (2nd ed).

Tower, Beeke Sell, *Klee and Kandinsky in Munich and at the Bauhaus*, Ann Arbor, UMI Press, 1981.

Winkler, Ernst, 'Paul Klee und die exakte Wissenschaft (Ein Kritik zu Paul Klee, *Das bildnerische Denken*, 1956)', in Paul Heinrich Diehl, *Grenzen der Malerei*, Vienna and Cologne, 1961.

## Background Reading

Abrams, M. H., *The Mirror and the Lamp: Romantic Theory and the Critical Tradition*, New York, 1958.

Arber, Agnes, *The Natural Philosophy of Plant Form*, Cambridge, 1950.

Blossfeldt, Karl, *Art Forms in Nature*, London, 1929, 1932. 2 vols.

Cook, Theodore Andrea, *Spirals in Nature and Art*, London, 1903.

Cook, Theodore Andrea, *The Curves of Life*, London, 1914.

Goethe, Johann Wolfgang von, *Goethe's Botanical Writings*, trans. Bertha Mueller, Honolulu, University of Hawaii Press, 1952.

Goethe, Johann Wolfgang von, *The Metamorphosis of Plants*, with an introduction by Rudolf Steiner, The Bio-Dynamic Farming and Gardening Association, Inc, USA, 1974. (For a convenient German edition of Goethe's major botanical writings see Johann Wolfgang Goethe, *Schriften zur Botanik und Wissenschaftslehre*, Munich, Deutscher Taschenbuch Verlag, 1975, 2nd ed.).

Grohmann, Gerbert, *The Plant, A Guide to Understanding its Nature*, trans. K. Castelliz, London, Rudolf Steiner Press, 1974.

Haeckel, Ernst, *The Wonders of Life, a popular study of biological philosophy*, trans. Joseph McCabe, London, 1904.

Haeckel, Ernst, *Art Forms in Nature*, New York (Dover Publications, Inc.), 1974.

Kayser, Hans, *Orpheus, vom Klang der Welt, Morphologische Fragmente einer allgemeinen Harmonik*, Potsdam, 1926.

Kayser, Hans, *Der hörende Mensch*, Berlin, 1930.

Kayser, Hans, *Harmonia Plantarum*, Basel, 1943.

Kayser, Hans, *Grundriss eines Systems der harmonikalen Wertformen*, Zurich, 1946.

Magnus, Rudolf, *Goethe as a Scientist*, New York, 1949.

Ritterbush, Philip C., *Overtures to Biology, The Speculations of Eighteenth-Century Naturalists*, New Haven and London, 1964.

Ritterbush, Philip C., *The Art of Organic Forms*, Smithsonian Institution, Washington DC, 1968.

Schmidt, Georg and R. Schenk (ed.), *Kunst und Naturform – Form in Art and Nature*, Munich, 1960.

Steiner, Rudolf, *Agriculture, a Course of Eight Lectures*, trans. George Adams, London, 1974.

Stevens, Peter S., *Patterns in Nature*, Boston and Toronto, 1974.

Thompson, D'Arcy Wentworth, *On Growth and Form*, abridged edition by J. T. Bonner, Cambridge, 1961.

Whyte, Lancelot Law (ed.), *Aspects of Form, A Symposium on Form in Nature and Art*, London, 1968 (2nd ed.).

# Index